S0-EKM-363

3 1215 00022 4268

HANDBOOK
of
ANIMATION
TECHNIQUES

DATE DUE

MAY 4 1994			

DEMCO 38-297

31215000224268

HANDBOOK
of
ANIMATION
TECHNIQUES

Eli L. Levitan

VNR VAN NOSTRAND REINHOLD COMPANY
New York Cincinnati Toronto London Melbourne

Copyright © 1979 by Litton Educational Publishing, Inc.
Library of Congress Catalog Card Number 79-12099
ISBN 0-442-26115-2

All rights reserved. No parts of this work covered by the copyright
hereon may be reproduced or used in any form or by any means—
graphic, electronic, or mechanical, including photocopying, recording,
taping, or information storage and retrieval systems—without written
permission of the publisher.

Printed in the United States of America
Designed by Loudan Enterprises

Published in 1979 by Van Nostrand Reinhold Company
A division of Litton Educational Publishing, Inc.
135 West 50th Street, New York, NY 10020, U.S.A.

Van Nostrand Reinhold Limited
1410 Birchmount Road
Scarborough, Ontario M1P 2E7, Canada

Van Nostrand Reinhold Australia Pty. Ltd.
17 Queen Street
Mitcham, Victoria 3132, Australia

Van Nostrand Reinhold Company Limited
Molly Millars Lane
Wokingham, Berkshire, England

16 15 14 13 12 11 10 9 8 7 6 5 4 3 2 1

Library of Congress Cataloging in Publication Data

Levitan, Eli L
  Handbook of animation techniques.

  Includes index.
  1. Animation (Cinematography)—Handbooks, manuals,
etc. I. Title.
TR897.5.L49   778.5'347   79-12099
ISBN 0-442-26115-2

R
397.5
.L49

To Rose
Who patiently watched television commercials
while her husband wrote and produced them.

Acknowledgments

My sincere thanks to the advertisers and their agencies for making their television commercials available for this book. All of the film presentations contain excellent examples of the animation and motion picture techniques described in the following chapters. This list tells who these nice people are: The American Oil Company, Joseph Katz Advertising—J. B. Goodman, Ginny Chapman; The American Tobacco Company, Gumbinner Advertising Agency—James McMenemy, Mort Kasman; Animation Equipment Corporation— John Oxberry, Ed Willette; P. Ballantine and Sons, William Esty Company—Joseph S. Forest; Boyle-Midway, J. Walter Thompson Company—Ed Wolfe, Jr., Albert Boyars; Cue Magazine—Edward Loeb; DuKane Corporation—Howard Turner; The Ford Motor Company, J. Walter Thompson Company—Harry Treleaven; General Electric Company—M. M. Masterpool, W. P. VonBehren; Martinson's Coffee, Inc., Al Paul Lefton Co., Inc.—Ray Sidor; National Broadcasting Company—Joel Friedman; Paramount Pictures Cartoon Studios—Abe Goodman, Leonard McCormick; Whitehall Laboratories, Ted Bates Advertising—R. C. Hettig, Douglas Gabrielle; J. B. Williams Company, Pharmaceuticals Division—Don Blauhut.

Contents

Introduction

"Building a better mousetrap" is no longer a sufficient guarantee that the world will beat a path to the builder's door. In today's highly competitive market, even the "better mousetrap" must be advertised.

Through the magic of the picture tube, television has provided a new medium for advertisers along with a new type of supersalesman. The commercial has replaced yesterday's "foot-in-the-door bell-ringer." The commercial film, with a viewing time ranging from ten seconds to one minute, introduces the product in the consumer's own living room under the most favorable conditions, delivers the message or "pitch," and promptly fades out. In order to keep the attention and patronage of the TV viewer during subsequent visits, new approaches and techniques must be introduced continually.

The impact and effectiveness of animation as a technique is acknowledged through its steadily increasing use by advertising agencies for commercial purposes, by industrial organizations for technical and training purposes, and by educational institutions for teaching a great variety of subjects.

The animation technique, although considerably older than any other motion-picture technique, is the least understood and perhaps the most misunderstood. Animation is capable of producing a wide variety of effects unobtainable with "live" motion-picture production and, when used as a technique for purposes other than entertainment, it is usually more effective than the "live" film. Interest is sustained for longer periods of time and a greater percentage of the film's subject matter is retained by the viewer.

Special animation and motion-picture equipment, tailor-made to fill today's requirements, make available a great number of techniques and effects. The amount and variety are limited only by the collective imagination of the talented men and women who plan and produce films.

This book describes in detail the process by which a series of individual drawings, photographs, or other graphic material, is transformed into an eye-arresting sequence of motion on a length of processed film. Also included in the pages that follow is a detailed analysis of the techniques and effects used most frequently and a description of the specialized equipment that is used to achieve them. The production processes are described in detail, from script to editing, opticals, and processing. The reader is taken by the hand and given a backstage look at these processes and techniques. This working manual and reference book answers the question usually asked by visitors to an animation studio: "What makes them move?"

This book is divided into two sections. The first analyzes and updates the state of the art and describes the conventional procedures leading to the filming of the mountainous pile of drawings generally needed to create the illusion of motion. The information in the pages following the description of the basic procedures bridges the two extremes—the conventional processes and techniques, and the changing technology that includes the new computer-generated animation and computer-controlled filming techniques.

The reader may be surprised to learn that the conventional processes, rather than being completely replaced or relegated to a minor role, are actually serving as the foundation for the newer electronic-imaging systems. There is now and probably always will be a place for each and room for both. The "old" will complement the "new" and vice versa.

The second part of the book describes the technical processes and the specialized equipment used for filming. The detailed explanations in this part of the book precede a close look over the film editor's shoulder into his world of film clips and sound tracks. A brief but comprehensive description of processing procedures is also included in this section. Following in logical sequence is a discussion of the versatile optical printer. Here, the many techniques described in earlier chapters fit into place like the pieces of a giant jigsaw puzzle. These techniques, along with transitional and special effects, offer a composite picture that provides a better understanding and appreciation of animation and its place in the motion picture industry.

In addition to the descriptions of the conventional animation techniques and the specialized equipment used by the industry, established procedures, production processes, and related terminology are explained and defined in language that is as nontechnical as possible. Cross-references help the reader through the more difficult areas. The emphasis throughout the book is on the practical applications of the processes, techniques, and equipment—what makes the systems *GO*. The photographs and illustrations that complement the text were carefully selected for their graphic representation of specific processes or techniques.

Intended primarily for those talented and imaginative people already in the animation and commercial film industry, this book, when used as a reference and guide, will open the door to more interesting film presentations and the development of additional eye-catching effects.

For those interested in photography, but who have a limited knowledge of the requirements of the animation and commercial film industry, these pages contain the information needed to help the amateur photographer attain professional status. Similarly, for the artist and cartoonist who would like to enter the commercial film field but who are not quite sure of their qualifications, this book, with its thorough analysis of the various techniques, shows the many different types of art work, other than animation, used in commercial film production. Advertising agency personnel will also find the contents especially useful as a guide for production and a basis for additional creativity on the pre-production level. As a text for use in schools and colleges offering courses in the communication arts, the book's subject matter provides a clear, detailed explanation and analysis of every phase of production. The processes, arranged in logical sequence, are explained in the simplest terminology possible.

Last, but certainly not least, the home television viewer, the all-important person for whom the commercial film is intended and whose acceptance assures its success, will find the book of considerable interest. The air of mystery surrounding the production of television commercials and motion pictures is cleared and the hows and whys of the techniques explained. The more complete understanding and appreciation of production processes should make subsequent viewing a more enjoyable experience.

Part I

THE ANIMATED FILM

The Animation Process

animate (ań-i-māt). vt. 1. to give natural life to; to make alive. 2. to give spirit or vigor to; to stimulate; rouse. 3. to impart an appearance of life to; as a cartoon. 4. to actuate; prompt.

animated cartoon or drawing. n. a series of drawings with slight progressive changes, made and arranged to be photographed and projected like a motion picture.

These definitions from Webster's New Collegiate Dictionary state concisely what the terms animate and animated cartoon mean, but the reader is left in somewhat the same quandry as the animation-studio visitor who, after being shown through the various departments, still had one last question: "Yes, but what makes them move?" This section of the book answers that question as well as many others on the subject.

Many of the production processes that make the animated cartoon the highlight and happiest part of any visit to local movie houses are similar to those for a feature film. The same all-purpose technique can be used to produce a wide variety of illusory effects that are unobtainable with other filming techniques. The words impossible and implausible are never used in connection with a technique in which the thin line that separates fantasy from reality and actuality from simulation vanishes altogether.

Basically, the "moving" takes place on a strip of processed motion-picture film—actually a series of pictures that have been exposed one at a time. Each exposure is called a frame of film. The illusion of movement is produced by the continuous projection of individual frames. The viewer sees 24 frames every second when watching a motion picture. In one minute of projection time, the viewer sees 1,440 individual pictures, or frames of film.

"Yes, but what makes them move?" The animator makes them move. Also, the script writer, the layout man, the background artist, assistant animator, inbetweener, inker, opaquer, checker, animation cameraman, optical cameraman, film editor, sound analyst, sound technician, and a small army of talented and dedicated personnel. Some use pencils; others use pen-and-ink or brushes; still others use cameras, moviolas, sound readers, microphones, tape recorders, and other equipment. The answer to the question "what makes them move" lies in the mountainous pile of drawings prepared under the animator's guidance. Each of the drawings, traced onto a transparent sheet of acetate and opaqued with specific colors, is placed over a rendered background and photographed in sequence by the animation cameraman on successive frames of motion-picture film. The exposed film, with its latent images, is processed, and the illusion of motion is created when the film is projected at a standard rate (24 frames per second). On the screen, the individual static drawings are transformed into smooth-flowing, continuous sequences of action. Every member of that army of talented artists and technicians helps make the move possible. The production of an animated film designed to entertain children of all ages as well as their grandparents and to produce anything from a chuckle to the heartiest belly laugh is a complicated, time-consuming procedure and a very serious business.

Animation was invented by Joseph Antoine Plateau, a Frenchman, who developed the phenakistoscope in 1831. This crudely designed device for showing sequences of motion combined the two features that make modern photography and projection possible. One of the two disks in the device carried the drawings and, mounted on a simple shaft, served as a projector. The drawings were viewed through slits cut into the

The script.

The sound track.

The story board.

Animation.

Casting.

Live action.

second disk. The two disks, mounted on a common shaft, led to the development of the camera shuttle and helped lend credibility to the persistence-of-vision theory. Three years later an Englishman named William George Horner invented a device called a zoetrope, or daedaleum (wheel of life), for showing moving drawings. Two years after the Civil War ended the first American patent for showing "motion pictorially" was issued to William Lincoln. The first animated cartoon was produced by J. Steward Blackton in 1906. The artist, an American, called it *Humorous Phases of a Funny Face*. The development of new procedures, techniques, and equipment paralleled the growth of the animation industry. Each new process had the same basic objectives: to speed production, reduce costs, and eliminate the tedium and monotony associated with many of the conventional procedures.

Following the same general pattern used for the production of motion pictures, an animated film begins with the preparation of a script. For animated cartoons as well as television commercials, the script is usually developed in the form of captions placed beneath the illustrations, which are arranged in comic-strip fashion. This storyboard serves as a guide for the production processes.

The first major step in the production of an animated cartoon is the recording of a sound track. An integral part of any motion picture, the sound track is especially important to an animated production. It gives the animator timings which indicate the number of frames allotted for a particular action within a scene or for a cartoon character's mouth movements (lip sync). In the world of fantasy that exists within the borders of the film frame, it provides the needed audio background to complement the visual effects and lends credibility to the animated-cartoon characters. Sound tracks recorded after the animation has been photographed are referred to as postsync tracks. In most instances, however, the recording of the sound track precedes any of the other production processes, not only with animated films made for entertainment purposes but also for television commercials that include animation sequences. If the recording process is to take place after the animation has been photographed (postsync), the film editor is expected to improvise and supply the animator with rough timings as a guide for the animation. A prerecorded track is preferable, however, and is used whenever possible.

In both instances the original recording on tape is transferred to film (either 35mm Magna-Stripe or 35mm magnetic full-base). The transfer of the sound track from tape to sprocketed film enables the film editor to use motion-picture equipment (moviolas, sound readers, etc.) to synchronize the sound track with the animation (on sprocketed film). The moviola is basically a projection device that allows the sound track and the picture portion of the film to be run simultaneously (to interlock). The sound reader, as the name implies, is used to reproduce and analyze the contents of the sound track. The synchronizer, in turn, is an accessory for measuring lengths of film. The results of the film editor's sound-track analysis are entered in the film's blank area alongside the magnetic stripe that carries the sound track. Words are reduced to syllables and rewritten phonetically. Accents and beats are also indicated in the clear area.

The corresponding frame and footage counts are then transferred to bar, or lead sheets. These sheets serve as a guide for every phase of production, indicating the exact frames in which actions take place, along with the timing for each word in the recorded dialogue. Timings for mouth actions, or lip sync, are particularly important, since the attention of the audience is usually focused on the cartoon character's face during exchanges of dialogue. Also included on these sheets, which are actually a visual synopsis of the entire production, are the musical beats and the specific frames in which camera effects such as zooms, fades, and cross-dissolves take place.

The animator, under the supervision of the director or layout man, does not make every drawing required for a complete action—only the key drawings, referred to as extremes. These drawings, registered on pegs in the animator's underlit drawing board, are necessary for showing the action and plotting its continuation. The animator's drawings contain spacing instructions that guide the animator's assistant (inbetweener) in preparing the inbetween drawings needed to complete the action.

When all the drawings have been completed and assembled, the action is checked. Flipping the drawings, a process similar to that used in viewing devices at amusement parks, immediately draws attention to flagrant flaws in the action. Another more accurate method for checking the fluidity of the sequence is to photograph the drawings on the animation stand (a camera suspended over a flat surface with a stop-motion motor and provision for registration pegs and underlighting). The process of photographing the animator's drawings is referred to as a pencil test. The exposed film, after processing, is viewed on a moviola. (Normally, film is processed and then printed to produce a positive image. For the pencil test, however, viewing the film negative is adequate.) If changes in the animation are necessary, the part of the action requiring correction is redrawn.

In the next phase of the production process the drawings are traced on sheets of transparent celluloid or acetate (cels) the same size as the drawing paper used by the animator. The inker traces each line

Musical backgrounds.

Backgrounds.

Job No._____ Scene No._____ Footage_____ft.____exp. Exp. Sheet #_____To #____
Animator_____ Assistant_____ Clean up O.K._____

Description_____
_____

BACKGROUND DEPT.

Still ☐   Pan moving ☐   Pan held ☐   Bkg. Used with Scs._____
To be rendered by Bkg. Dept. C. O.'s _____ Cels_____
Overlays_____ _____Underlays_____
Remarks:

TIMING DEPT.

_____
_____
                                                    Timed by:

ASSISTANT

_____
_____

INBETWEEN DEPT.

_____
_____
(To be filled in by Inbetweener) No. of dwgs. in Sc._____ Inbetweened by:

INKING DEPT.

Cels Used From Other Sc's_____
Cels Used With Other Sc's_____
Shift Charts_____Tracing Guides_____
Remarks:_____

PLANNING DEPT.

_____
_____
                                                    Planned by:

COLORING DEPT.

List cels to be drybrushed_____
List cels to be airbrushed_____
Remarks:_____
                                                    Matched by:

CAMERA DEPT.

(Timer: Check camera used)   Zoom ☐   Approach ☐
Fields used_____ Remarks:_____
Cut From Sc._____ | Cut To Sc._____ _____
☐ Ft. Diss From Sc. | ☐ Ft. Diss To Sc. | _____

Production charts accompany each scene from one department of
an animation studio to another. The information included on these
charts enables each department to function at peak efficiency.

meticulously with a crow-quill pen in either black ink or another color selected by the animator. After the inker has traced all of the drawings in the scene onto cels, the opaquer applies opaque watercolors to the reverse side of each cel in accordance with the instructions included on the model drawings. Opaque colors applied to the reverse side of the cel keep the ink lines from running or smearing and hide the crude appearance of visible brush marks. The inked and opaqued cels are in turn checked for numerical continuity and color consistency. In the last of the prefilming processes each cel is matched to doors, windows, and other props rendered on the backgrounds which are prepared by skilled artists specializing in that area of production. These prefilming checks are in effect a dry run designed to avoid subsequent retakes.

Exposure sheets, prepared by the animator, guide the cameraman during the filming process. An exposure sheet is basically a visual synopsis that includes frame-by-frame information pertinent to the scene. The animation cameraman places each of the numbered cels on the registration pegs set into the compound table of the animation stand. In some cases, as many as four or five cels are positioned over the background, which is registered on a separate set of pegs and can be moved (panned) independently. Panning instructions, along with start and stop positions for effects such as zooms, fades, or cross-dissolves, are also included on the exposure sheets. Zooms and pans must be plotted incrementally before the stop-motion filming begins. The exposed film, along with its latent images, is sent to the laboratory for processing.

PENCIL TEST CORRECTIONS

EXTREME:

No Corrections. O.K. to Clean Up ☐   Correction done ☐

CLEAN UP:

O.K. for Production ☐   Shoot new test ☐   Shoot part test ☐   Correction done ☐

2ND CLEAN UP:

O.K. for Production ☐   Shoot new test ☐   Shoot part test ☐   Correction done ☐

On the reverse side of the production chart, the director, after viewing the pencil test, makes notes regarding changes and corrections in the animation, timing, sync, etc.

Inking.

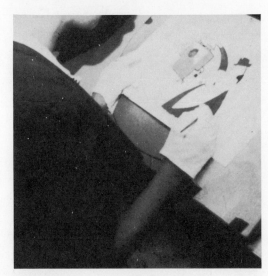

Opaquing.

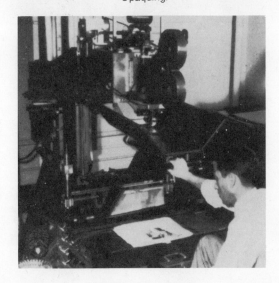

Animation photography.

If the animation is to be combined with live-action sequences, as is often the case in television-commercial production, if titles are to be superimposed, or if special illusory effects are required, the additions are produced with the optical printer. The optical printer, a projection unit which operates in synchronization with a motion-picture camera, can photograph several lengths of previously processed film simultaneously to produce a composite effect. The preliminary work (photographing the titles, mattes, etc.) needed to achieve the effect, however, is done on the animation stand.

The dailies or rushes are screened when the processed film is returned and, if no revisions are needed, the film editor synchronizes picture and sound. In the final stage of production, music and effects are mixed with the dialogue track to form a composite track, which in turn is combined with the optical negative to yield a composite print.

Although animation is a technique that is sufficient unto itself, imaginative use, especially when combined with other motion-picture techniques, makes possible a wide variety of illusory effects. These effects, in turn, become stepping-stones for the development of new techniques and additional effects. Secure and unchallenged as an entertainment medium, animation has also justified its reputation as a teacher *par excellence* and, in television, as a supersalesman.

Titles.

Moviola.

Packing release films for distribution.

Blank frame of film with sound track.

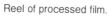

Reel of processed film.

Optical printer.

Bar Sheets

After the film editor has analyzed and timed the sound track, the animation director makes out bar sheets—a complete visual synopsis of the entire production—to be used as a guide by the animator and the film editor. Each line on a bar sheet, also referred to as a lead sheet, represents a frame of film, or a twenty-fourth of a second. Each box represents a foot of film.

Bar sheets show, in terms of single frames of film, the exact length of each syllable in each word of the dialogue in the animated portion of the commercial; they also show exactly how many frames of film a word is to occupy so that the animator can draw the action to fit.

When the animation director has accounted for the content of each frame, the bar sheets indicate the entire action described in the story board. The animator is always guided by the frame count. He cannot, for example, use 100 frames to animate a scene or action if the dialogue for that scene takes only 60 frames of film.

Sound effects, musical beats, and optical or camera effects are also indicated on the bar sheets, as are live-action sequences. However, for the live action, the director simply writes "live" on the bar sheet; obviously, no sound-track analysis is necessary for live actors.

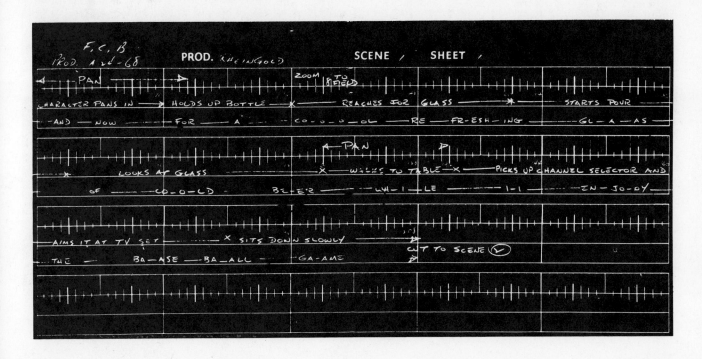

Cartoon Characters

Cartoon characters are basically caricatures of real people with whom we come in daily contact—fat people, thin people, tall people and short people, each with individual characteristics. One word suffices to cover the general categories—types.

Before attempting to interpret a character from the sound of his voice, a layout man should listen to the sound track many times—always with his eyes closed and his imagination open. This will help him to visualize and then draw a cartoon character that fits the voice on the sound track. The result will be a good combination of sight and sound.

The voice of our cartoon character, Mr. Wimple, used as the example throughout this book, is that of a well-known radio and television actor whom the animator may have seen. But if the animator drew a caricature of the actor as he really is, it would not be at all in character with Mr. Wimple, the voice the actor has projected.

It may be disillusioning but we know the owner of the Popeye voice, and he looks no more like Popeye than the average animator does. Therefore, we again strongly suggest that a sound track be listened to with closed eyes and open mind.

BASIC CONSTRUCTION

Shown here is the basic construction of Mr. Wimple, the character to be animated. The two circles used in the construction and drawing of the head can be used to draw almost any type of cartoon head for animation purposes.

When laying out or animating cartoon-character situations, an animator would do well to imagine himself as a performer acting out the same situation. An animator's cartoon characters cannot portray an emotion through facial expressions unless the animator himself is capable of portraying that emotion. Most animators keep a mirror handy to study their own expressions so that they can duplicate them when drawing cartoon characters.

Although it is generally accepted that most expressions are portrayed with the eyes and mouth, it would be unfair to minimize the variety of expression that can be achieved with the hands. Most people would be tongue-tied if asked to place their hands behind their backs while describing a spiral staircase. Try it and see. An animator should feel free to have his characters gesture with their hands while speaking. The added movement gives a feeling of freshness to animation, which might otherwise appear stiff and amateurish. Both layout man and animator should also remember that a shrug of the shoulders or a shake of the head can often accomplish more than several sentences of dialogue.   .

After completing the basic construction chart of the cartoon character to be used in a scene or picture, the layout man should indicate the colors to be used for later opaquing of the cels. The drawing containing these color markings is known as the color model. The lines separating areas to be opaqued in different colors are known as separation lines and should be closed or connected to other lines.

Construction drawings.

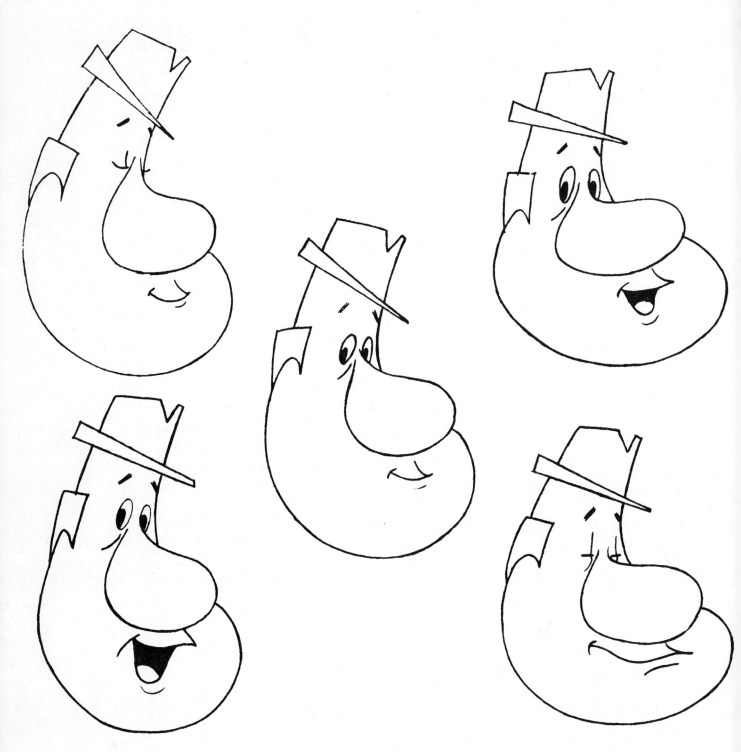

These drawings were made by the animator after he had worked out Mr. Wimple's basic characteristics. These studies of key facial expressions will be used by studio personnel as models for the commercial. The animator keeps them pinned to his wall and uses them as guides during the animation. If the commercial is the first of a series featuring the same cartoon character, photostats are made so that anyone who works on the later animation will have the same models to follow. The full-figure studies on the following page are also used as models.

These full-figure studies are also used as models.

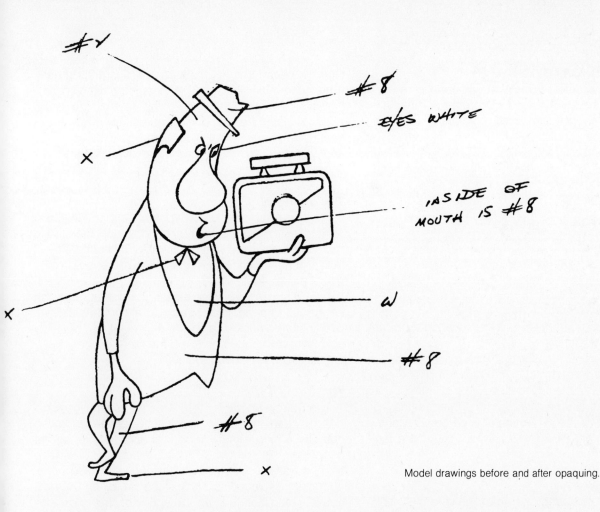

Model drawings before and after opaquing.

TYPES OF CHARACTERS

Cartoon characters usually fit into one of several basic types. The types used most often in animation are: cute, heavy or tough, screwball, and goofy. Each of these types is distinguished from the others by many individual characteristics. Beginning layout men and animators should keep the following notes handy and refer to them when designing or laying out new cartoon characters.

The Cute Type

The most important distinguishing characteristics of the cute type are the physical proportions and attitude. The proportions are similar to those of a baby. The head is large in relation to the rest of the body. The forehead is high, and the eyes are placed about halfway down the head. The ears, nose and mouth are smaller than an adult's.

A very short neck causes the head to look as though it were sitting right on top of the shoulders. The body itself is on the pear-shaped side and a bit longer than normal; the stomach bulges slightly; the arms and legs are short and rounded. The completed drawing of the cute type of character should always suggest a feeling of delicacy.

The Tough Type

The heavy or tough character, usually the villain, has many distinguishing features and characteristics that set him apart from all other types.

Built along bigger lines than other characters used in the same picture, the tough or bully type usually has a tremendous chest which tapers down to a small waist. Normal-sized feet are topped by short, heavy legs. The head and facial characteristics differ greatly from those of all other types. Although the head is comparatively small in relation to the rest of the body, heavy jowls and a jutting chin are usually quite prominent. Small ears, heavy eyebrows, small, beady eyes, and a protruding lower lip are the other facial characteristics that stand out above a heavy, thick neck.

The Screwball Type

The screwball and goofy types have many physical similarities. The main difference between them is in the body mass itself. The goofy type is shaped almost like a banana, while the screwball type is built along pear-shaped lines.

The screwball type has exaggerated features, such as a low forehead, long head and a normal-sized but overly skinny neck. Big feet and skinny legs that support the pear-shaped body are the more important distinguishing body characteristics.

The Goofy Type

The goofy character usually has a smaller-than-normal head that is angled slightly forward from the body by a long, skinny neck. His hair may or may not hang over his forehead, but his eyes almost always have a half-closed, sleepy look. An oversized nose, buck teeth, a receding chin, and a prominent Adam's apple, which bobs up and down when the character talks, complete the head and facial characteristics.

Some of the other distinguishing features are stooped shoulders, a sunken chest, long arms, big hands and a protruding waistline. Baggy pants and oversized, clumsy feet complete the picture.

Backgrounds

Backgrounds have an important function in an ani-mated cartoon made for theatrical release. Back-grounds not only serve as a setting for the action in a scene, they sometimes subtly help to put over a gag or comic situation. Painted by accomplished artists and designers, some backgrounds made for animated theatrical films could be framed and hung.

In commercial animated production, backgrounds play an entirely different part. Since the emphasis in these films is on the "sales pitch" or message, the rea-soning of the client and the ad agency is that anything on the screen not absolutely essential to the commer-cial would be distracting. Therefore, background de-tail in commercial animated films is kept to a minimum; abstract and stylized backgrounds are the rule.

The layouts on this page show how the backgrounds for an animated commercial film are developed.

Upon completing the background layouts, the lay-out man and background artist discuss and agree on the technique to be used in rendering the backgrounds.

There are two types of backgrounds: still and pan. A still background is one that remains in a fixed position during an entire scene. A pan background is one that is made to move during the photographic process. Pan

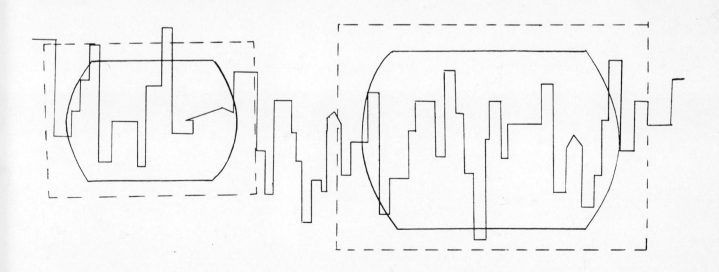

Background layouts.

backgrounds may move horizontally, vertically or diagonally, depending on the action and general movement of the character being animated.

Inasmuch as the story board showed the cartoon character, Mr. Wimple, walking in the opening scene, the animation director and the layout man decided that an abstract, pan background was desirable. To give some interest and movement to the background, they added the soft silhouette of a city skyline, with the buildings placed far enough back to eliminate any problems in perspective.

Another background was needed for the close-up scenes in the production. For these scenes, the background artist was asked to make a solid-tone, still background, consistent with the building colors used in the pan background.

Pictured here are two frames showing how the cartoon character looks against the pan and still backgrounds in the completed film.

The Exposure Sheet

The ledger-like sheets reproduced on these pages are known in the animation industry as exposure or *X* sheets. Like bar sheets, exposure sheets account for every frame of animation in a commercial. Both are used as a guide during the production processes; but the bar sheets are used by the animation director, film editor and animator, while the exposure sheets are used by the inbetweener, inker, colorer, planner, checker and cameraman. The animation director makes out the bar sheets before production begins, whereas the animator makes out the exposure sheets as he animates. The bar sheets remain in the anima-tion director's possession at all times during the production of the commercial, but the exposure sheets go with the scene as it progresses from one department to the next.

Exposure sheets contain information and instructions required for each production process that follows animation. The sheets indicate the exact order in which the cels are to be photographed by the cameraman; they also include a description of the sound and the action taking place, as well as background notes, camera instructions, and other general information pertaining to the scene.

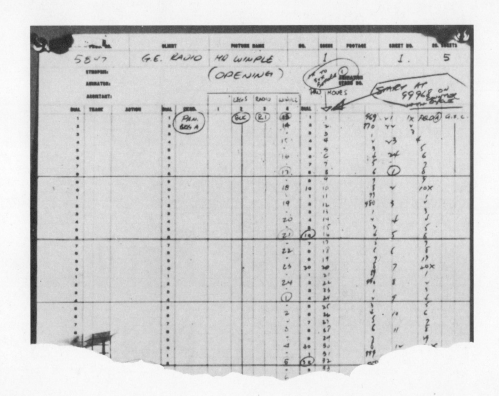

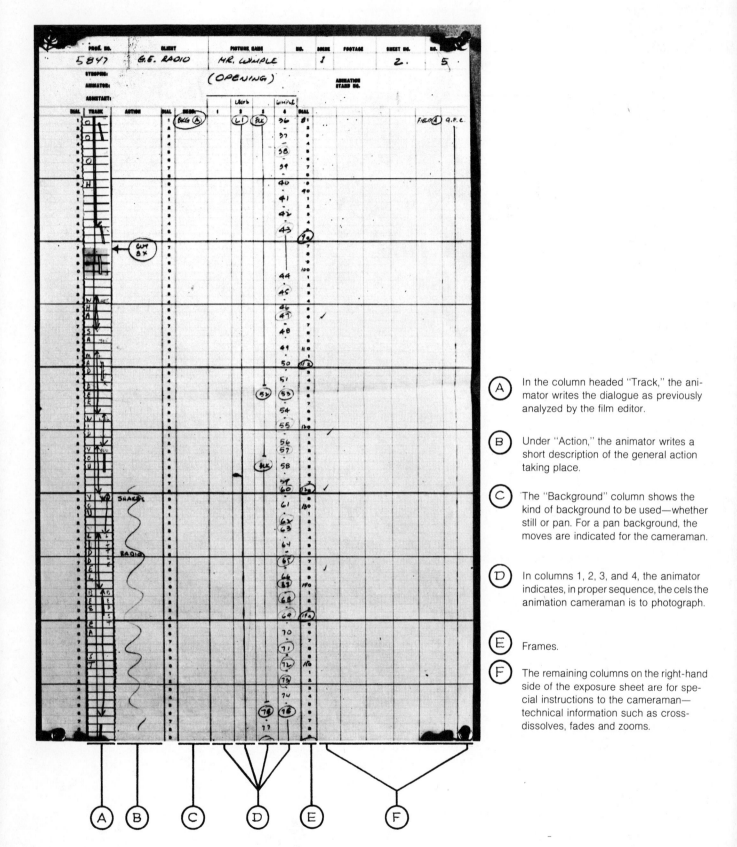

(A) In the column headed "Track," the animator writes the dialogue as previously analyzed by the film editor.

(B) Under "Action," the animator writes a short description of the general action taking place.

(C) The "Background" column shows the kind of background to be used—whether still or pan. For a pan background, the moves are indicated for the cameraman.

(D) In columns 1, 2, 3, and 4, the animator indicates, in proper sequence, the cels the animation cameraman is to photograph.

(E) Frames.

(F) The remaining columns on the right-hand side of the exposure sheet are for special instructions to the cameraman—technical information such as cross-dissolves, fades and zooms.

CEL LEVELS

The number of cel levels (the number of separate drawings to be photographed at the same time) used over the background must be consistent throughout a scene. This is the only way to ensure uniform density over the background of the scene. If this were not done and some frames in a scene were photographed with, for instance, two cel levels over the background, and others with three or more levels, the result would be flickering on the screen.

In order to avoid such an undesirable effect, a scene that has a maximum of three cel levels, for example, must have three cel levels over the background for each frame of the scene during the photographic process. It is the animator's responsibility to instruct the camera department, through his notes on the exposure sheets, where additional cels must be added. He does this by first recording on the exposure sheets all of the cels to be used in the scene. Then, if he finds the number of cels used over the background inconsistent, he indicates on the exposure sheets where blank cels must be added.

It is the maximum number of cels over the background at *any* point in the scene that establishes the cel level to be used for the whole scene. When the animator finds he has four levels exposed as the maximum at any point in a scene, that scene becomes a four-level scene. This same rule applies to one- two- and three-level scenes.

Five-level scenes, or anything over that number, should be avoided if possible. Although the cels or acetates used are completely transparent and only .005 of an inch thick, each cel used over a background will tone it down somewhat. Five cel levels will gray a background down considerably.

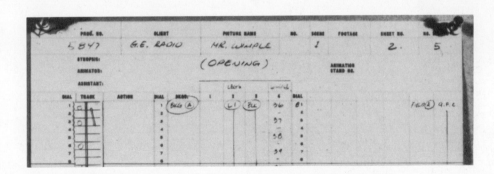

Section of an exposure sheet for a three-level scene. A blank cel has been inserted in column 3 to keep the number of cel levels in the scene consistent.

EXPOSURE NUMBERS

The animator should number all drawings used in a scene as simply as possible. Obviously, the number assigned to a particular drawing on animation paper should also be used for the cel on which the drawing is traced.

If more than one cel level is animated in a scene, each level should be numbered differently. A good system for identifying cel levels is to use numerals only—1, 2, etc.—for the first cel level; a number and an alphabet letter—1A, 2A, etc.—for the second level; and for each additional level use a different letter. For example, the third level would be identified as 1B, 2B, etc. and the fourth as 1C, 2C and so on.

Mixing numbers in an animation sequence can only cause great confusion, a needless waste of time and the likelihood of errors.

ONES, TWOS AND THREES

Because of the differences in the comparative speeds of certain actions or movements, animation is drawn to be exposed on either ones, twos or threes. This refers to the number of times each drawing in an action is photographed. A drawing that is exposed on threes, for instance, is photographed three times, that is, the same drawing is repeated on three consecutive frames of film. When an action is drawn to be exposed on ones, that means there is a different drawing for each successive frame; if drawn to be exposed on twos, there is a different drawing for every second frame only.

Obviously then, only half as many drawings are required for an action animated on twos as are necessary for a similar action animated on ones. Since most animated action on twos will be just as smooth as a similar action on ones, almost all animated action should be planned for exposure on twos.

Exposure sheet on which each cel level is identified by a different letter: the ideal procedure recommended by the author.

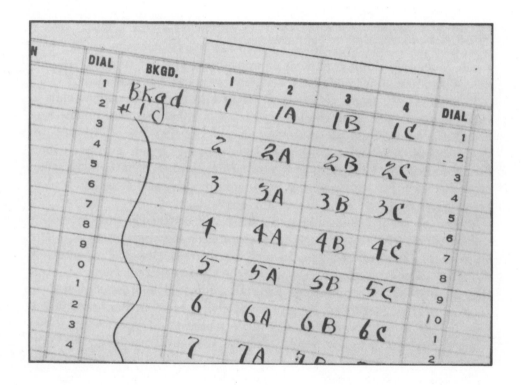

However, there are some instances when animation on twos is not preferable. When the action is fast and the drawings do not overlap, as in violent or widely spaced animation, the action should be planned for exposure on ones. When a cartoon character or object comes in contact with a pan background that is moving on ones—one frame for each background move—the animator should plan the action for exposure on ones also.

If, however, the character or object being animated is not making contact with anything specific on the background, the animation may be on twos, even if the background pan is moving on ones. An illustration of this occurs in the opening action of the commercial serving as our example. Since the character, Mr. Wimple, is in the foreground and no definite relationship exists between his walk and the movement of the pan background, he is animated on twos, while the background moves on ones.

When the scene being animated calls for an extremely slow or closely spaced action with very little movement between drawings, it is possible to animate for exposure on threes. In such cases, the thickness of a pencil line should be the maximum space separating the inbetweener's drawings. Closely spaced drawings must be very carefully animated and inbetweened to avoid a jiggling motion of the closely placed lines when the animation is seen on the screen. No action should be planned for exposure on threes when the background panning or any other camera movement is required during the action.

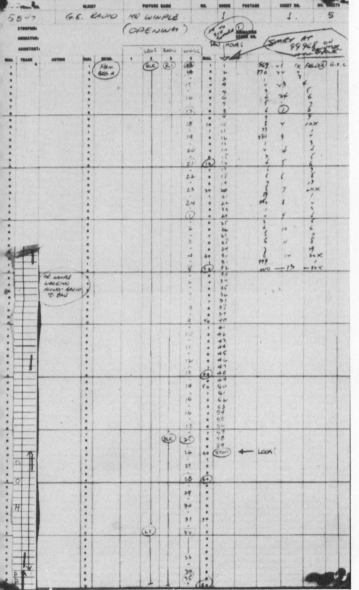

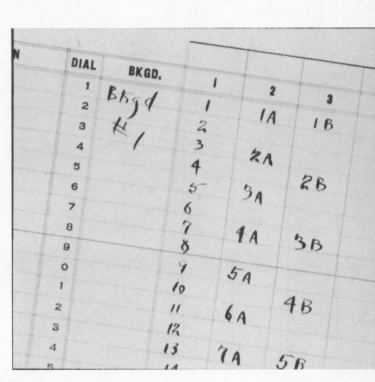

Exposure sheet showing Mr. Wimple being animated on twos while the background moves on ones.

Exposure sheet showing one cel level moving on ones, another on twos, and a third on threes.

THE HOLD CEL

The use of the hold cel, a cell that is held still for several frames during some portion of an animated sequence, is one of the most effective means of avoiding unnecessary inking and coloring. A hold cel is made when, during the course of an animated action, the character's movement is brought to a complete or partial stop for any length of time.

Imagine, for example, an animated sequence in which a cartoon character stands still while speaking. In such a case, the animator can make a separate drawing of the head and body of the character and indicate on the exposure sheet that it is to be held for the length of time the character remains in the still position. Then the animator need only draw each new mouth action instead of the full head and figure. And later, the inker and colorer will have only one cel of the head and body to trace and color instead of the great number that would be required if the inker had to keep retracing the head and body for each new mouth action.

Hold cels can be used in many situations. In the accompanying illustration, the drawings of Mr. Wimple's arms and body have been held while the head continues to be animated.

Not only do hold cels save work, but the results obtained through their use are infinitely better than those achieved through retracings or tracebacks, as the danger of jiggling ink lines, which might result from continual retracing, is completely eliminated. A great work-and-time-saver, the hold cel should be used wherever possible.

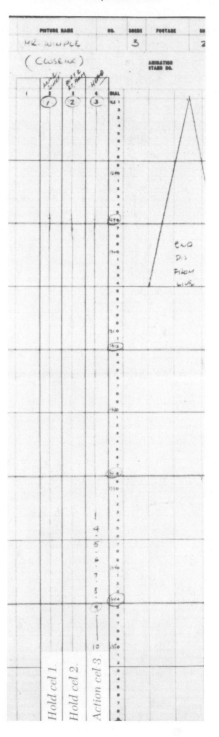

Section of exposure sheet.

34

Hold cel 1.

Hold cel 2.

Action cel 3.

The three cels placed in position over the background, as they will appear on the finished film.

Animation

An animator's value to a studio largely depends upon how well he knows all phases of animation, for he can only take full advantage of all established short cuts if he has sound all-round knowledge of animation studio procedures.

Some of the most frequently used time and labor savers include the clever use of repeat actions, the use of animation on twos whenever possible, combining drawings for the purpose of reducing the number of cel levels, and the elimination of unnecessary retracing through the use of hold cels.

By taking advantage of such short cuts and other efficient methods, the animator will not only save considerable time of his own but also help cut the studio's production costs.

THE ANIMATION BOARD

The animation board differs from other drawing boards in two ways: 1) provision is made for the registration of drawings through the use of pegs; 2) the center portion is made of glass and is lighted from underneath.

The animation boards shown here have two sets of pegs, one set at the top and the other at the bottom. With this arrangement, it is possible to animate on either set of pegs and still have another on which to register a background or other drawing that is to move independently.

The peg arrangement ensures a great degree of registration accuracy for the studio worker, but those working at home can achieve positive registration through the use of crosses and circles. This method is widely used throughout the advertising and printing fields.

Some animation boards are on a swivel so that they can be turned in any direction. The swivel animation board is usually used only by the inker for whom it was originally designed in order to make it easier to trace certain types of lines, such as circles or arcs.

An animation board on a swivel. The sheet of animation paper, placed over the glass section, is held in position by the pegs.

Close-up of another animation board. The metal plate above the top pegs keeps several sheets of animation paper flat.

Exposure sheet showing how the action of the pendulum could be continued indefinitely by repeated photographing of the five drawings.

EXTREMES

An extreme is a key drawing made by an animator. Key drawings do not usually make up an entire action, but they are sufficient to guide the inbetweener from one position of the character or object being animated to another. Other extreme drawings continue the action from the point of the last extreme drawing.

The illustrations show both extreme and inbetween drawings; they also show the spacing guides the animator places on his extreme drawings for the inbetweener to follow. These two illustrations apply to the animation of cartoon characters as well as to objects.

In example A, let us imagine the swinging of a clock pendulum as the action being animated. Normally, in any animated scene, each of these positions would be a separate drawing on a separate sheet of animation paper. Here, however, we have combined them in one illustration for clarity and ease in identification.

Drawings 1 and 5 are the extreme drawings made by the animator. Notice that on the spacing guide he has called for evenly spaced movements. The inbetweener is then responsible for making drawings 2, 3 and 4 exactly as shown in example A.

In example B, drawings 1 and 5 are again the extremes. This time, however, the animator wishes to slow the action of the pendulum as it reaches the end of its arc. In his spacing guide, he has indicated exactly the amount of slowdown he desires. Here, too, drawings 2, 3 and 4 are the inbetween drawings. Notice, however, the difference in spacing from example A. When the animator wants the spacing of the drawings for an action to change, such spacing notes are indicated on the last extreme drawing before the change in spacing is to occur.

Should the animator wish to continue the swinging action of the pendulum for a required film length, he would simply indicate the numbers of the drawings on the exposure sheet. No new drawings would have to be made. For instance, if the action starts with the pendulum at one end of the arc, as in example A, the first drawing exposed is number 1. The animator would then write numbers 2, 3, 4 and 5 in that order on the exposure sheet. Having reached the other end of the arc, the animator would continue with drawings 4, 3, 2 and back to number 1. Then he could start the whole process over again. Thus, by using only five drawings, the animator could continue the cycle of action indefinitely.

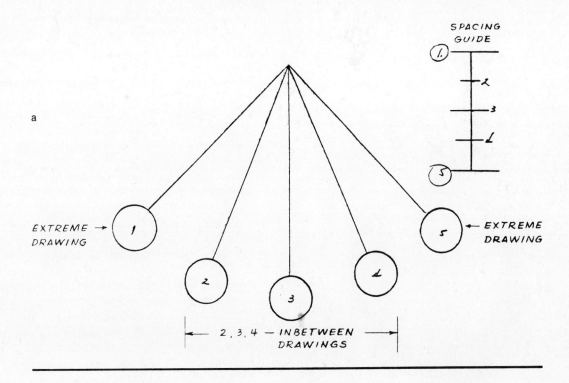

a

EXTREME → DRAWING

EXTREME DRAWING

SPACING GUIDE

2, 3, 4 — INBETWEEN DRAWINGS

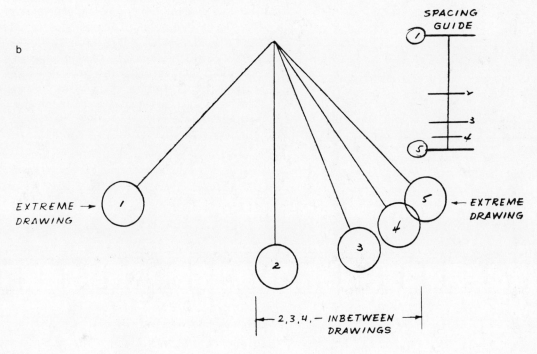

b

EXTREME → DRAWING

EXTREME DRAWING

SPACING GUIDE

2, 3, 4, — INBETWEEN DRAWINGS

TIMING

Correct timing is of the utmost importance. The animator must keep in mind that an animated action should take the same amount of time the same action would take if it were done live.

For example, if a live performer lifts a heavy object, he must expend considerable energy. His movements are relatively slow as compared to other actions requiring less effort. If this same action is animated, the animated character's movements must also be relatively slow.

The exact film length of most actions to be animated is determined by the film editor's analysis of the sound track. By referring to the animation director's bar sheets, which have the action broken down into the exact number of frames required, the animator can see the exact film length and the time allotted to any particular scene or action.

However, sometimes it is necessary for the animator to determine the length of an animated sequence for which there is no sound-track analysis. At such times, the best results can be obtained through the use of a specially made stop watch that shows time in seconds and corresponding film footages.

For accuracy, the animator should clock an action several times and then use the over-all average as the timing for that action. The animator, for instance, may get a reading of six seconds on the first timing, seven seconds on the next, and six and one-half seconds on the third. In this case, the animator should plan the action to the average, or the six-and-one-half second timing. (See the timing table in the section on Lip Synchronization.)

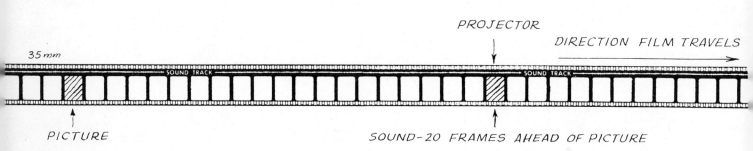

PROJECTOR

DIRECTION FILM TRAVELS

35 mm

SOUND TRACK — SOUND TRACK

PICTURE

SOUND–20 FRAMES AHEAD OF PICTURE

The term *advance* refers to the number of frames of film between any specific point in the sound track and the corresponding picture portion. In the 35mm. composite print, the sound track precedes the corresponding picture information by 20 frames. The sound track advance in the 16mm. composite print is 26 frames. The advance is necessary because the projection gate through which the picture information passes is ahead of the gate through which the sound track is scanned by the exciter lamp. The exciter lamp converts the sound track's modulations or light waves into sound waves and, subsequently, into audible sound. The advance places the picture and sound track in their respective gates in the projection equipment at the same instant.

Singing or dialogue should never begin on a scene's first frame of animation. The first sound must be spaced so that it is not heard until at least the sixth frame. If the scene is the first one on a reel of film, this spacing is achieved by starting the sound track on the leader strip which always precedes the first frame of a reel.

THE BEAT

A beat, as used in animation, refers to the audible or visual marking of a specific interval or period of time. Beat is used to mean both the musical beat or tempo and the breakdown of that tempo into taps. A 24 beat would mean one tap for each second, or every 24 frames of film.

If no musical background accompanies an animated scene and the sound track is clear, a beat should be established by the animator and used as the rhythmic basis for the animated action. Should the animator decide to plan his action to a 12 beat, that would be the equivalent of two taps for every 24 frames of film or two taps per second.

As the scene or picture progresses, the beat should be quickened to 11, or slightly more than two taps per second, then to ten, and finally to a nine beat or almost three taps per second. An action does not usually become so fast or violent that it becomes necessary to animate to anything faster than a nine beat. But if an exceptionally fast action is called for, an animator can use an eight or even a seven beat, but practically never any beat faster than a seven. The seven beat might be used for such animated actions as chases, runaway horses, imminent collisions, or other actions leading to the climax of a scene.

If, when timing with a stop watch, the animator should have difficulty in breaking a beat down into taps, the following method may be used with fairly accurate results. If one tap to a beat is the required timing, the animator should say the word "one." For two taps to a beat, a two-syllable word, like "seven," should be used, with one tap for each syllable of the word. For three taps to the beat, the animator should use the word "animate," and for four taps to the beat, the word "animation," in each case he should tap once for each syllable of the word.

FIRST FRAME
OF ANIMATION

35mm

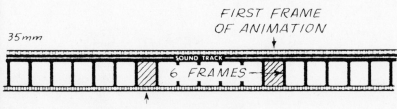

SOUND —
14 FRAMES OF LEADER FOOTAGE →

FIRST FRAME OF PICTURE
WITH WHICH SOUND IS HEARD

LIP SYNCHRONIZATION

Lip sync, or mouth action, is as important in animation as the basic accompanying action itself. The rules governing the animation of mouth actions are few and simple; and the simpler the animation of mouth actions, the better the results.

It is not necessary to put each vowel or consonant into lip-sync animation. In fact, it is almost impossible to animate an action for each syllable in a sentence, and it should not be attempted. The result of such an attempt would only be a meaningless pile of animated drawings and much wasted effort.

The animator must first absorb the over-all feeling of the dialogue before he can decide which words, syllables or sounds should be accented and emphasized. If the animator looks at himself in a mirror while repeating the recorded dialogue, it will help him to select and later to draw appropriate facial expressions for complete sentences. Having made his decisions, the animator's next step is to roughly pencil in the key positions for the mouth actions to be accented. The inbetween drawings will usually carry the balance of the animated dialogue.

When a cartoon character is being animated on twos, it is not necessary to draw the mouth actions on ones unless the character is speaking rapidly. Mouth actions can work as well on twos as they do on ones if the animator accents and emphasizes the right words.

The mouth actions shown here are the ones used most frequently in animated cartoon dialogue. Each group of mouth actions shows: 1) the start of the formation of a sound, 2) the position of the mouth during the actual pronunciation of the sound, and 3) the closed-mouth position that follows. The vowels are shown in the first five groupings. These mouth actions are slightly less exaggerated for singing.

Surveys have shown that dialogue spoken during a television commercial must be considerably slower than dialogue spoken in a radio broadcast. In television viewing, both the eye and ear work at the same time, so the efficiency of one or the other may be considerably lessened.

Therefore, the table given here should be followed diligently when timing unrecorded dialogue. The right-hand column gives the maximum number of words that should be used in the time shown in the left-hand column.

MAXIMUM WORDS IN A GIVEN TIME PERIOD

Time	Maximum Words
½ second	1
1 second	2
2 seconds	4
3 seconds	7
4 seconds	9
5 seconds	11
6 seconds	13
7 seconds	16
8 seconds	18
9 seconds	20
10 seconds	22
15 seconds	33
20 seconds	44
25 seconds	55
30 seconds	65
35 seconds	77
40 seconds	88
45 seconds	99
50 seconds	110
55 seconds	120
1 minute	130
1½ minutes	195
2 minutes	260
3 minutes	390
4 minutes	520
5 minutes	650
10 minutes	1,300
20 minutes	2,600
30 minutes	3,900
40 minutes	5,200
50 minutes	6,500

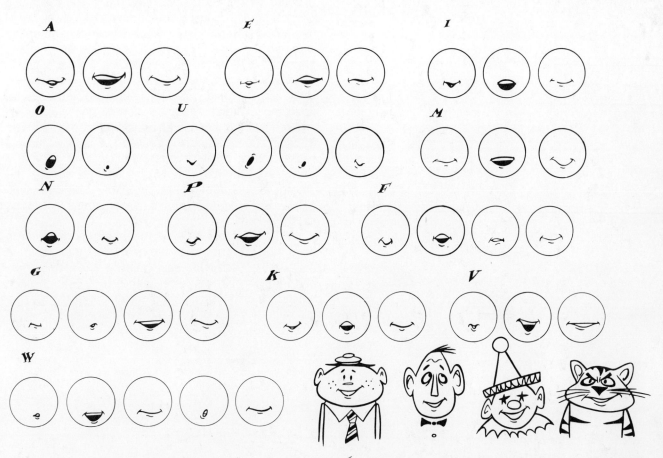

SAME MOUTH ACTIONS CAN FIT DIFFERENT TYPE HEADS

mouth action	also used for
a	r
e	c
i	l
o	y
u	q
f	s
g	t, z
k	d, h, x
m	—
n	—
p	b, j
v	—
w	—

ACCENT AND ANTICIPATION

When an animator is working on a scene that has a musical background, he should be constantly aware of beats and accents. The best way to accent an action is to use a change of pace. If, for example, an animated character is running to a definite beat, but the action is all evenly spaced, there will be no accented position. However, a change of pace, either slowing down or speeding up the character's action will not only emphasize the beat but provide an anticipatory action as well. Speeding up the animation between accents will have a similar effect. In either case, a change of pace is a necessity; and the greater the desired accent, the greater the change of pace should be. This basic rule can be applied to almost all animated action, including mouth actions.

Here are some other good rules for the animator to keep in mind. The faster the beat, the more accurate the hit or accent must be. Accuracy is especially important if the beat is faster than a nine beat. In such cases, the hit must occur exactly on the frame with the tap. Where a slower beat is used, such as a 12 or 16

ANTICIPATION

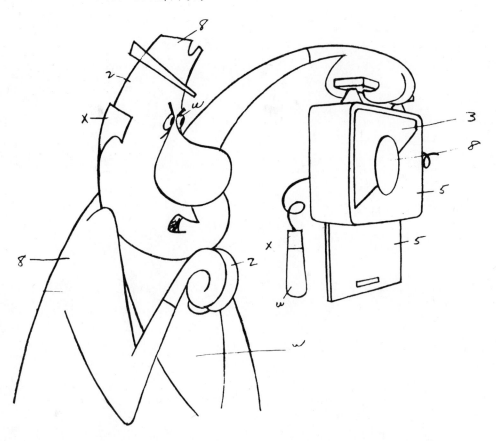

beat, the accented action may hit two frames before the frame of the tap. These rules also hold true when an animated action is being timed to a sound effect rather than a musical beat.

An accented pose becomes much more emphatic when it is preceded by a preparatory action: an anticipation. Anticipation plays a very important part in animation. The holding of a static pose before an animated action begins can be called an anticipation. A slower action preceding or leading up to the action to be accented is also an anticipation. The take, described in the next section, is a wonderful example of anticipation and accent because it takes full advantage of the principles described here.

An accent becomes more emphatic as the time gap between it and the anticipatory action increases. The greater the number of frames between the two, the greater the impact of the accent. The number of frames between the anticipation and the accent will, of course, depend on the previously determined film length of the over-all action as recorded on the sound track.

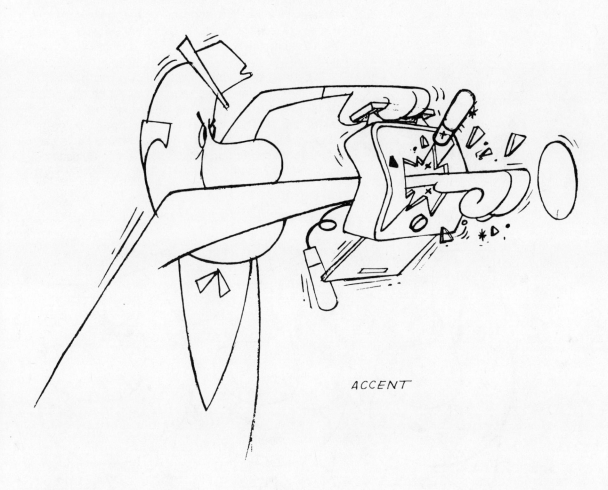

ACCENT

TAKES

The cartoon take, a reaction indicating an element of surprise, is probably one of the most frequently used actions in animation and one of the most important. There are several types: subdued takes, violent takes and double takes. Each has its definite place and function.

A cartoon character might react in any number of ways during a take. The reaction might be only in his facial expression. Or, at the other extreme, in violent takes, the cartoon character might fly up in the air, stagger, fall backwards or "freeze" completely. In each of these takes, a good anticipatory action helps to accent the take itself.

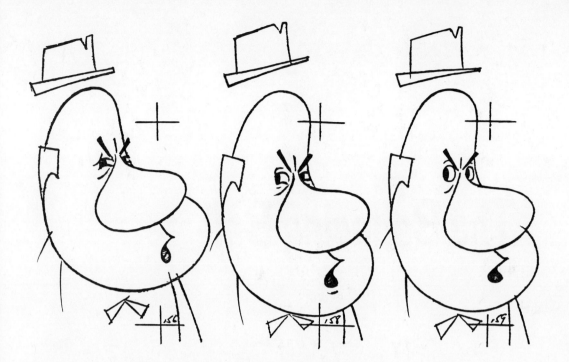

On these pages are drawings which illustrate a double take. Only the animator's extreme poses have been selected to show the sequence of action. A double take is used more often than any other take. It occurs when a cartoon character first reacts mildly to something he has seen or heard; then, with fuller realization of the cause of the initial reaction, the character reacts a second time, this time more violently. This violent reaction causes the first take to become an anticipation, a build-up for the more accented movement, and the over-all action is thereby given more emphasis than could be obtained through the use of a single take.

The Bouncing Ball

The bouncing of a ball can serve as an example for many of the principles used in animation.

A bouncing ball follows a definite arc or line of action, which is influenced by the laws of gravity. We know, for instance, that when a person jumps either horizontally or vertically, it is only a matter of time before he is back on the ground, no matter how high the jump. And while the person is in the process of jumping, certain movements occur. Although some of these movements may be classified as illusions, slow-motion studies show that these "illusions" often have substance in reality.

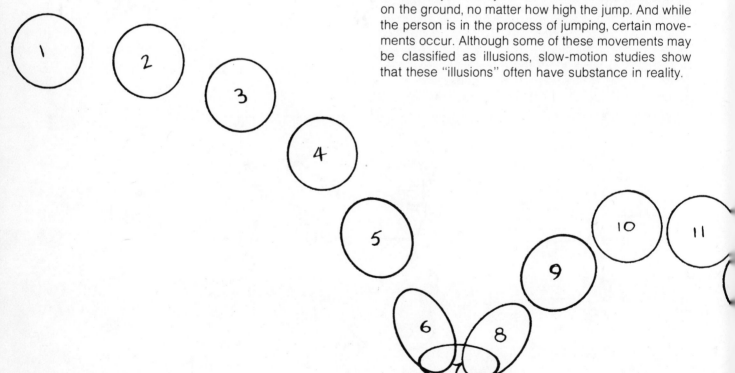

If an animated cartoon character is to look believable, these same movements must occur. However, in animation, these movements are often exaggerated. For instance, when a cartoon character jumps, the entire body mass seems to stretch out, so that it is similar to the bouncing ball action in positions 8, 9, 15, 16, 21, and 25 in the illustration. The recoil of the jumping action is similar to the shape of the ball in positions 5, 6, 12, 13, 18, 19 and 23. The cartoon character then assumes normal proportions once again, as in positions 1, 2, 3, 4, 10, 11, 17, 22, 26 and 27, the positions at the top of the bounce. Notice that in positions 7, 14, 20 and 24, the ball has been flattened or squashed by its contact with the ground. This is the hit position.

While the ball's bouncing has been drawn as a smooth, continuous action for the purpose of illustrating the above paragraph, the timing of the ball in mid-air also helps to explain another principle that is important in bringing realism to animation. The ball does not move at a constant speed throughout its bounce action. The ball moves faster coming down than while going up to the top of the arc. Having reached the top of the arc, the ball slows down considerably, just as it does at the bottom of the arc in its flattened out or hit position.

Proper timing, and flattened out and elongated positions—squash and stretch—can make the difference between smooth, realistic action and stiff, amateurish-looking movement. Therefore, their proper use is one of the most important aspects of good animation.

A spacing chart or action path can be an invaluable guide in animation. Plotting the general movement of the animation should be done at every opportunity. Combining the arc or path of action with lines showing the exact spacing of the object or figure being animated will help to achieve a smoother animated action.

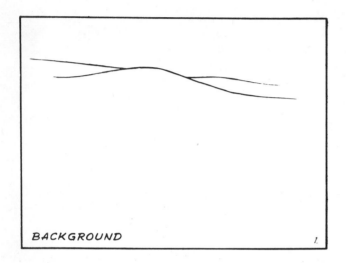

BACKGROUND   1.

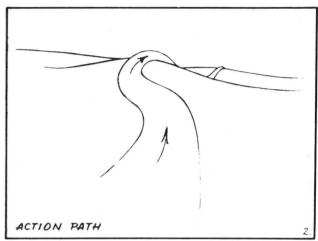

ACTION PATH   2.

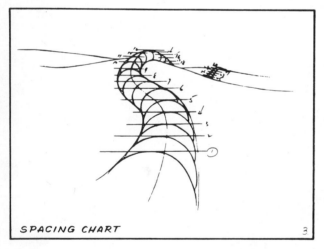

SPACING CHART   3.

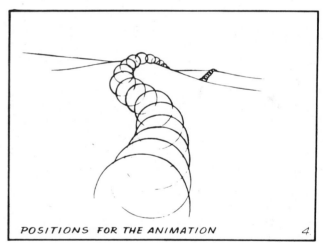

POSITIONS FOR THE ANIMATION   4.

SQUASH AND STRETCH

An animated cartoon character's head and body are built around masses of circles and ovals. Exaggeration of these masses so that they squash or stretch can help give added expression to the face and figure. However, when an animator uses squash and stretch, he should remember to visualize all of the forms or masses as solids with normal dimensions.

Illustrated here is a good example of squash and stretch elasticity in a cartoon character. Notice that the basic construction of the character has been exaggerated so as to achieve greater facial expression but the character's identity has been maintained.

Movement Cycles

HOOK-UP

WALK

STRUT

RUN

HIT POSITION

The figures shown here represent the movement cycles used most often in animation: the walk, the strut and the run.

Over the first and last drawings of each cycle are the words *hook-up*. The term hook-up is used in animation to indicate that the first and last drawings in a cycle are the same and interchangeable. By repeating an entire cycle of drawings, an action can be used over and over for as much film footage as may be required in a scene or action.

The figures at the beginning and end of each cycle are in hit positions, the positions in which the foot makes solid contact with the ground. The animator should draw these positions first since they are the ones that eventually become the key drawings in the action being animated.

An important rule to follow in animating any movement cycle is that *the slower the movement of the character being animated*, *the more upright his position should be.* For instance, a walk is always slower than a run; in a walk, the body may lean forward in the direction the character is facing, but the character is still relatively upright as compared to one who is running.

In any movement cycle, except an extremely fast run, the arms always move in the opposite direction to that of the legs. In other words, when the right leg is in a forward position, the right arm is back and vice versa. The faster the action, the more violent the movement of the arms, but the arms continue to move in opposition to the direction of the legs.

HOOK-UP

HIT POSITION

traveling peg bar
controls and counters

zoom counter

platen

Compound tables are assembled to meet the specifications of the
user with as few as one and as many as six traveling peg bars.
All peg bars have hand cranks and counters that register in hun-
dredths of an inch.

For an extremely fast run, however, the rule governing arm movement in relation to leg movement *does not* follow. Since the action of the arms would be so fast as to be confusing, it has been established, after a great deal of testing, that the best procedure to follow in animating arm action for extremely fast runs is to place both arms extended forward in a reaching position and to keep them that way.

When planning a walk to a musical accompaniment, the animator should avoid having the character's heel come down on the beat. The action will always look better if the hit comes on the flat-footed position.

In any movement cycle, the cartoon character always faces in the direction opposite to the one in which the background is moving. When two or more characters are walking or running in a scene and each of the characters is on a separate cel level, the animator should continually check their actions and positions in relation to each other as well as to the background. This kind of checking also enables the animator to match the characters to any objects or props on the background.

SLIDING CELS

The dimensions of the standard cels used in most animation studios is 10½ by 13 inches, or slightly larger than the dimensions of the 12 field. Sliding cels are similar to these standard-size cels in many ways.

The length of a movement cycle is determined by the "beat" on the accompanying sound track. If a cycle is to be photographed on twos, or two frames for each of the inked and opaqued cels, a 12-drawing cycle is used with a 24 beat. A 24 beat is slow and indicates that there is only one beat for each second of projection time. A 16 beat exposed on twos would, therefore, require eight drawings and a 12 beat, only six drawings.

Each of the seven positions of a movement cycle is shown here. Used in a theatrical animated cartoon, the cycle was drawn for a 14 beat. During the photographic process, drawing 1 follows drawing 7 and makes possible the repetition of the cycle.

They have the same thickness, .0005 of an inch, and the same degree of transparency. They differ only in length and general usage. The width of the sliding cel is the same as the width of the standard-size cel and fits between the top and bottom peg bars of the compound table. When a cel is registered to the top peg bar, for example, it does not interfere with the positioning of other cels on the bottom pegs or the independent movement of either peg bar. The length of the sliding cel, however, varies considerably depending on the use for which it is intended.

REPEAT ACTIONS AND MOVEMENT CYCLES

The panning of repeat actions and movement cycles, registered to the traveling peg bars, is one of the more important functions of the sliding cel. When animating a walk, run, or other repeat action, the animator draws only one complete cycle of the action. The first and last drawings of the movement cycle or repeat action are known as hook-up positions. If seven drawings are needed for the animation of a complete cycle, for example, the last drawing (7) acts as a transition for the repeat of the cycle and makes possible the subsequent continuation of the action during the photographic process.

A completely different relationship exists between the background and a movement cycle that is inked and opaqued on normal size cels and the same cycle on sliding cels. When a movement cycle animates in one position or specific area in relation to the field, the illusion of movement is achieved by panning the background. The drawings for the cycle animating in place are inked and opaqued on standard-size cels and the pan background is moved in the direction opposite to the one in which the cartoon character is facing. By repeating the movement cycle, the action can be photographed for the film footage specified on the exposure sheets, or indefinitely for that matter.

Where it is necessary to show a cartoon character moving or panning into or through a scene, however, the movement cycle is inked and opaqued on sliding cels that are registered to the traveling peg bars.

The background in such cases remains in a stationary position throughout the panning action of the sliding cels. The illusion of movement is achieved by panning the traveling peg bars on which the movement cycle is registered. By photographing each of the sliding cels in sequence and advancing the peg tracks for each frame according to the instructions on the exposure sheets, the cartoon character appears to be gradually moving into or through the scene. No additional drawings are needed for the panning movement other than those used to animate the character in place. It is not necessary to animate the complete movement from one side of the frame to the other as the character passes through the scene. A full field of blank cel area on either side of the inked and opaqued cartoon character keeps the number of cel levels over the background consistent and eliminates the need for exposing blank cels at the beginning and end of the panning action.

To summarize briefly, movement cycles that animate in place are inked and opaqued on standard-size cels and are used with panning backgrounds. The same cycles, moving into or through a scene, are inked and opaqued on sliding cels and used with still backgrounds. Although variations may sometimes occur, they would be considered the exception rather than the rule.

DIAL	BKGD.	
1		①
2		2
3		3
4		4
5		5
6		6
7		7
8		①
9		2
1 0		3
1		4
2		5
3		6
4		7
5		①
6		2
7		3
8		4
9		5

A seven-drawing repeat cycle is exposed on ones in this illustration. The hook-up drawings are encircled.

DIAL	BKGD.	
1		①
2		2
3		
4		
5		3
6		
7		4
8		
9		5
1 0		
1		6
2		
3		7
4		
5		①
6		
7		2
8		
9		3

The same seven-drawing repeat cycle in this illustration is exposed on twos. Here again, the hook-up drawings are encircled.

The inking instructions for movement cycles are usually indicated in the hook-up drawing.

The animation cameraman is shown placing one of the sliding cels on the traveling pegs. Note the length of the sliding cel.

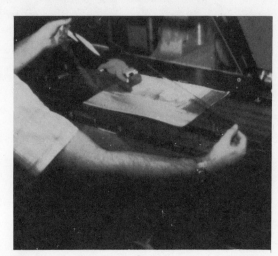

The animation on the sliding cel in this photograph has been panned across the stationary background and is moving out of the scene. Here again, the blank area of the sliding cel eliminates the need for exposing a separate blank cel in order to maintain a consistent density over the background during the panning.

Although sliding cels are generally used for panning a repeat action into or out of a scene, the sliding cels used in this scene were photographed in a normal center peg position. Previously used in another scene from the same picture, the sliding cels remained in a hold position while a pan background created the illusion of movement.

SLIDING CELS AND THE BOUNCING BALL

In the 1920's, B. S. C. (Before Sliding Cels), the bouncing ball that was used in community-sing animated cartoons was actually a white paper disc glued to a stick which was painted black in order to blend with the background. The words of the song were painted white on a long piece of black cardboard attached to a drum-like mechanism. This mechanism was turned by hand to reveal two lines of the song at a time. Another person raised and lowered the white paper disc in sync with the piano's tinkling notes while the camera, mounted on a tripod, ran continuously. The animation, used as the background for the song's lyrics, was photographed separately and both pieces of film were later combined optically. The entire process, popularized by the Max Fleischer studios, was truly fascinating but, nevertheless, crude when compared with methods used today for achieving similar effects. But, that was the way the ball bounced in the days before sliding cels and traveling peg bars.

With today's techniques, the same effect can be achieved with a half-dozen sliding cels registered to the traveling peg bars. The background, animation, and the titles are all photographed with the bouncing ball action. The elimination of the "double run" and opticals not only saves a great deal of time but automatically reduces the possibility of errors during the photographic process.

In the days of vests and celluloid collars, the bouncing ball "sing-along" cartoons were quite popular with movie-goers. This photograph shows the actual production process for the lyrics and bouncing ball action. While fashions have changed the ball is still bouncing today, although the early production methods have been replaced by sliding cels and modern production methods.

The layout for the bouncing ball animation is registered to the bottom traveling peg bar. Each of the six positions for the bounce action is inked on a separate sliding cel, approximately 40 inches in length. The guide for panning the six sliding cels is registered to the bottom traveling peg bar.

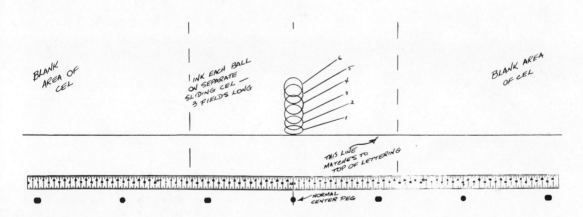

The vertical movement of the bounce action is achieved by inking and opaquing each of the balls in a slightly higher position on the cels in relation to the lettering.

In the lowest or hit position, the ball is oval shaped or flattened out slightly in order to give a feeling of solidity and to help add realism to the over-all bounce. The horizontal movement for the bouncing ball, as it moves from one syllable to another, is achieved by panning the traveling peg bars. By photographing these sliding cels in the sequence indicated on the exposure sheets and panning the traveling peg bars and the sliding cels for each frame, the ball can be made to arc in moving from one syllable to the next. When the end of a line is reached, the ball is returned to its starting position in one graceful arc before beginning the bounce action over the next line of the song.

By using the film editor's analysis of each syllable of the song on the recorded sound track, the animator and animation cameraman can accomplish in hours the filming process that took days with the old method.

These examples show the versatility of the sliding cel and the traveling peg bars. The many other uses for the sliding cel cannot all be included here. Many of the time saving techniques used in animation today are possible only because of the sliding cel registered to the traveling peg bars.

The floating peg unit consists of a set of three standard pegs mounted on a flat metal plate. Unlike the sliding peg bars built into the compound table, the floating peg unit remains in a fixed position, completely independent of table movements. This unit makes possible the movement of cels and subject matter positioned on the compound table, while other cels registered to the floating pegs, remain in a stationary position in relation to the moving cels.

"Bouncing Pill"

The one-minute Sominex film presentation, made for Pharmaceuticals, Inc., features the bouncing ball and demonstrates its practical application in the commercial film.

The ball, or pill in this case, appropriately titled "Bouncing Pill" on the Parkson Advertising Agency production schedule, bounces over the words of the Sominex musical jingle after some animated antics in synchronization with the sound track. The title, "Take Sominex tonight and sleep—safe and restful, sleep—sleep—sleep," is lettered in white on a sliding cel and registered to the top sliding peg bar. This sliding cel pans through the scene in sync with the sound track and the action of the bouncing ball.

The animation of the white bouncing pill and the panning title are photographed separately on the animation stand over a black card which serves as the background. High contrast film is used for photographing the two actions. The separate filming of the animation and panning title enables the optical cameraman to achieve a dropped shadow effect under the lettering without getting a similar dropped shadow effect under the bouncing pill. (The section entitled "The Optical Printer" includes a detailed explanation of the dropped shadow effect and the reasons for its use.) The achievement of this effect would not be possible if the title and animation were combined on the same length of film during the original photography on the animation stand.

For the optical combination of the live action film with the title and bouncing pill animation, the optical cameraman photographs the live action film with the high contrast negative of the panning title. The high contrast negative, after processing by the laboratory, contains black lettering in the clear area of the film frame.

During the second optical run the white pill on the high contrast positive print is burned in over the previously exposed film. In the final step of the optical process, the camerman copies the high contrast print containing the white lettering in an off-center position to complete the dropped shadow effect and the optical combination.

The bouncing ball action for the entire sequence was achieved with a mere half-dozen sliding cels. A seventh sliding cel was used for the panning title. The slogan for another commercial sums up the difference between the old and new methods used for the technique—"More bounce to the ounce."

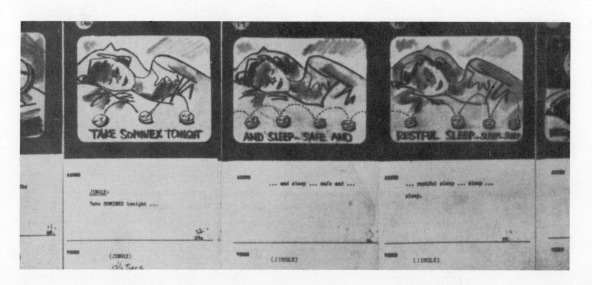

Part of the story board used in the production of the Sominex commercial is shown here.

TAKE SOMINEX TONIGHT   AND SLEEP   SAFE AND RESTFUL   SLEEP...SLEEP...SLEEP

The guide for panning the titles used in the Sominex commercial is taped in position on the layout. The sliding cel containing the lettering is registered to the top traveling peg bar.

ACTION	TRACK	TOP 5	4	3	BALL 2	BTM 1	DIAL	BKGD	TOP PEGS	BTM PEGS	FIELD	CAMERA EFFECTS	N/S	E/W
					6		1		10	288	1×2			
							2		20	284				
PILL IS	LETTERING						3		30	280		CAR STATION		
BOUNCES	PANS						4		40	277				
TO	IN						5		50	274		SHOT LETTERING		
FIELD	FIELD						6		60	271		AND		
							7		70	268		ON STATION		
							8		80	265				
							9		90	262				
					2		10		100	259				
					3		1		110	256				
					4		2		120	253				
					3		3		128	250				
					2		4		130	247				
							5		138	245				
	TAKE ⊗				1	HIT	6			244	⌒			
							7			243				
					2		8	HOLD		241				
					3		9			237				
					4		20			236				
					5		1			233				
					4		2			230				
					3		3			227				
					2		4			225				
							5			223				
	SOM — X				1	HIT	26			222	⌒			
					2		7			220				
					3		8			217				
					4		9			214				
					3		30			211				
					2		1			208				
	IN —				1	HIT	32			206	⌒			
					2		3			206				
					3		4			201				
					2		5			198				
	EX ⊗				1	HIT	36			196	⌒			
							7			195				
					2		8			194				
					3		9			192				
					4		20			190				
					5		1			188				
					4		2			186				
					3		3			184				
					2		4			182				
							5			181				
	TO — X				1	HIT	46			180	⌒			
							7			179				
					2		8			177				
					3		9			175				
					4		50			173				
					5		1			170		PAN BACK		
					4		2			167		TO START		
					3		3			165		OF NEXT		
					2		4			163		SWING		
							5			161				
	NIGHT ⊗				1	HIT	56			160	⌒			
							7			162				
					2		8			166				
					3		9		132	170				
PAN					4		60		144	174				
IN					5		1		152	178				
AND					6		2		164	184				
SLEEP							3		180	187				
					4		4		196	194				
					5		5		210	196				
					4		6		224	200				
					3		7		238	204				
					2		8		250	208				
							9		258	212				
	AND X				1	HIT	70		262	214	⌒			
							1			212				
					2		2	HOLD		210				
					3		3			202				
					4		4			204				
					5		5			201				
					4		6			198				
					3		7			195				
					2		8			192				
							9			190				
	SLEEP ⊗				1	HIT	80			188	⌒			

ACTION	TRACK	TOP 5	4	3	BALL 2	BTM. 1	DIAL	BKGD	TOP PEGS	BTM PEGS	FIELD	CAMERA EFFECTS	N/S	E/W
					1		8 1			189	1 vFL	PAN		
					2		2		HOLD	190		BACK		
							3			191		TO		
					3		4			192		START		
							5			193		OF		
					4		6			194		NEXT		
							7			195		LINE		
					5		8		163	196				
							9		165	197				
					6		70		165	198				
							1		171	199				
							2		177	200				
							3							
							4							
							5							
							6							
							7							
							8		308	207				
							9		314	208				
		⊗					100			210				
							1			211				
							2		331	213				
							3		337	214				
							4			216				
							5		347	217				
							6		357	218				
							7		357	219				
							8		363	220				
							9		367	221				
							11 0			222				
					5		1		377	223				
							2			224				
					4		3		386	225				
							4		389	226				
					3		5		391	227				
							6			228				
					1		7			229				
							8		HOLD	230				
							9			231				
SAFE	⊗				1	HIT	120			234				
							1			231				
					2		2			229				
					3		3			226				
					4		4			223				
					5		5			219				
					4		6			215				
					3		7			214				
					2		8			209				
							9			207				
AND	X				1	HIT	130			206				
							1			205				
					2		2			203				
					3		3			201				
					4		4			198				
					5		5			195				
					4		6			192				
					3		7			189				
					2		8			187				
							9			185				
REST-	⊗				1	HIT	140			184				
							1			183				
					2		2			181				
					3		3			179				
					4		4			177				
					5		5			175				
					4		6			173				
					3		7			171				
					2		8			169		PAN BACK		
							9			167		TO START		
FUL	X				1	HIT	150			166		OF NEXT		
							1							
					2									

A part of the exposure sheets used for the photography of the bouncing pill sequence.

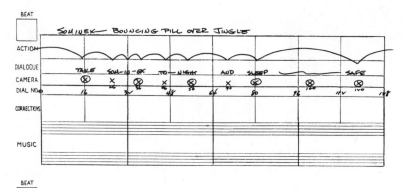

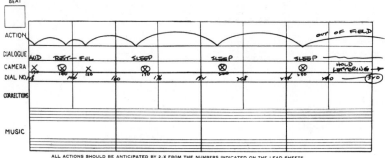

ALL ACTIONS SHOULD BE ANTICIPATED BY 2-X FROM THE NUMBERS INDICATED ON THE LEAD SHEETS.
INDICATE ON THE LEAD SHEETS, BY DIAL NUMBER, ALL ACTIONS OFF THE BEAT AND STARTS AND ENDS OF ACTIONS.

FORM 2964 F. S. 2800 1-60

Shown here is the lead sheet, or bar sheet, prepared by the animation director. The beats and timing are the result of the film editor's analysis of the sound track.

These film clips contain portions of the film sequence showing the
action of the bouncing pill over the titles in the Sominex commercial.

Effects

The cartoonist or animator can only learn how to draw effects through observation. Everyday actions must be carefully studied. For example, how does a ball bounce? Is its downward speed greater than its upward speed? What happens when a drop of water hits a solid surface? How does a cloud of dust dissipate?

Scientists offer pages of explanation to answer these questions, but drawing these actions realistically is something else again. There are no set rules for an animator to follow. Animators have individual styles and draw similar actions differently. The only requirement is that the action, regardless of the style, must look convincing and realistic when it appears on the screen.

Effects are very important because they help lend reality to a scene. For example, the accompanying illustration uses speed and vibration lines to add reality to the basic actions. Other animation effects often used are: dust, water splashes, smoke and fire, as well as blur effects which help to indicate great speed. These visual effects become even more realistic when accompanied by appropriate sound effects.

When drawing effects the animator should follow the same rules for indicating color that he follows when animating the main action. He should close all lines on drawings where more than one color tone is to be used so that the inker and opaquer can follow the action.

FLIPPING

In this photograph we see an animator flipping through the drawings in a scene. After arranging all the drawings in sequence, with the low numbers on the bottom, the animator can flip through them and see an entire action unfold before his eyes. An experienced animator can approximate the exact timing of the animation sequence.

Any faults or flaws in the animation become immediately apparent through flipping. Individual drawings that need additional work can then be pulled out for correction.

The drawings on the corner of every other page, from 67 to 121, are so arranged that they can be animated by flipping. Practice with them and see if you can approximate a set timing.

SHADOWS

Unless some special effect is desired, shadows under cartoon characters and objects being animated should be kept to a minimum.

Shadows are used to show the relationship between a character or object in the air and the ground line of the background. The basic rule governing the size of a shadow in animation is simple: the higher off the ground the character or object, the smaller the shadow and vice versa.

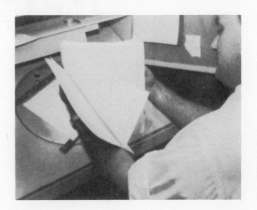

The beginning of a walking cycle. The hand and leg were inked in throughout the cycle in order to emphasize the animation.

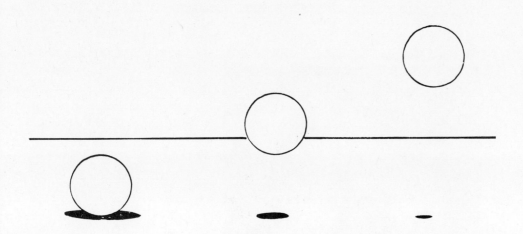

The Inbetweener

The hands shown in the accompanying photograph belong to an inbetweener. Special attention should be given to the position of the left hand. This hand is used to manipulate the drawings in such a way that at least four are visible at the same time. Through such control, the action of the animation can be seen as a continuous flow rather than as individual drawings.

The right hand, of course, holds the pencil and draws in lines as the movement of the animator's extreme drawings become apparent.

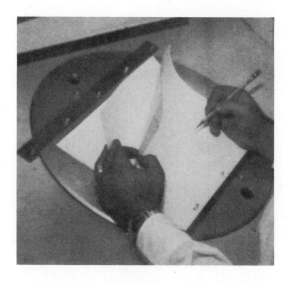

The inbetweener

The Inker

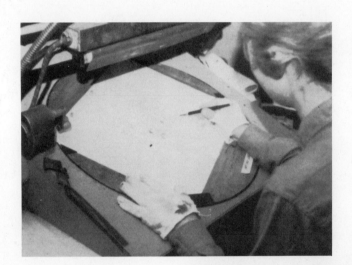

All drawings originally made on animation paper must be meticulously traced on cels. This is the inker's job. He uses a crow-quill pen or a fine brush, whichever he prefers, and a quality, waterproof ink that will not spread or creep.

It is common practice for the inker to wear white lintless-cotton gloves in order to keep the cels as free from smudges as possible.

The inker

The pens and inks used by the inker. Pictured from top to bottom are the superflexible crow quill pen #62, used for fine lines; the Esterbrook #7628, for heavier lines; the #63 crow quill, for normal inking; and the #64 crow quill pen, for inking extremely fine lines. Black India ink is in the bottle on the left. The other bottle contains black opaque water color which is used for filling in larger areas.

The Opaquer

The opaquer

The opaquer uses a brush to apply the colors, which range from black through varying tones of gray to white. The gray tones are numbered from one to ten. The lower the number, the lighter the color.

Although cells are clear and transparent they do have a slight density. As a result, when the blank portion of one cel is placed over the opaqued portion of another, the cel on top darkens the opaqued color of the cel beneath it by one full shade of gray. Therefore, if the same color value or density is desired on the opaqued portions of both cels, the upper cel must be opaqued one shade darker than the cel beneath it. For example, if the lower cel had been opaqued with #1 gray, the cel over it would be painted with #2 gray.

An opaquer applying colors to an inked cel. A light beneath the glass insert on the animation board makes it easier for the opaquer to work accurately. On the table are the brushes and water colors used by the opaquer.

The opaquer does not work on the inked side of the cel but on the reverse side. He does this for two reasons: 1) it permits faster work because he does not have to worry about meeting the ink lines precisely—a slight overlapping on the reverse side does not show on the inked side; 2) the only way to avoid the crude appearance of visible brush marks is to opaque the reverse side; when the cel is turned over its surface makes the opaque look shiny which eliminates any signs of brush marks.

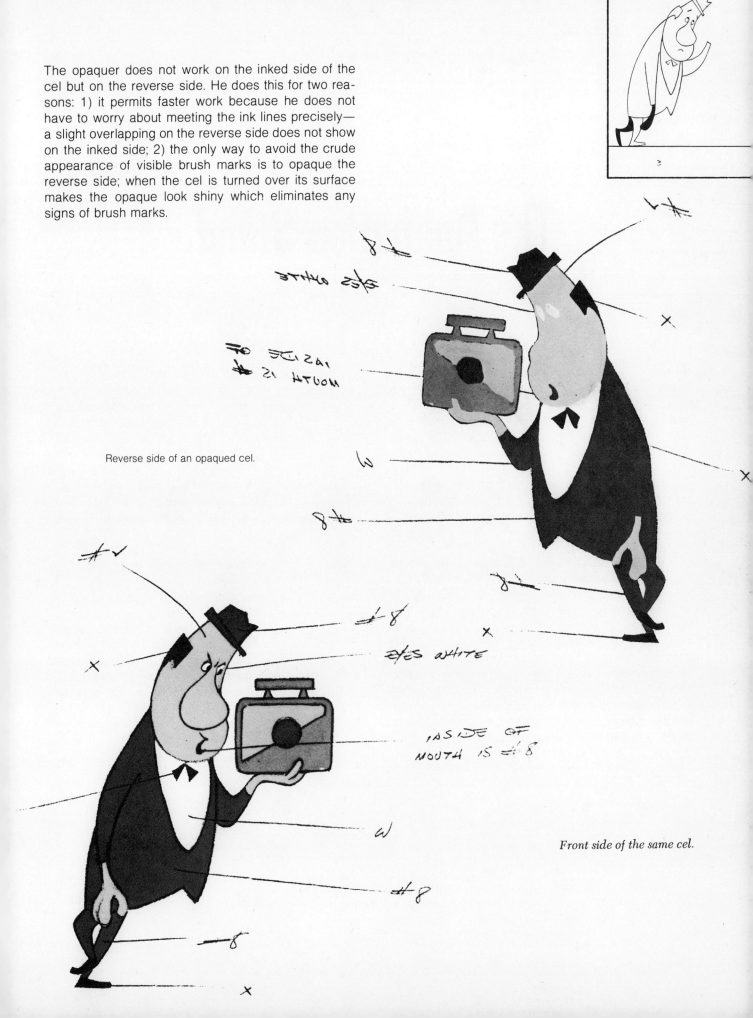

Reverse side of an opaqued cel.

Front side of the same cel.

The Animation Stand

Certain names are synonymous with the artistic development of animation. Walt Disney, Max Fleischer, Paul Terry and others have contributed greatly toward making animated films the potent force they are today—a medium for amusement, education and commerce. No discussion relative to the development of the animation industry, however, could be considered complete without mentioning another pioneer, John Oxberry. Although Oxberry began in the animation industry as a cartoonist, he has been responsible for the development of much of the technical equipment in use today.

The artistic development of animation might never have progressed beyond the cradle stage without the mechanical and technical contributions of such men as John Oxberry. They taught the infant to crawl and then to walk. And today, thanks to the highly specialized animation equipment these men developed, the animation industry takes giant strides with modern production methods and effects unattainable a brief 25 years ago. In developing equipment to meet today's requirements, the design of all components was correlated in order to achieve maximum accuracy, versatility and speed in animation photography.

Close coordination of the functions of the animation stand, camera, stop-motion motor, and compound table—the movable working area on which the art work is placed—has always been the basic aim behind all design and redesign of equipment for animated-film production. From the outset, the goal has been a combination of the best ideas of the past with unique new ideas. This could be realized only by developing components that complemented one another in order to make maximum flexibility in over-all studio production possible.

Because production of animated films depends, essentially, on accurate control of the movements of the camera and the art work, an important question was raised: Which movements should be assigned to the camera and which to the art work?

Sound engineering principles dictated that camera movements should be minimized since minor alignment errors are greatly magnified on film. Therefore, newly designed equipment confines camera movements to the vertical and allots all horizontal movements to the compound table top. This provides great latitude in mechanical design and opens countless new avenues for the director in planning animated sequences.

The working area or table top of an animation stand. A finished cel is being placed over the background. The two sets of pegs on the table top exactly match those on the animator's drawing board.

The glass platen, the frame of the table top, is now in shooting position and the art work is ready to be photographed.

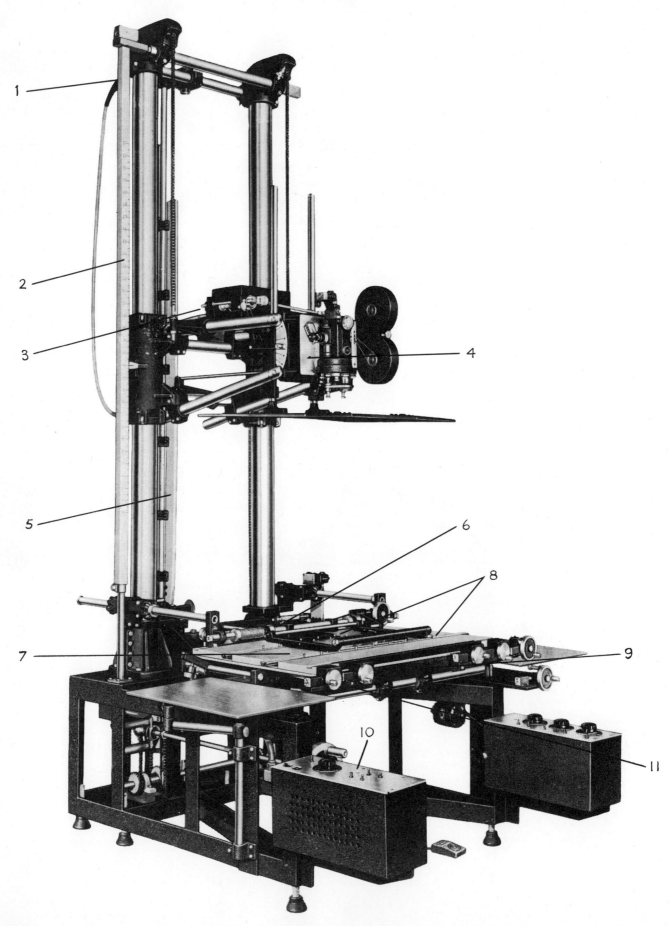

Listed here are the more important parts of the animation stand and their various functions:

1. Automatic cut-offs. These establish the extreme positions of the zoom mechanism.

2. Field-position bar. Numerical markings on this bar indicate the size of the area to be photographed. For example, a number 9 position would indicate a field size 9 inches wide.

3. Stop-motion mechanism. Although the camera mounted on the animation stand is a motion-picture camera, this specially constructed motor drive, a stop-motion mechanism, permits the cameraman to photograph one frame of film at a time.

4. The camera.

5. Follow focus cams. These cams automatically adjust focus, thereby relieving the cameraman of the tedious task of changing focus for each move in relation to the field-position bar.

6. Floating pegs. Because these pegs remain in a fixed position at all times, they give an accurate registry of the original table position regardless of any subsequent table movements.

7. The table top. The table top is the movable working area of the animation stand on which the art work is placed.

8. Traveling pegtracks. These tracks, top and bottom, enable the cameraman to move the art work or cels with a greater degree of accuracy. The two controls at the front of the table are attached to counters for more accurate positioning.

9. The compound table. The table top is set on the compound movement in such a way that any movement can be made, including the rotation of the table, without interfering with any of the other movements.

10. The control panel. A motorized unit that permits the cameraman to make table-top moves, spins and zooms by motor rather than by hand turning or cranking.

11. Split-nut control. This enables the cameraman to engage or disengage any of the compound movements so that the table can be moved freely by hand to any desired position.

The GE Commercial

The drawings reproduced on these pages were made during the production of the GE one-minute commercial. They are arranged in their proper sequence as exposed (recorded) on the exposure sheets. Although most of them are the animator's extremes, some inbetween drawings are included to show how a particular action was developed. (The term *expose*, as used in these pages, refers either to the process of photographing, that is to expose a frame of film, or to the recording of cel numbers on exposure sheets in the sequence in which they will be photographed.)

Exposure sheet 1 of Scene 1 shows that three cel levels are exposed over the background. One of these cel levels, the blank cel, is exposed in order to keep a uniform density over the background throughout the scene. The blank cels were indicated on the exposure sheets by the animator after he had exposed (recorded) all the cels to be photographed and found the cell levels inconsistent.

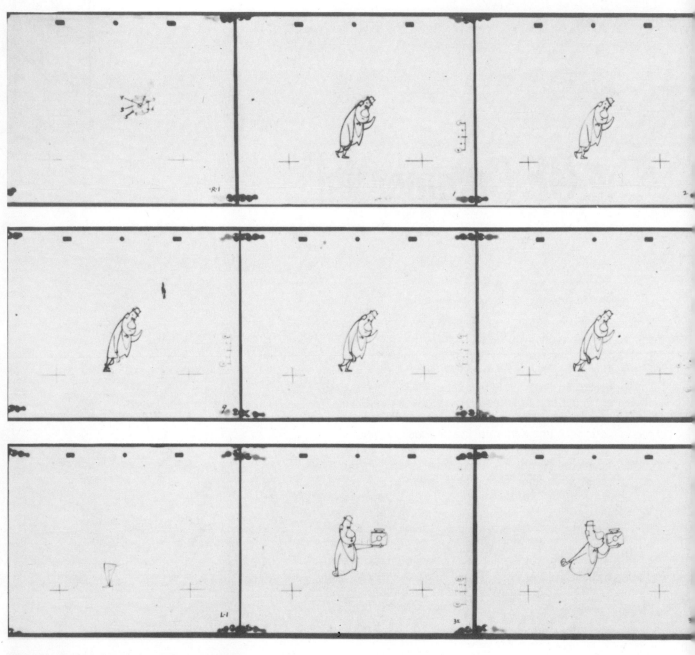

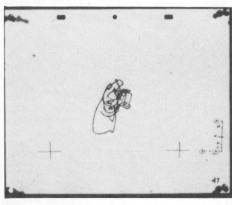

SCENE 1

All the extreme drawings, as well as several important inbetween drawings, used in the opening animation sequence of the one-minute commercial are shown here. A total of 114 drawings were used for the entire Scene 1 action. Of this total, 35 were animator's extremes or key drawings. The 229 frames of film for the opening scene have a projection or screen time of approximately 9½ seconds.

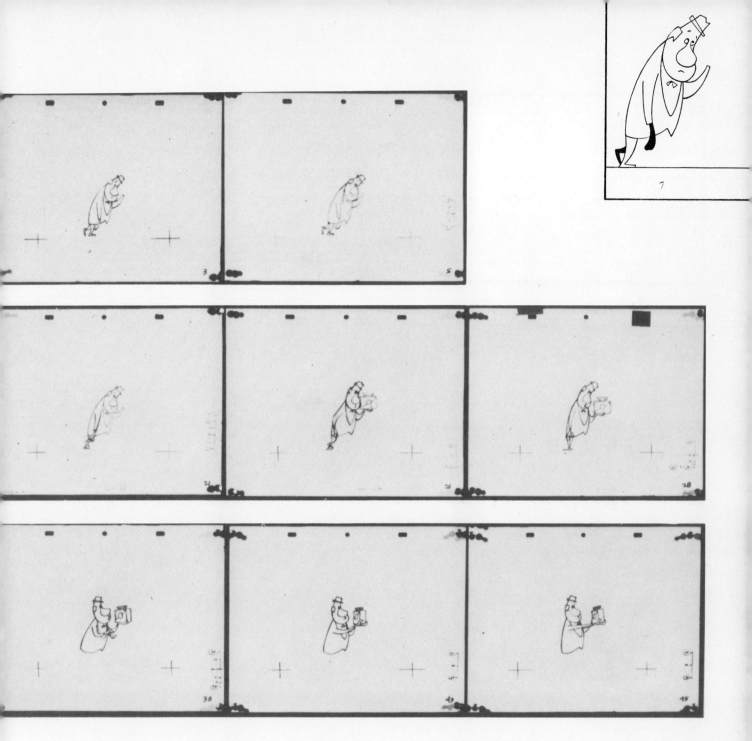

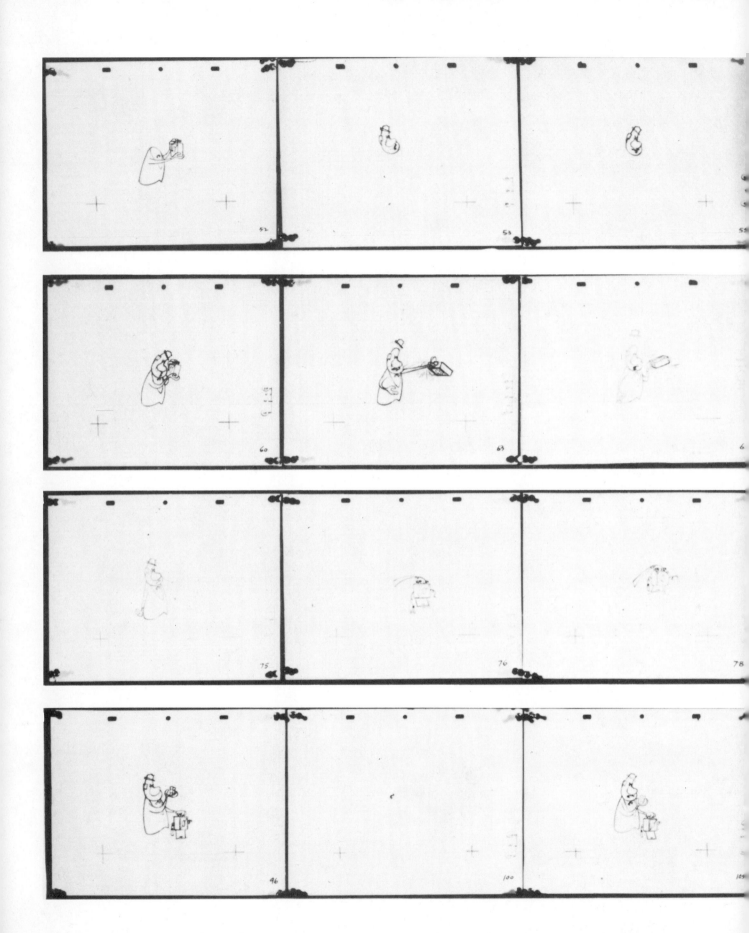

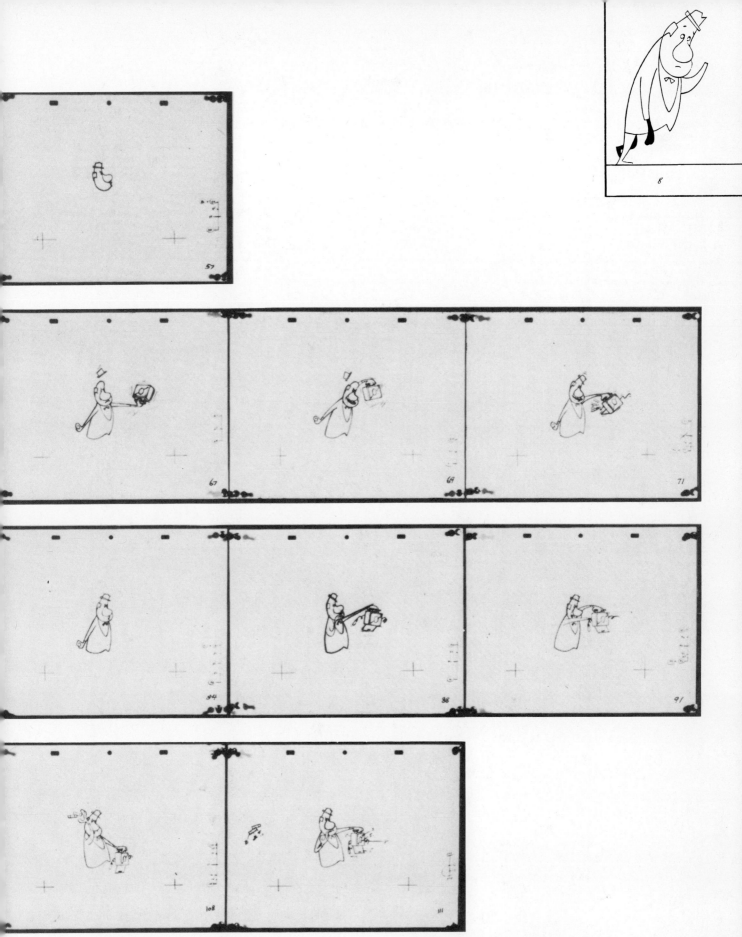

Exposure sheet 1, Scene 1.

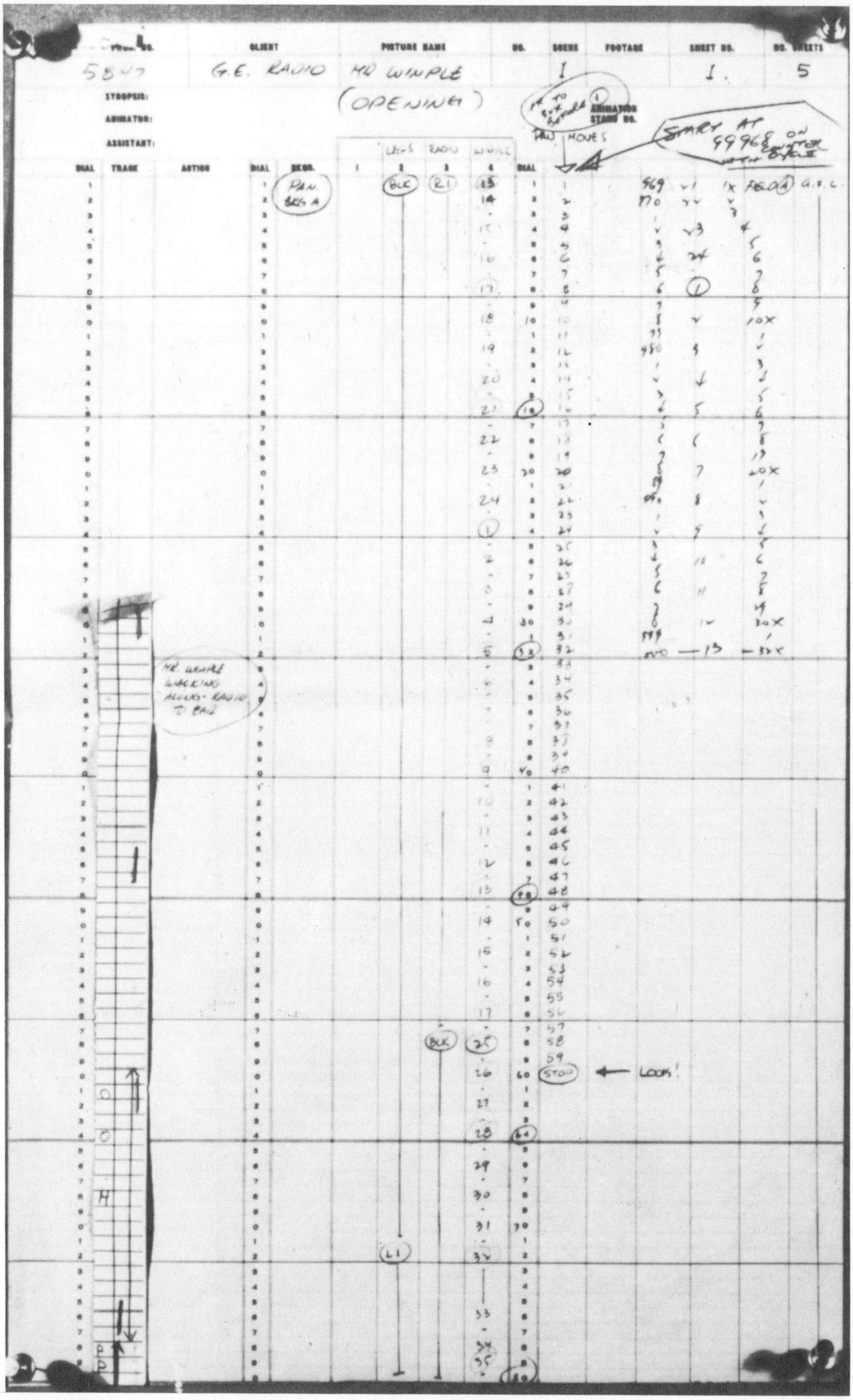

Column 4 exposure sheet 1 shows a series of drawings numbered from 1 to 24. These drawings make up the cycle of Mr. Wimple walking. The twenty-four drawings actually combine to make only two steps; however, drawing 1 has been animated so that it hooks up with drawing 24 to start the cycle over again. By repeating the cycle, it is possible to show Mr. Wimple walking. In fact, by using the same twenty-four drawings over and over again, he could be kept walking for the entire length of the one-minute commercial, or indefinitely for that matter.

Column 3 on exposure sheet 1 shows a hold cel numbered R-1 exposed along with the walk cycle. Cel R-1 is Mr. Wimple's hand holding the radio. The drawing for this cel was designed by the animator to match any of the twenty-four drawings in the walk cycle, thereby eliminating the necessity of retracing the hand and radio on each of the twenty-four drawings. Continuous retracing of the hand and radio might have resulted in uneven ink lines which produce a jiggling effect when seen on the screen. Through the use of R-1, the hold cel, this possibility was avoided.

For this twenty-four-drawing cycle, the animator drew the hold cel, R-1, and extreme drawings 1, 5, 9, 13, 17 and 21. Drawings 2, 3, and 4, shown in the accompanying illustrations, were made by the inbetweener, as were the remainder of the drawings of the repeat cycle which are not shown here.

The animator's notes on the right-hand side of the extreme drawings are guides for the spacing of the inbetweener's drawings. Compare the spacing notes on the repeat cycle of the walk with the spacing called for by the animator on drawing 28 where the walk cycle has ended and the cartoon character has begun to slow down before coming to a full stop. As can be seen on the spacing chart on drawing 28, the inbetweened drawing 29 is evenly spaced between extreme 28 and the combination of two other extremes, 32 and L-1. The next inbetweened drawing, 30, is evenly spaced between drawing 29 and extremes 32 and L-1, as is drawing 31. The animator, by means of this spacing, has slowed down his action to the desired smooth and well-timed stop.

In the column under "Action," the animator has written a brief description of the animation alongside the corresponding drawings. For this portion of the scene, the animator has simply indicated, "Mr. Wimple walking along—radio to ear."

With Mr. Wimple at a full stop, the animator has again made use of the hold cel. This time, a separate drawing, L-1, has been made combining Wimple's legs and feet. No matter what the cartoon character's head and body actions may be, the inker will not have to trace Mr. Wimple's legs and feet on any drawings for the length of time he remains in a static pose.

These have been drawn so that they can hook up and thereby make repetition of the cycle possible.

Spacing guide for the walk cycle.

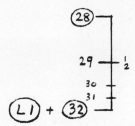

Spacing guide for drawings 28–32.

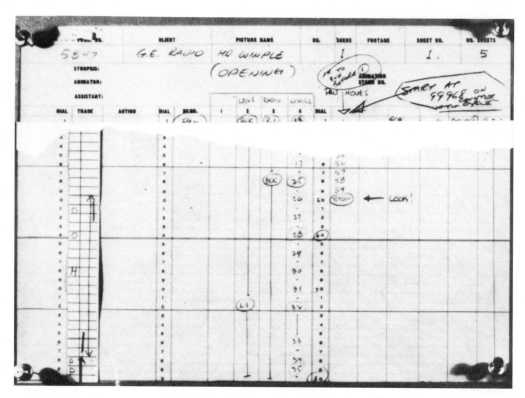

Bottom of exposure sheet 1, Scene 1.

Top of exposure sheet 2, Scene 1.

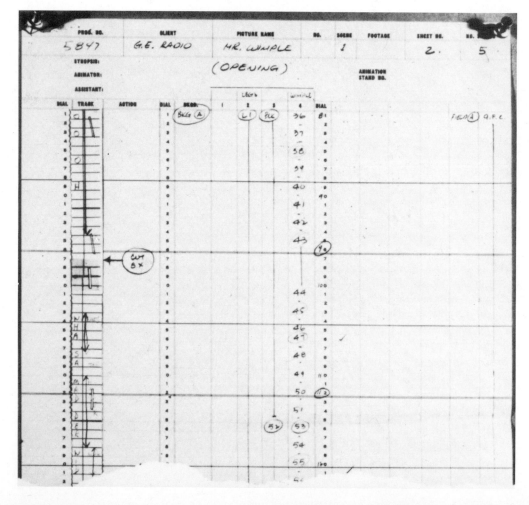

The column under the word "Track" contains the sound-track dialogue, as analyzed by the film editor. At frame 60 on exposure sheet 1 (for frame numbers, look at the column under "Dial"), our cartoon hero makes his first sound, a history making "Oh, Pooh!" Up to this point, with the exception of a musical beat during the walk cycle, the animator had not been concerned with any sound track sync. Mr. Wimple had remained silent while listening to the radio he held in his hand. For the length of the walk cycle, the accompanying music on the sound track was full of static and rather annoying, to give contrast to the fine tone and dependability of the GE transistor radio shown later in the one-minute commercial.

At drawing 52, Mr. Wimple's head is the only part of the cartoon character still animating. As in the case of hold cels R-1 and L-1 used previously, drawing 52 is also made to be used as a hold cel on a separate level.

The reason for exposing a blank cel at the beginning of the scene now becomes obvious, since, at this point, all three cel levels are being used. Column 1, which would have been used if the animator had needed four levels at any time during the scene, remains empty on the exposure sheets. Column 2 lists L-1, the cel with Wimple's legs. The hold cel of Mr. Wimple's body, drawing 52, is in column 3, while column 4 lists the head and mouth actions.

Column 2 on exposure sheet (legs).

Column 3 on exposure sheet (radio).

Column 4 on exposure sheet (Wimple).

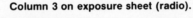

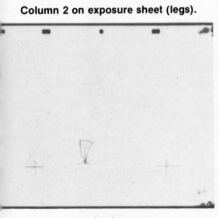

L-1, drawing for hold cel.

Blank cel inserted to keep color tones consistent throughout the scene.

47, drawing for action cel.

L-1, drawing for hold cel of legs.

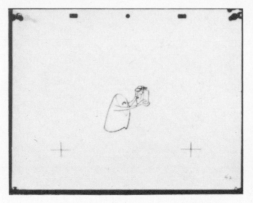

52, drawing for hold cel of body and radio.

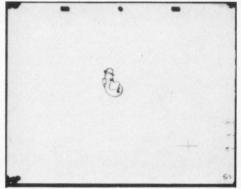

53, drawing for action cel of head.

85

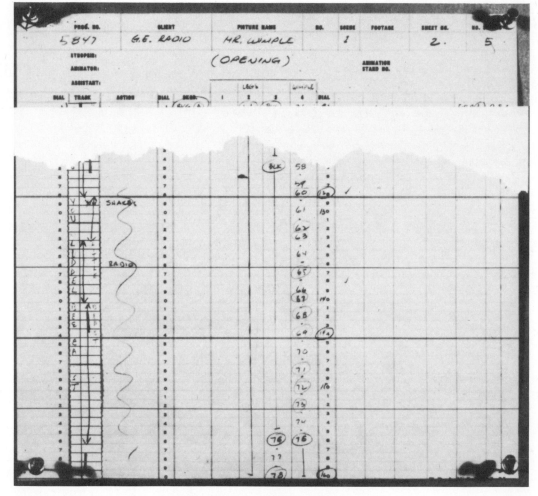

Bottom of exposure sheet 2, Scene 1.

Top of exposure sheet 3, Scene 1.

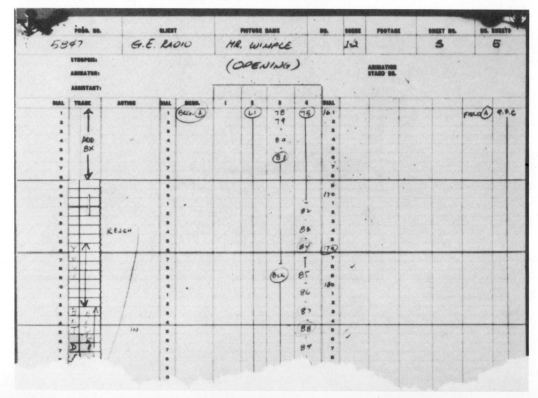

Beginning with drawing 60, Mr. Wimple's body is no longer in a stationary pose. Therefore drawing 52, the hold cel of the body, is replaced with a blank cel in order to keep the number of levels used over the background at three.

At this point of the opening scene, Mr. Wimple is quite angry. The soundtrack column shows him saying: "What's the matter with you, you little beast?" This speech is, of course, directed at the old radio model he has been holding.

Drawings 60 through 71 show Mr. Wimple shaking the radio angrily. Beginning with drawing 75, the violent shaking of the radio has subsided. Mr. Wimple's body, drawing 75, becomes a hold cel and only the arm holding the radio continues animating.

Up to this point, the hold cels have been exposed on the lower levels, those closest to the background. The hold cel of the body, drawing 75, however, is exposed on the top level so that the arm holding the radio does not have to be matched to the body. The drawing of the arm is extended beyond the line of the body so that the hold cel of the body covers the area which otherwise would have had to be matched. If hold cel 75 had been exposed on the third level, drawings 76 through 81 would all have had to be matched to hold cel 75. Drawing 81, the last of the arm-movement drawings, would also have had to be retraced and matched to each of the three drawings of Wimple's body following hold cel 75.

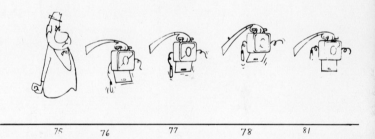

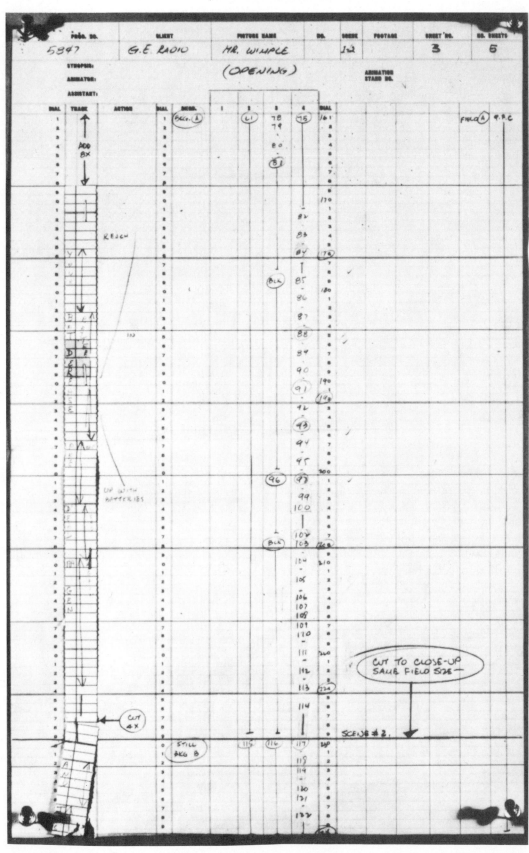

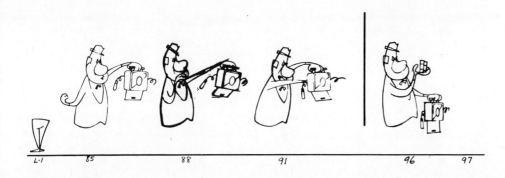

Beginning with drawing 85, Mr. Wimple reaches into the radio and removes the batteries. On the sound track, at frame 176 of exposure sheet 3, the cartoon character begins to speak again. He says: "Your batteries are dead again." These five words of dialogue require forty-seven frames, continuing to frame 223 of exposure sheet 3.

Attention is directed, at this point, to the dialogue spelling on the "Track" column of the exposure sheet. This is not an example of poor spelling by the animator. These words were spelled phonetically, as they sounded on the sound track, in order to indicate the basic sounds and syllables to be accented and emphasized in the animation of the lip movements. The sounds were indicated at the exact frames where they occur.

Mr. Wimple, having removed the batteries from the radio, is in a still position at drawing 96, and a hold cel is made of that static pose. Only his mouth is animating in drawings 97 through 102. At the end of his little speech, Wimple looks down at the dead batteries he is holding and throws them over his shoulder and out of the scene.

With the exception of the walk cycle at the beginning, Mr. Wimple's legs, drawing L-1, have been held in a still position throughout the scene, resulting in a saving of many hours of needless retracing and opaquing by the inker and colorer. The other hold cels used in various places throughout the scene have added to the great saving in production time and costs.

The lines and numbers on model drawings R-1, L-1 and 111 indicate the colors to be used by the opaquer in coloring the various areas of the cels. These colors, black, white and shades of gray, are selected by the animation director and layout man after several sample cels have been opaqued and tried out over the background to be used with the scene.

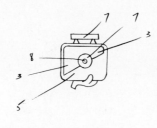

R-1, color model.

L-1, color model.

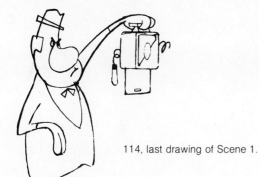

114, last drawing of Scene 1.

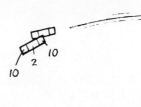

111, color model.

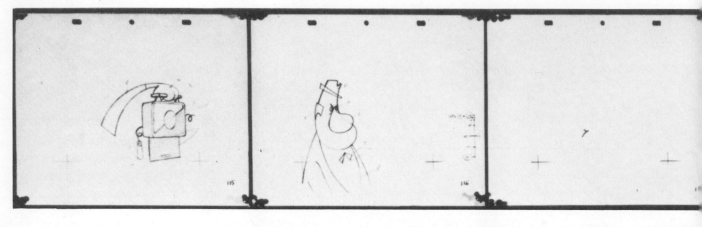

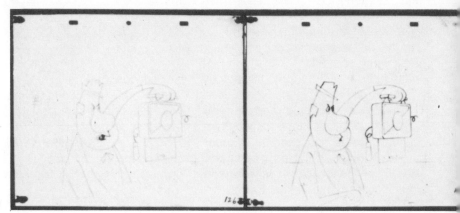

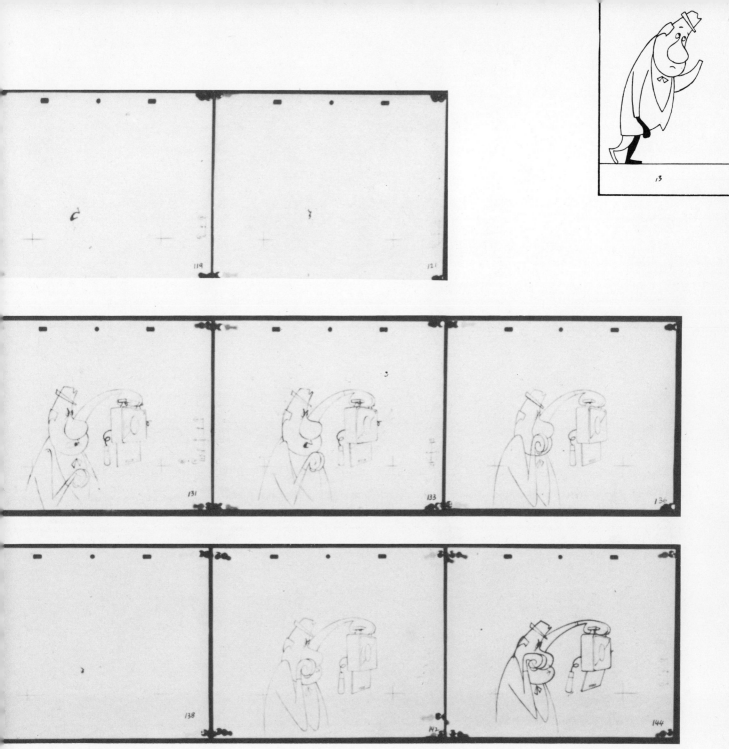

SCENE 2

The drawings shown here are from Scene 2. The total number of drawings required for this scene, including the animator's extremes, was 60.

All of the drawings required for the entire opening animation sequence, Scenes 1 and 2, covering 24 feet of film, totaled 174. At the end of this second scene of animation, there is an optical cross-dissolve to the live-action section of the commercial. The projection time from the start of Scene 1 to the middle of the cross-dissolve to the live action is exactly 16 seconds.

Opaqued cels from Scene 2. The first cel has been placed over the background.

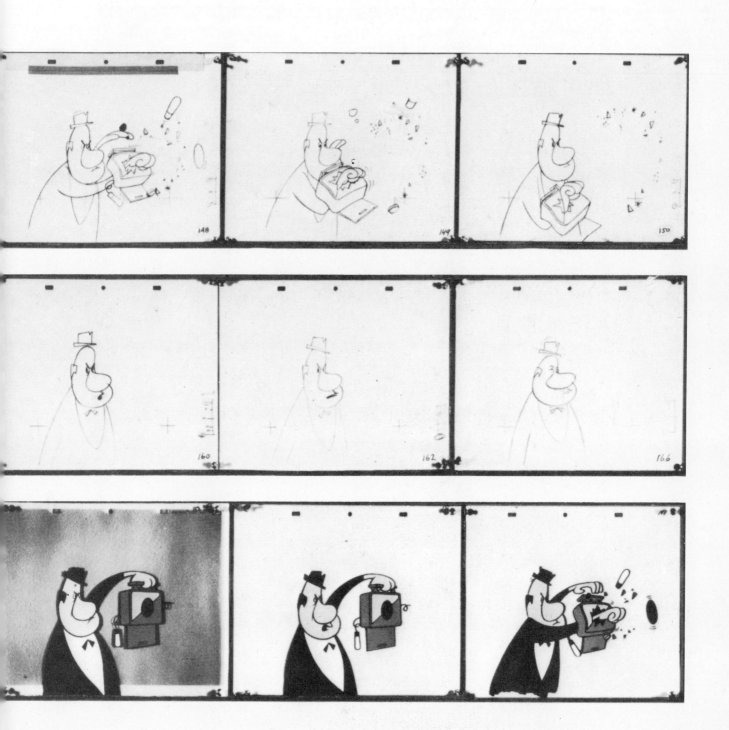

Immediately below frame 229 of exposure sheet 3, a heavy line has been drawn across the page. This indicates a cut and the beginning of a new scene. This new scene, Scene 2, is a continuation of the action in the preceding scene.

Scene 2 is a close-up: a scene that is shot so that the subject matter appears in an unusually close relationship to the camera. For instance, a normal camera shot of an actor might show his complete figure, but a close-up shot of the same actor would show only the head, hands or some other area to be emphasized.

The still background for this scene is a solid color or tone matching the color of the buildings in the pan background used in Scene 1.

Scene 2 begins with frame 230. The animation again uses three cel levels.

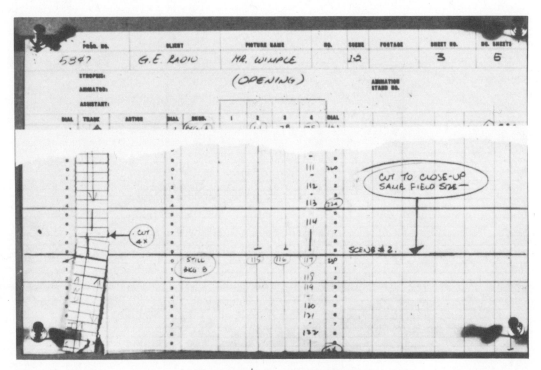

Bottom of exposure sheet 3, Scene 1-2.

Top of exposure sheet 4, Scene 2.

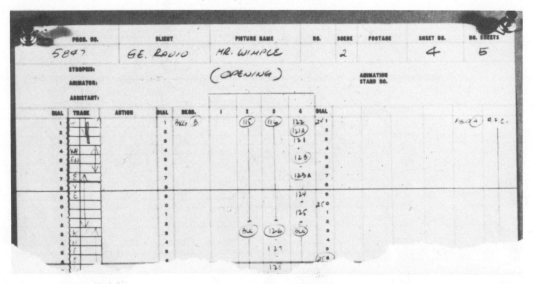

The first drawing, 115, in column 2, the cell level nearest the background, has the hand, arm and radio in a static pose similar to that shown in drawing 114, the last drawing used in Scene 1. Drawing 116, exposed in column 3, consists of Mr. Wimple's head and body. Beginning with drawing 117, the third or top level has the mouth actions for the dialogue which opens the scene. Mr. Wimple is saying, "And just when I need a radio most." This arrangement of cel levels continues to frame 253. At that point, all three levels are combined on one cel, drawing 126, and two blank cels are exposed in order to keep the color density of the scene consistent.

In the sequence of action beginning with drawing 126, a good example of anticipation is shown. The expression on Mr. Wimple's face helps support the animated action that follows.

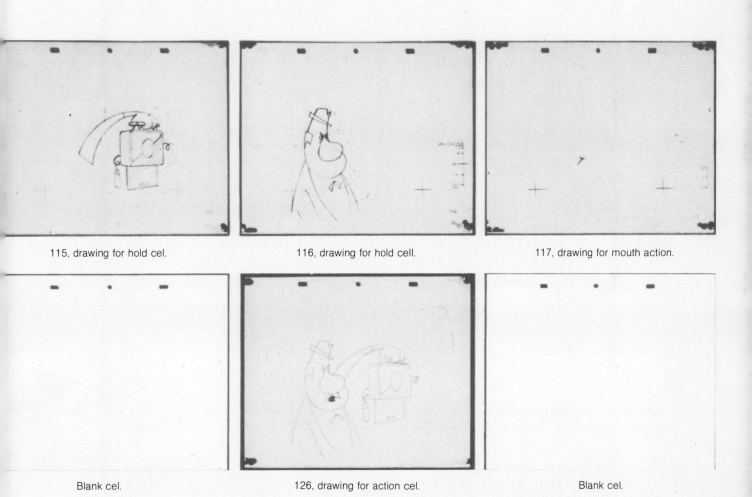

115, drawing for hold cel.

116, drawing for hold cell.

117, drawing for mouth action.

Blank cel.

126, drawing for action cel.

Blank cel.

Exposure sheet 4, Scene 2.

At frame 275, there is another hold cel, drawing 137. It was made in order to avoid additional retracing and opaquing. Mr. Wimple's mouth actions are drawn and exposed on a separate level.

The word "most," ending the dialogue, is spoken as the anticipation builds up to the accent. The climax is reached with the sound effect of the crash, which is synchronized with the animation so that it is heard at the point when Mr. Wimple's fist smashes into the radio.

Because of the comparatively violent action of the smashing of the radio, all cel levels have been combined, starting with drawing 142. The animated effects beginning on drawing 148 and continuing through drawing 152 help emphasize the main action and are very important to the animation. The facial expressions and poses in the drawings used before and after the violent action also help lend reality to the animated sequence. The vigorous manner in which Mr. Wimple says "Phooey!" not only ends the dialogue in the scene but causes his hat to bounce off his head, as shown in drawings 157 to 166. Although this hat action was not indicated in the story board, the animator added it to emphasize the sound effect of the Bronx cheer which accompanied the word "Phooey."

Little auxiliary actions, such as the hat's bounce have almost the same effect in amination as facial expressions and hand gestures. They help accent and emphasize other actions which otherwise might be dull and routine.

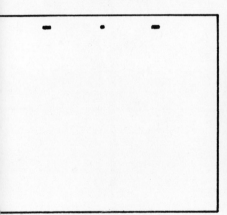

Blank cel.

137, drawing for hold cel.

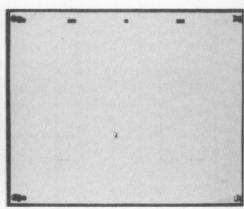

138, drawing for action cel.

157

160

162

166

Exposure sheet 5, Scene 2.

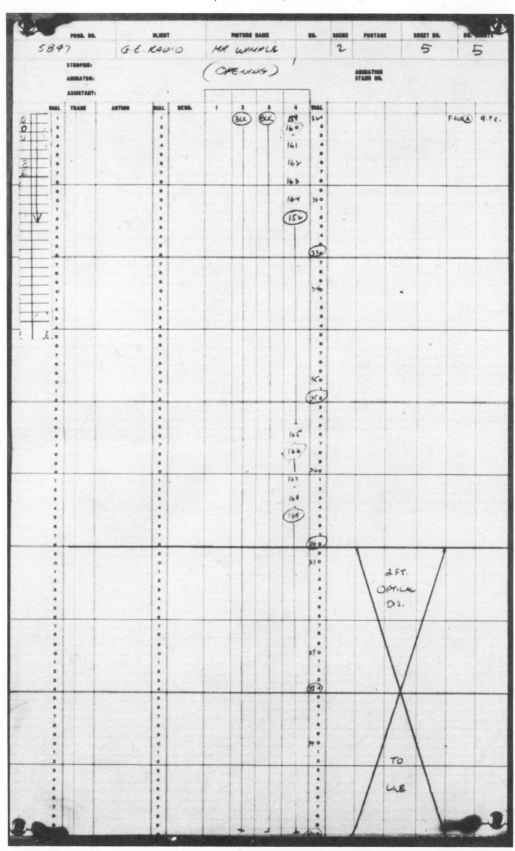

98

At frame 369 on exposure sheet 5, a cross-dissolve to the live-action part of the commercial is indicated. The cross-dissolve to live is written on the exposure sheet by the animator as a direction to the animation cameraman. In this case, the cross-dissolve does not require any drawing or additional work by either the animator or the animation cameraman, since the animated scene ends with Mr. Wimple in a static pose. The animation cameraman will simply photograph the hold-position cel for the number of frames in the cross-dissolve. If, for example, the desired length of the cross-dissolve is one foot, the cameraman will photograph the hold position for 16 frames. A two-foot cross-dissolve would require 32 frames.

The cross-dissolve itself will be done by the optical cameraman, who will first copy the film made by the animation cameraman. Then starting at the exact frame where the cross-dissolve is to begin, the optical cameraman will fade out the animation in the required number of frames. When the fade-out has been completed, the optical cameraman will then reverse the direction of the camera and go back to the frame where the fade-out began. He will complete the cross-dissolve by fading in the live-action scene over the same portion of the film containing the fade-out of the animation. This method of overlapping two scenes is one of the most widely used effects in motion pictures, both live and animated.

Last drawing of Scene 2 held for cross-dissolve.

169

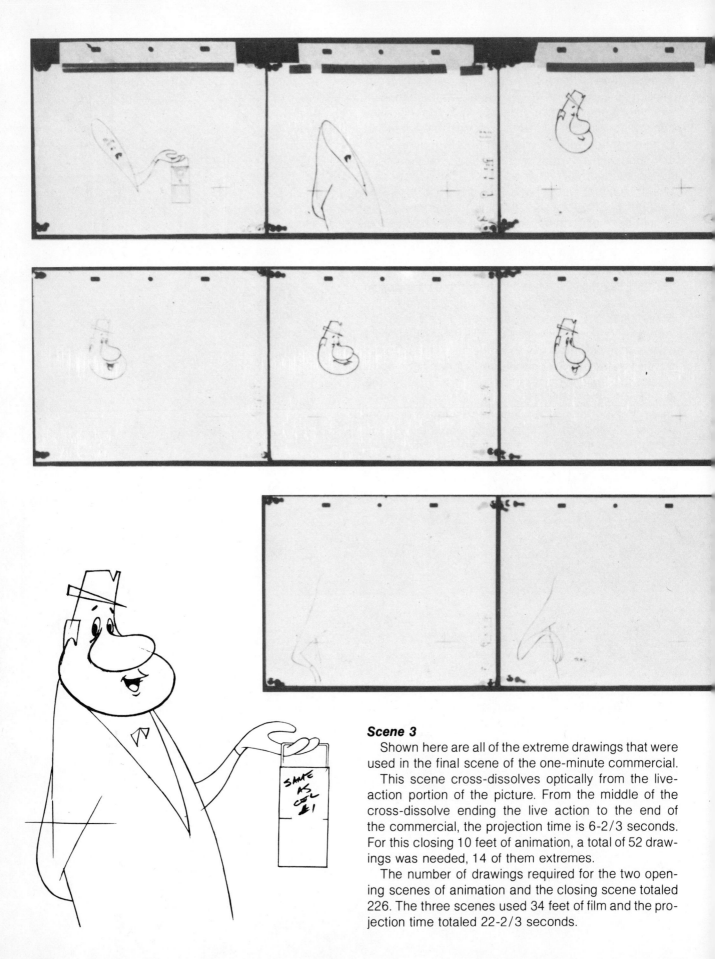

Scene 3

Shown here are all of the extreme drawings that were used in the final scene of the one-minute commercial.

This scene cross-dissolves optically from the live-action portion of the picture. From the middle of the cross-dissolve ending the live action to the end of the commercial, the projection time is 6-2/3 seconds. For this closing 10 feet of animation, a total of 52 drawings was needed, 14 of them extremes.

The number of drawings required for the two opening scenes of animation and the closing scene totaled 226. The three scenes used 34 feet of film and the projection time totaled 22-2/3 seconds.

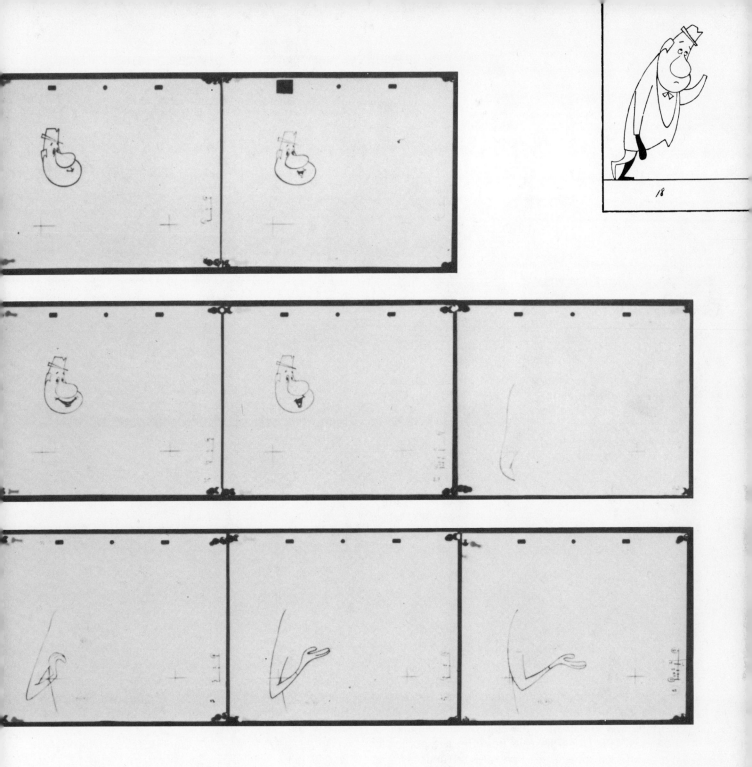

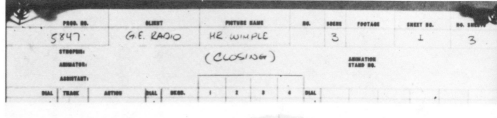

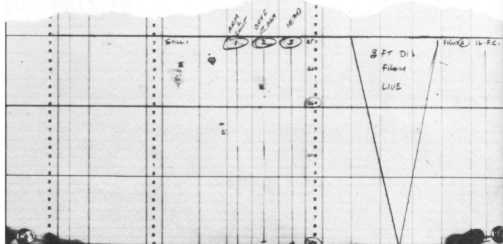

Opaqued cels 1, 2, and 3 over their background.

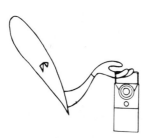

1, drawing for hold cel.

2, drawing for hold cel.

3, drawing for action cel.

The same procedure followed in cross-dissolving to the live sequence from the animation at the end of Scene 2 is now exactly reversed in cross-dissolving from the live sequence to the start of the animation of Scene 3. The cross-dissolve from the live portion of the commercial begins at frame 1257 and ends at frame 1304, exactly 48 frames or three feet later.

The same background used in Scene 2 is again used in Scene 3, the closing scene of animation. A three-level scene, drawing 1 is exposed in column 2, or the level nearest the background. On this hold cel, Mr. Wimple's hand is shown holding the new GE transistor radio featured in the commercial. Because the transistor radio used in this scene is the product being advertised, it was drawn realistically, from a photograph of the actual radio used in the live sequence, as compared with the stylized drawing of a radio used in the two opening animation scenes. Drawing 2 in column 3

on the exposure sheet, another hold cel, has Mr. Wimple's body and right arm. Only the head is animating. Beginning with drawing 3, the head is exposed in column 4, the top level.

On the sound track, Mr. Wimple says: "What a Jim Dandy gift." This dialogue begins at frame 1351 of exposure sheet 2 and ends forty-five frames later on exposure sheet 3, frame 1396. In preparing for the dialogue, drawings 4 through 10 contain another good example of anticipation. Although Mr. Wimple has not yet begun to speak, the facial expressions become the anticipation of the dialogue that follows. Wimple's eyes slowly open and his smile widens in pure contentment before the first syllable is uttered. The subtlety of this anticipation contrasts with other anticipations in the film which preceded more violent animated actions.

102

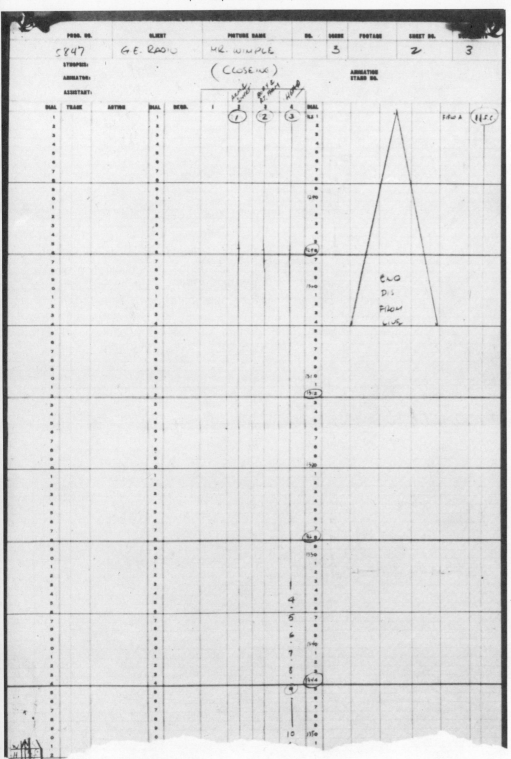

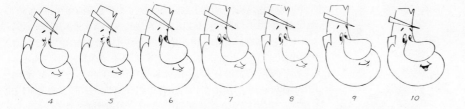

Anticipation series.

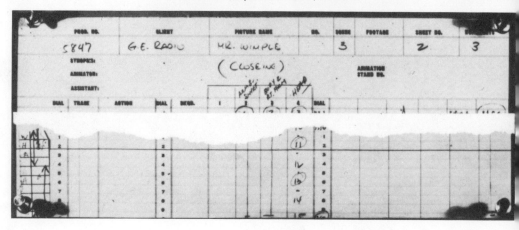

At drawing 11, Mr. Wimple begins to speak. His right hand, motionless during the anticipation and at the start of the dialogue, begins animating at frame 1365, drawing 33. These hand gestures help emphasize Mr. Wimple's dialogue. At frame 1404, after the dialogue has ended, Mr. Wimple goes into a static pose which he holds for the balance of the scene.

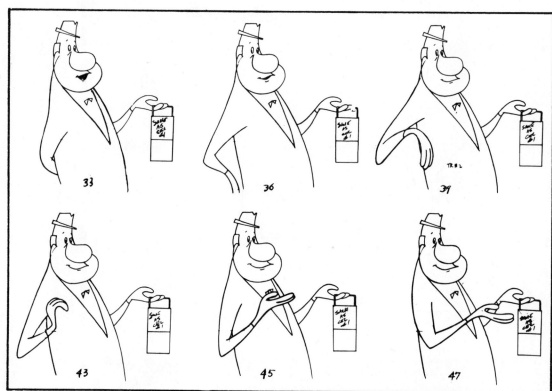

At frame 1440, the last frame of the one-minute commercial, the animator has written a note on the exposure sheet directing the animation cameraman to photograph forty-eight frames or three additional feet of film of Mr. Wimple in the final static pose. This is what is known as bumper footage. It is added to the end of each commercial as a standard operating procedure.

PROD. NO.		CLIENT	PICTURE NAME		NO.	SCENE	FOOTAGE	SHEET NO.	NO. SHEETS
5847		G.E. RADIO	MR. WIMPLE			3		3	3

SYNOPSIS:
ANIMATOR:
ASSISTANT:

(CLOSEUP)

ANIMATION
STAND NO.

DIAL	TRACK	ACTION	DIAL	DESG.	1	2	3	4	DIAL			
						①	②	16	176		HOLD	①⑤⑥
								17				
							33	18				
							34	19				
							35	20	190			
							36	21				
							37	22				
							38	23				
							39	24	820			
							40	25	850			
							41	26				
							42	27				
							43	28				
							44	29				
							45	30				
							46	31	890			
							47	32	893			
							48					
							49					
							50		900			
							51					
							52					
									908			
									910			
									920			
									928			
									930			

HOLD 3 FT EXTRA
TO DIAL # 1488

Limited Animation

Limited animation is the film technique designed for the low-budget production. Although the technique can be regarded as a compromise between the slide motion film and the fully animated cartoon, the processes for the production of the limited animation film are similar to those used in full animation.

Cartoon characters are designed, backgrounds rendered, and the drawings containing the animation are inked and opaqued before being photographed on the animation stand. Where a fully animated film may require several thousand drawings and cels, it is possible to produce a limited animation film of similar length with only a small fraction of that number of drawings.

Each of the drawings used in this type of production is designed to produce the maximum effect with a minimum of animation effort. In most cases, the eyes and mouths of the cartoon characters animate while the head remains in a static pose. Similarly, legs and arms move, during walking or running cycles, while the body, inked and opaqued as a hold cell, remains motionless.

The opaquing process is also simplified and the number of colors is held to a minimum. Backgrounds are kept simple and as free from unnecessary detail as possible. The panning of cels and backgrounds, combined with camera and compound table movements, does much to create the effect of full animation.

Where limited animation is included as a part of a training or industrial film, the cartoon characters add a considerable amount of interest to the serious subject matter in that type of film presentation. Films shown at sales meetings and conventions, known as "sleepers" for obvious reasons, also include one or more limited animation sequences in order to create and maintain interest. Because of the low cost of production and the versatility of the technique, the limited animation film has been and will, undoubtedly, continue to be a popular motion picture technique.

All of the drawings used in the CUE commercial.

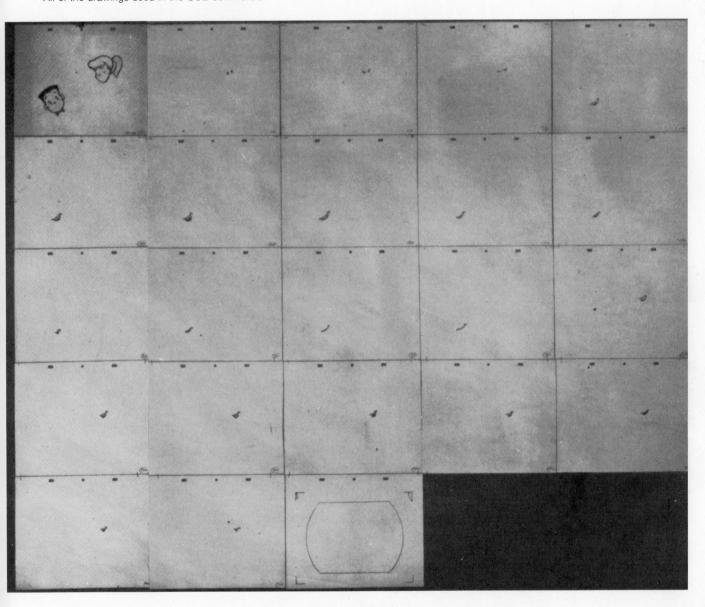

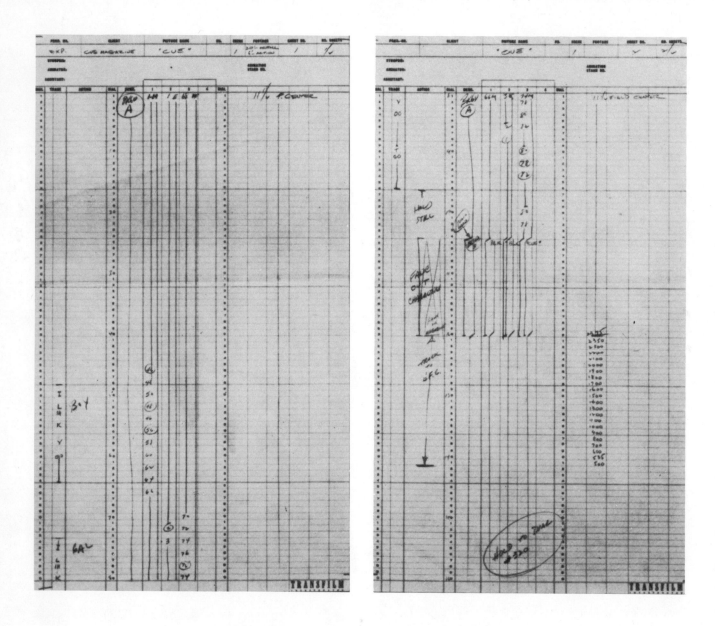

The exposure sheets used for photographing the animation.

The 22 drawings used for the discussion of the limited animation technique tell a ᴄᴜ(t)ᴇ story. Another ᴄᴜ(t)ᴇ story is attached to the exposure sheets in the form of a note from the sales department. The note, however, merits an explanation.

Sponsors, in the early days of television, were on the constant alert for new ideas for commercials. Animation directors and animators filled that need easily. The absence of potential sponsors, a frequent occurrence in those days, was only a minor consideration and provided no great obstacle for the ingenious masters of the pencil. The flow of ideas continued and very often commercials were made even for nonexistent products. The argument that began with "Animation is a form of expression" was irrefutable. Ideas were freely expressed.

A firm grip on a pencil, a supply of paper, an active imagination, and a cooperative animation cameraman formed an all-powerful combination. All of this creative energy provided a monumental job for the film editor, who received endless rolls of film from the laboratory. These non-scheduled and non-profit productions provided the film editor with many anxious moments. These films also provided the animation industry with many new techniques, gratis. The material from one of these no-budget productions is used here to illustrate the limited animation technique. The writer is in no small way responsible for the idea contained in the 22 drawings to be discussed.

The idea for the production originated during a discussion of magazines. *Cue Magazine* was one of the periodicals mentioned. The comment by one of the animators, "I like *Cue*," was immediately followed by the observation from another animator, "I like *Cue*, too." The light bulb drawn over the heads of comic strip characters to indicate the birth of an idea flashed on and another unauthorized and unrequested film was in production.

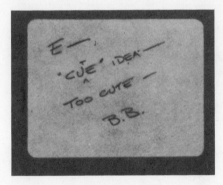

The note from upstairs.

Several decisions were reached during the brief production conference that followed. The decision concerning the animated action was unanimous. A teen-age boy would look up at a teen-age girl, sigh, and say, "I like you." The teen-age girl would then close her eyes and reply, "I like *Cue*, too." In synchronization with the word *Cue*, the animation of the boy and girl would fade out and be replaced by an actual magazine. A zoom to a close-up of the name on the cover of the magazine would follow the cross-dissolve and remain on the screen until the end of the "spectacular."

It was also agreed that no script, story board, background, or cels could be used for this no-budget film. The last condition specifically stipulated that pencils could be used providing the number of sheets of animation paper for the entire production be held to 25 or less. Characters were designed and put into production almost before the conference ended.

Several hours later, the unbeatable team of Bill Hudson and Eli Levitan delivered 22 drawings and a copy of *Cue Magazine* to the animation cameraman. The following day, the processed film was handed over to a bewildered film editor. Screened for the studio sales department, the production was greeted by overwhelming silence. The two proud producers mistook the reaction for speechless approval until the following morning when a rejection note was delivered to two dejected masters of the pencil. *Cue's* loss was the animation industry's gain.

For the actual production, the drawings were photographed with underneath lighting. This is the same method that is used for filming a sequence of drawings in order to review the acceptability of an action before the drawings are inked and opaqued. The heads of the girl and boy on drawing A served as the background for the animation.

The boy's mouth actions, drawings 1M and 46M to 66M, appear in column 1 on the exposure sheets. Only ten drawings were used for these mouth actions and the formation of the phrase, "I like you." Several of these drawings were repeated during the short speech.

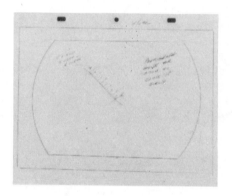

The layout and Pantograph guide used for the zoom to the close-up field.

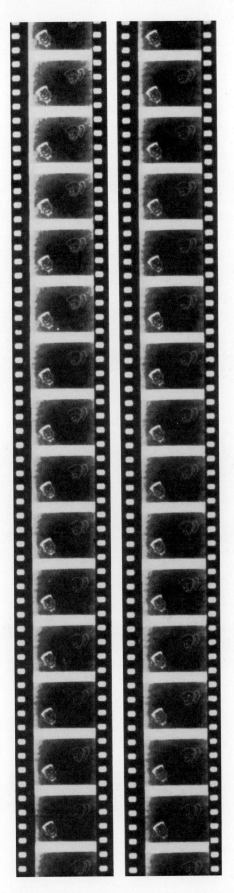

During the girl's reply, her eyes close, drawings 1E to 3E, exposed in column 2, and then reopen in a reverse action that uses the same three drawings. In column 3, drawings 68M to 82M contain the girl's mouth actions. Of the eight drawings used for these mouth actions, several are repeated during the phrasing of "I like *Cue*, too."

In synchronization with the word *Cue*, the animation cross-dissolves to the actual magazine. Following the fade out of the animation, normal top lighting is used for fading in the magazine and completing the cross-dissolve. The top lighting arrangement is used until the end of the production.

At dial 121, the first frame after the cross-dissolve, a zoom to a close-up of the magazine is indicated on the exposure sheets. The calibrations for the camera zoom from the 11½ field to the 5 field is shown on exposure sheet 2. The calibrations show the ease in and ease out at the beginning and end of the zoom and the constant speed maintained for the intermediate moves to the close-up position. The east-west and north-south compound table movements to the 3-west, 4-north position, the close-up showing the name of the magazine, were made by using a pantograph guide.

A total of 22 drawings were used for the production of this limited animation sequence. In all fairness, one magazine should be included as part of the art work. Although the entire action was limited to the animation of eyes and mouths, the effect was comparable to full animation.

A great time and budget saver, the limited animation technique has been increased in use greatly in recent years. The rise in popularity is directly attributable to the versatility of this all-purpose technique.

A portion of the limited animation discussed in this section is shown in these film clips.

GUIDES AND GIMMICKS

While most animated actions are the result of conventional animation processes, many actions and movements are achieved with other methods. Guides and gimmicks are used frequently in order to satisfy the varied animation requirements of the commercial film user.

A mountainous pile of drawings and cels is no longer a yardstick by which animated actions are measured. In many instances, effects that seem to be fully animated are achieved with surprisingly few drawings. As time and budget savers, the value of these guides and gimmicks is incalculable. The savings, however, are not made at the expense of the quality of the animation. As a matter of fact, in some instances, because of the nature of the subject matter, a smoother action can be achieved with these guides than with conventional animation processes. Besides, animators are a lazy group of individuals, generally speaking.

The sequences discussed in this section contain some excellent examples of animation short cuts. Each of the animated actions is taken from an actual scene that was used in the production of a theatrical or commercial film.

The use of these guides and gimmicks is limited only by the imagination of the animator. As the man in the cigarette commercial says, "Every man should think for himself."

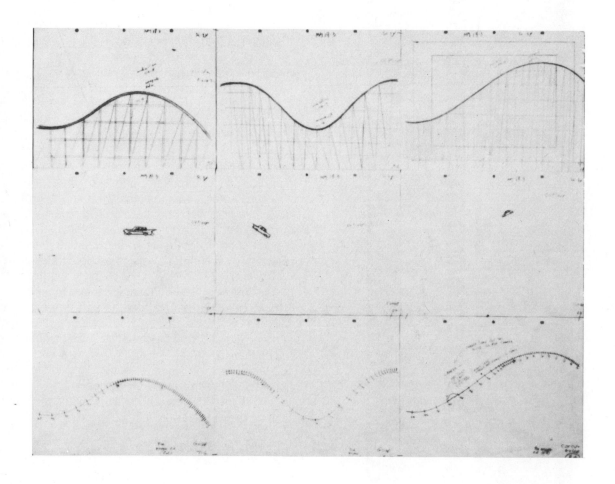

The Cutout

The cutout is a great time and budget saver in animation. Used in all animation techniques, it has many functions and, in certain instances, is almost indispensable. The cutout is made from an animator's drawing and is inked and opaqued on thin illustration board instead of a cel. The illustration board, after the inking and opaquing processes have been completed, is cut out along the outer ink lines. The cutout is usually pasted on the background and held in one position for the amount of film footage indicated on the exposure sheets. It may also be moved by hand, from one position to another, according to the positions indicated on an accompanying guide.

Very often, because of the colors involved, it is inadvisable to use more cel levels than are absolutely necessary in order to avoid the inevitable darkening of the background. In these situations, the cutout is used in place of the hold cel and results in a great saving in the inking and opaquing processes.

Cutouts are used very often in place of conventional animation. They are not used at the expense of reduced quality in animated action. The overall effect of some animated actions where cutouts are used is usually smoother than the action obtainable with conventional animation methods. An excellent example of the effectiveness of the cutout is contained in a scene from a Paramount Pictures cartoon studio production. In Scene 34, picture MM 19-3 of the "Modern Madcap" series, several automobiles move over a roller coaster in a continuation of an action from the preceding scene of the picture.

The cars used in the scene are drawn by the animator and the cutouts are made by the inker and opaquer. The three cels containing the framework of the roller coaster (T-1, M-1, and B-1) are the only cels used in the entire scene. These cels are photographed over a light blue card which serves as the background.

Each of the cutouts is moved on a different cel level. As each car passes behind the framework of the cel over it, the illusion of depth in the scene is increased considerably. The entire action of the scene consists of the moving cutouts of the cars. The guides for moving these cutouts are made by the animator. Guide T-G is used for moving cutout 1. The moves for cutout 2, on the middle cel level, are indicated on guide M-G. Guide B-G is used for moving cutout 3 over the bottom cel level.

The cutouts, in position over the three cels, are shown in this frame from the scene.

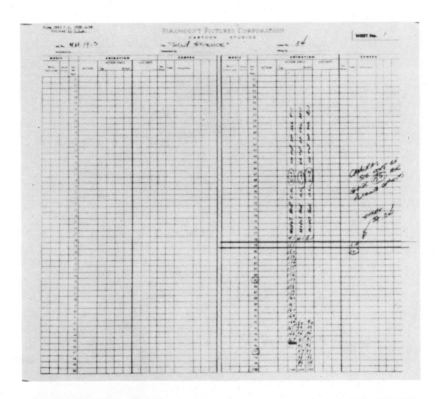

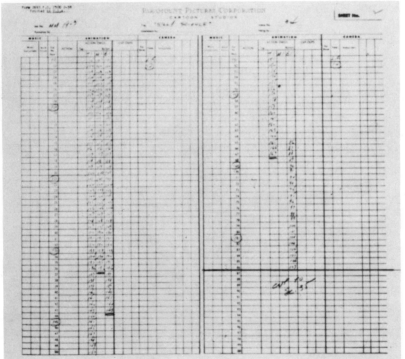

The exposure sheets indicate the position for the cutouts.

Each of the three cars is moved by the animation cameraman for each frame of the scene. Because of the manner in which the cutouts are exposed, more than the three cars actually used appear to be moving through the scene. Spaced at different intervals, for the 6 feet and 12 frames of movement, the effect is interesting and unusual.

If each of the cars was inked and opaqued for every movement in the scene, the result would be a mountainous pile of cels. Some guides dreamed up by animators for the movement of cutouts give animation cameramen nightmares. They do show what can happen as the result of the combination of a lazy disposition with an active imagination. In any case, not only is the pencil saved for other animated actions but a great deal of time and effort as well.

Used in a scene from Paramount Pictures' "Modern Madcap" series, the gimmick described here is another good example of an animation short cut.

For the animated action of the carousel in the scene, cutouts of cars are used in place of the conventional horses. The three cutouts of the cars are inked and opaqued and then taped to strips of illustration board. These strips move in slots cut in the guide or gimmick.

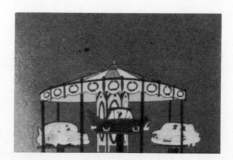

One of the frames taken from the scene.

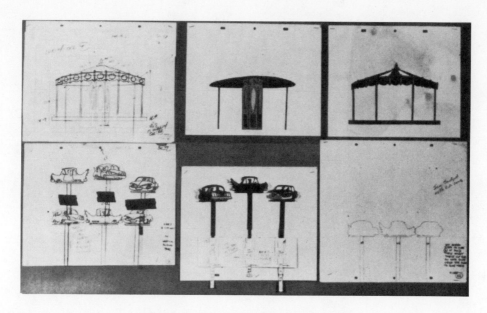

The layouts, cutouts, the underlay and overlay.

The positions for the vertical movement of the cars are indicated at the bottom of the three strips and register to the guide lines. Cutouts 1 and 3 move up and down simultaneously, while cutout 2 moves in the opposite direction. The first few moves, in either direction, are held for two frames in order to slow down the vertical movement of the cars at the extreme positions. The intermediate moves are on ones, or one exposure for each position of the action.

The gimmick for the movement of the cutouts is positioned on the bottom pegs. The tone card background and the hold cels of the carousel are registered to the top pegs in the normal center position. Cel BB, the back part of the carousel, and cel T, the front portion, are the only two cels used in the entire scene.

The need for matching the cutouts of the cars to the posts on the carousel is avoided by inking and opaquing the front and back parts of the carousel on separate cels and moving the cutouts between the two cel levels. Finally, overlay X, a tone card, is taped across the lower portion of the carousel to conceal the gimmick and the "mechanism."

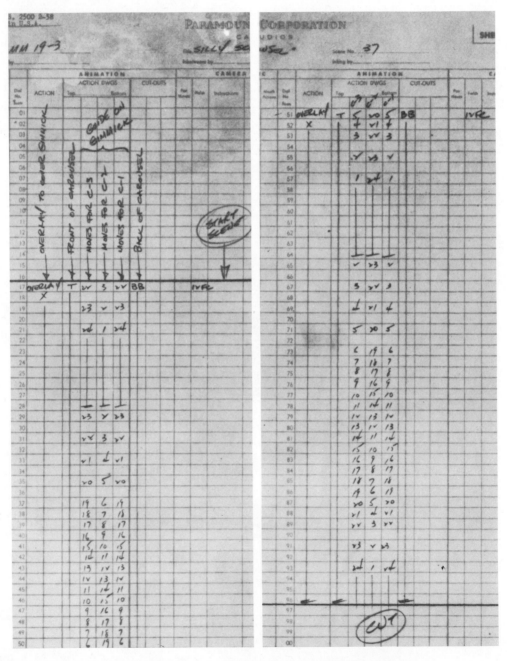

The exposure sheet contains the moves for each frame of the scene.

The Guide

A completely different kind of guide is used in scene 3 of the Aero Shave commercial. With this guide, the accomplishment of a difficult animated action was made relatively simple. The tracing chart also eliminated a great deal of work for the entire production staff.

In order to achieve the "bounce" effect of the word "Moisture," one drawing of the lettering, 3L, was made in the hook-up position of the eight-drawing repeat cycle. This key drawing was used for inking each of the letters in the word "Moisture" in the different positions of the animated cycle.

TRACING GUIDE   No _____

Job No. _AERO SHAVE_   Scene No. _3_

CEL. NO.	TRACE DRAWINGS AS FOLLOWS: POSITIONS ON GUIDE (XX)										
	M	O	I	S	T	U	R	E			
(3L)	3	✓	1	✓	3	↙	5	↙			
4L	↙	3	✓	1	✓	3	4	5			
5L	5	↙	3	✓	1	✓	3	4			
6L	↙	5	↙	3	✓	1	✓	3			
7L	3	4	5	↙	3	✓	1	✓			
8L	✓	3	↙	5	↙	3	✓	1			
9L	1	✓	3	4	5	↙	3	✓			
10L	✓	1	✓	3	4	5	↙	3			

The guide used by the inker for tracing the various combinations of letters to form the hook-up cycle in the example given here.

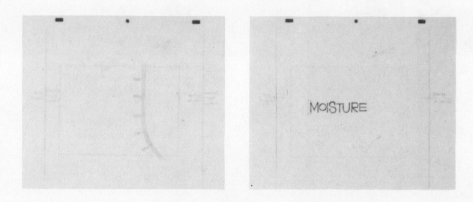

Layouts for background and lettering.

Two guides were used for inking the eight cels of the cycle. The two vertical registry lines and the five positions for tracing each of the letters was called guide X. The same two vertical registry lines on guide X were retraced on guide XX. Only one position, however, was drawn on these vertical lines. The word "Moisture," in its hook-up position, was also drawn on guide XX.

The upper part of the animation paper containing the peg holes was folded over so that the guide XX could be moved freely along the vertical lines and taped down in each of the five positions on guide X. The production cels, 3L to 10L, are registered to the normal peg position and each of the letters in the word "Moisture" is inked in the position indicated on the tracing chart.

The word "Moisture," drawn on guide XX, contains the combination of letters shown on the first line of the tracing chart. The letter M is in position 3, O is in position 2, I is inked in position 1, S in position 2, T in the 3 position, U in the fourth position, R in 5 and the letter E ap-

The exposure sheets used for photographing the animated lettering.

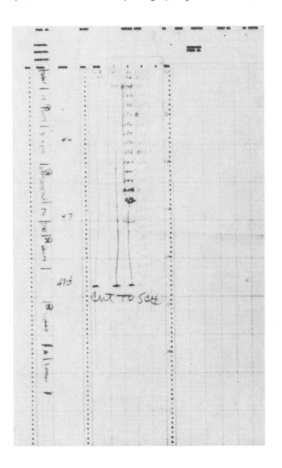

These film clips show the animation of the word "moisture" in the Aero Shave commercial.

pears in position 4. The tracing chart shows the positions for the other letters in the cycle action.

A separate eight-cel repeat cycle of "bubbles," B-3 to B-10, animates around the word "Moisture" during the movement of the lettering. During the eight-cel repeat cycle of the word "Moisture," a hook-up occurs in each of the animating letters. The letter M, for example, animates downward from the 3 position on cel 3L to the 5 position on cel 5L. At this extreme point, the letter M starts upward to the 1 position on cel 9L. The letter M, on 10L, the hook-up cel, is in the 2 position and the cycle is ready to be repeated with the letter M in the 3 position on cel 3L. The other letters in the word "Moisture" animate in similar cycles during the repeat action.

The smoothness of the action and the great saving of time and effort in all of the production departments of the studio more than justify the use of this type of animation short cut.

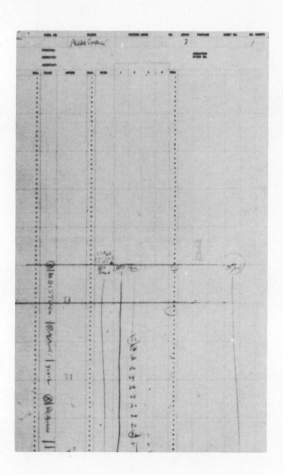

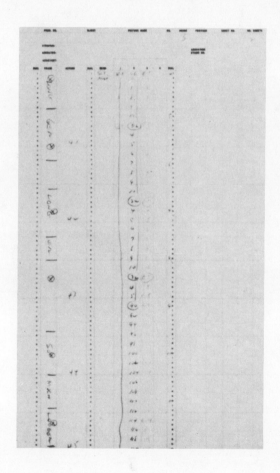

The Gimmick

The comment, "What some people won't do to keep from working," applies to the animator responsible for the gimmick shown here. Used in a scene from a Paramount Pictures cartoon studio production, the story board simply showed four Pilgrims walking through a wooded area after the landing on Plymouth Rock. The gimmick made by the animator for the walk cycle of the four characters, however, was an inspired effort. As a budget saver, the time required for the production of the gimmick was completely justified.

After the background layout had been completed and the characters designed, cutouts were made of each of the four figures and attached to long strips of illustration board. The pointed ends of the strips served as the registry marks for the positioning of the cutouts by the animation cameraman for each frame of the scene.

Each of the cutouts was photographed in the eight positions shown on the gimmick. A hook-up at the end of each cycle enabled the animator to repeat the walk for the entire length of the scene. The gimmick itself was registered to the bottom pegs in the normal center position. The pointed strips of illustration board, attached to the cutouts, were fitted into slots cut in the gimmick. These slots helped keep the cutouts in place during the photographic process and provided the animation cameraman with an additional registry point for positioning the cutouts according to the guide numbers.

The layout of the background and the overlay cel "C."

Above right:
The background and gimmick are shown here without overlay sliding cel "C." The overlay was used to conceal the gimmick and the non-existent legs of the four figures during the walk cycle.

Below right:
The complete set-up of the scene is shown in this photograph. The background and the pan moves, the gimmick with the characters taped in position, and the overlay cel "C" are all shown in relation to each other.

The pan background and the overlay sliding cel "C" were both registered to the top sliding peg bar. Overlay cel "C," the only cel used in the scene, contained the foliage that concealed the character's legs during the walk cycle.

Old Glory flying from the top of a flag pole is always a thrilling sight. To achieve such an effect in animation, the gimmick described here was used quite successfully. The blue area of the flag containing the stars was painted on a thin piece of illustration board and taped to underlay XX. Two pieces of cardboard pasted on underlay XX served as the track for the panning of the stripes in the flag. Vertical bands of color painted on the horizontal stripes simulated the folds in the flag and added realism to the action.

The hook-up positions for the panning stripes, 0 and 32, were identical and made possible the continuous movement needed for the scene. An area matching the shape of the flag was cut out of overlay X. Also used as the background for the flag, the mast was painted on this overlay by the background artist. A smooth animated action was achieved through the use of this clever gimmick. For the keen-eyed observer, the 33 stars in the flag were not a mistake by a careless artist. The gimmick was used in a picture showing the evolution of the flag. The flag shown in this scene was flown after Oregon was admitted to the Union as the 33rd State in 1859.

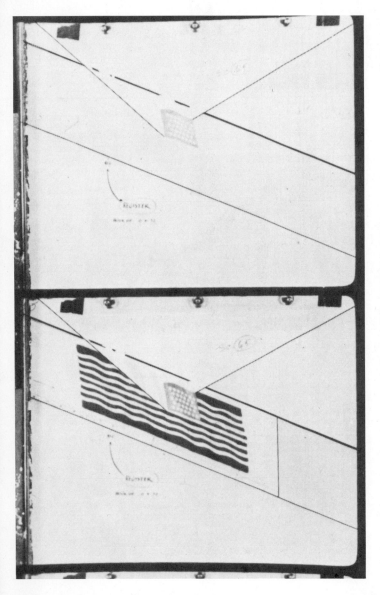

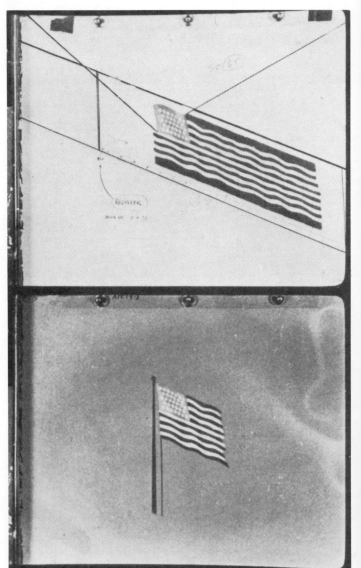

The components.

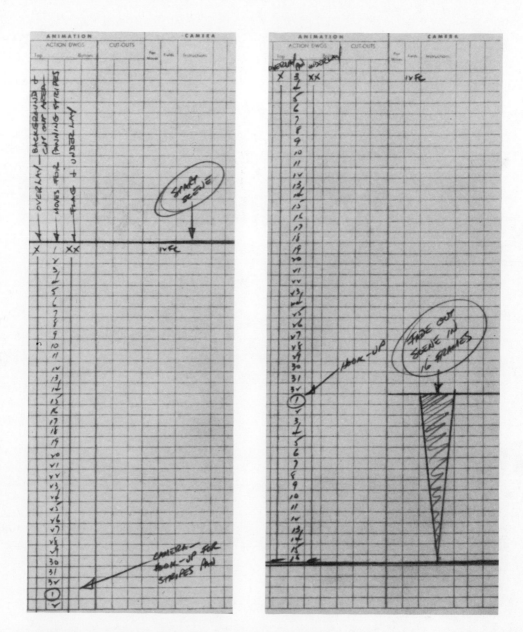

The exposure sheet shows the position of the overlay and underlay in relation to the gimmick. Note the hook-up positions for the panning of the stripes in the flag (1 and 32).

Animation and Live Action

The trend towards individuality and the unusual in commercial films is reflected by the theory, "if one is good, then two must be better."

Because of the constant search for new effects and methods of presentation by clients, advertising agencies, and production studios, motion picture techniques are combined to provide the viewer with an almost unlimited variety of effects. The use of animation techniques with live-action motion picture processes is generally recognized by researchers as the most effective combination.

Practically all of the technical processes described in detail in earlier sections are used in the commercial film that uses the combination of animation techniques and live action. Wipes, fades, and cross-dissolves are used freely for making transitions from animated scenes to live action and from live action to animation.

One of the frames from live-action sequence.

One of the animated drawings.

The matte made for the above drawing.

Animated wipes, other than those pictured on the wipe charts, are specially prepared to fill story board and script requirements. These animated wipes produce unusual effects and interesting visual transitions between animation and live action sequences.

The matte also plays an important part in the combining of techniques and makes possible the use of cartoon or other animation with live action without danger of a double-exposure effect. The superimposure of titles over live action scenes has also become routine in the combination of techniques.

These effects and processes are but a few of the many that are used for combining techniques and achieving the great variety of effects needed to satisfy today's commercial story board requirements. Combining not only creates additional visual interest but helps keep a firm hold on the viewer's attention, the fundamental objective of all commercials.

CARTOON ANIMATION AND LIVE ACTION

Although the processes used for combining live action sequences with cartoon animation are relatively simple compared with other techniques, a great amount of planning and preparation is needed for this type of commercial.

Before actual production can begin, the animation and live action directors must review the story board and decide on the approach or treatment of the film's subject matter. During this planning stage, the animation layout man designs the cartoon character that is to be used in the commercial. The sample or model cel of the inked and opaqued cartoon character plays a key part in the discussion between the two directors. Since the spotlight is to be shared, the clothes worn by the actors and the colors for the background or set used in the live filming are carefully selected in order to complement the colors used for the cartoon character.

The positioning of the actors is also of extreme importance, since a tracing of one of the projected frames of the live action film is used as a layout and guide by the animator. Standard production procedures are followed in the animation, inbetweening, inking, and opaquing departments. In the camera department, however, the photographic process differs slightly. In the first of the two filming processes, the cels are photographed on Eastman Background X 5230 or DuPont 936 B film, both ideally suited for animation purposes. During this first filming, the animation is photographed over a black card and normal top lighting is used.

For the second of the two filmings, the animation cameraman uses a high contrast film, Eastman 5362, for making the mattes needed for the optical combination of the animation with the live action film. Photographed with underlighting, a silhouette effect results when the opaqued cells are placed over the opal glass in the center of the compound table. This filming process is similar to the one used when photographing the drawings for a pencil test.

The high contrast positive, after processing by the laboratory, shows the animated action in silhouette on the clear celluloid film base. The high contrast negative shows the animation as the clear area and the balance of the frame, competely black.

During the optical process, four separate pieces of film are used for the combination of the animation with the live action film.

1. The live action film
2. The animation
3. The high contrast positive matte
4. The high contrast negative matte

The optical cameraman, in the first phase of the combining process, photographs the live action film with the high contrast positive matte. If the film were taken out of the optical camera and processed immediately after this run, the print would show the live ac-

The inked and opaqued cel.

The composite.

tion scene with a black silhouetted area in the place where the animation is to appear.

In the next step of the combining process, the film in the optical camera is returned to the frame where the animation begins. The camera shutter remains closed during the run-back. The two pieces of film containing the animation and the high contrast negative matte are then photographed over the film previously exposed on the first run. This completes the optical combination.

The film after processing will present the cartoon character and live performers in a co-starring role. The mattes, not visible in the final print, completely eliminate the possibility of a double-exposure effect.

While the home television viewer may not be aware of the great amount of planning, preparation, and effort behind the actual production of this type of commercial, the channel selector, nevertheless, remains in place for the entire projection time—a tribute to the effectiveness of the technique.

The live action and cartoon animation film clips shown here were taken from different film presentations. Both films were especially combined in order to show the effectiveness of the combined techniques.

The animation in column 1 was taken from a Paramount Pictures animated cartoon and photographed over a black card which served as the background. Normal top lighting was used for this filming.

Columns 2 and 3 show the mattes made by photographing the animation with under lighting. The high contrast positive is shown in column 2 and the high contrast negative in column 3. Column 4 shows the live action film as it appeared in a commercial.

If the film in the optical camera was processed after the live action scene was combined with the high contrast positive matte, the animation would appear in silhouette as shown in column 5. The completed effect, following the optical combination of the animation with the high contrast negative matte, is shown in column 6.

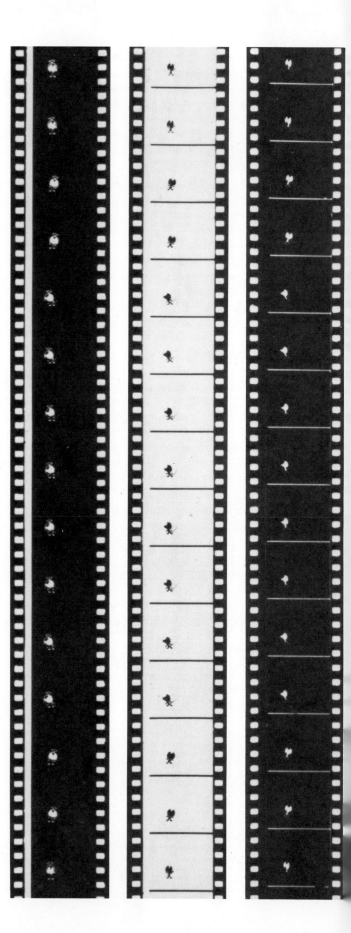

Miniatures, stop-motion, and animation.

Live-action combined with animation. Matteing processes were used to produce this eye-arresting sequence for a Green Giant commercial. Initially, a single frame from the live-action scene was projected onto the compound table of the animation stand. The tracing was subsequently used as the layout for positioning the animation.

The Visual Squeeze

The visual squeeze is a relative newcomer to commercial television when compared with older and more established film techniques. With this technique, an advertiser is able to "squeeze" more audio-visual information into a one-minute commercial than can be included in any other film presentation of similar length.

The idea for the technique originated with the animated "flip books," a concept as old as animation itself. In its original form, the illusion of motion in flip books was created by flipping a sequence of pictures. The pictures, assembled in book form, were bound or stapled together at one end in order to obtain a semblance of registry.

A modernized adaptation of the flip book, used as a training device during World War II, was indirectly responsible for the subsequent development of the visual squeeze technique. The tachistoscope, a specially constructed projection device used for training recruits in aircraft and ship identification, flashed images for only 1/150th of a second. The flash image method proved so highly effective for teaching that the idea was reactivated by advertisers and adapted for commercial films. The picture used in a commercial visual squeeze presentation, in contrast to tachistoscope projection, is projected and seen on the screen for several seconds.

The production of the visual squeeze film, unlike other films using animation techniques, does not begin at the motion picture studio. Instead, a still photographer takes as many as 500 pictures of the subject matter for a one-minute commercial. Only about a tenth of the many photographs taken are used in the actual production.

The pictures selected by the animation director are assembled and then registered to the pegs on the animation board. Exposure sheets, similar to those used for photographing animation, are prepared by the animator. The frame counts for the photographic process are determined by the film editor's analysis of the sound track. Although the film footage varies with each picture, it is unusual for any of the stills to remain on screen for more than a few feet.

In order to achieve an even greater variety of effects, animated actions are sometimes combined with the still photographs. In other film presentations using the visual squeeze technique, fully animated scenes are used as inserts in order to illustrate the more technical subject matter.

Very often, the figures in a sequence of still photographs are cut out and pasted on cels. Animation principles are used for the positioning of these cutouts in order to create an even greater illusion of movement. These cels are then photographed against an art background on the animation stand. The art backgrounds not only provide a novel setting for the live figures but also eliminate the need for props during the original still photography.

The success of practically all motion pictures depends on the near perfect synchronization of picture and sound. For the visual squeeze technique, the relationship *must* be perfect. The failure to obtain a critical sync in matching picture to sound can mean the difference between a good presentation and a dud. The sound, or effect, accompanying the change from one photograph to another must hit on the exact frame where the change occurs. The copy for this type of film presentation, usually in meter, is sung or recited to the beat of an original musical score written especially for the commercial.

The subliminal process, in which a picture of a prod-

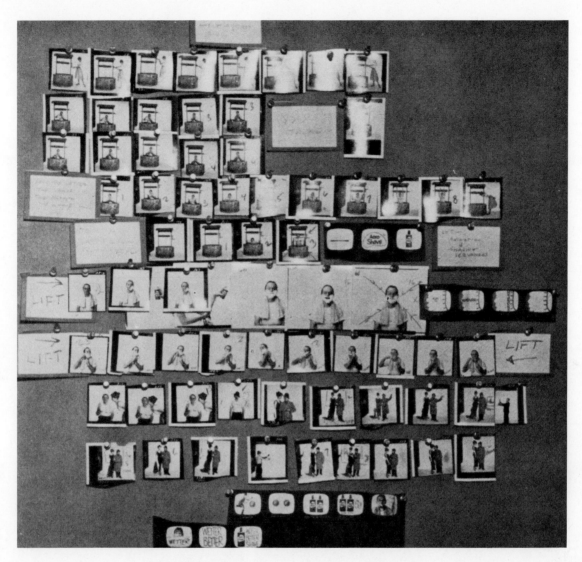

Photographic story board of Aero-Shave commercial.

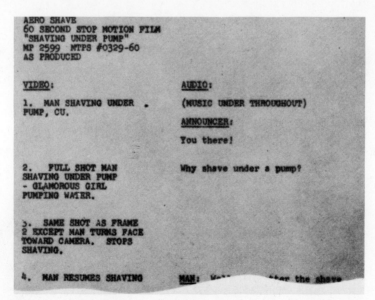

The script.

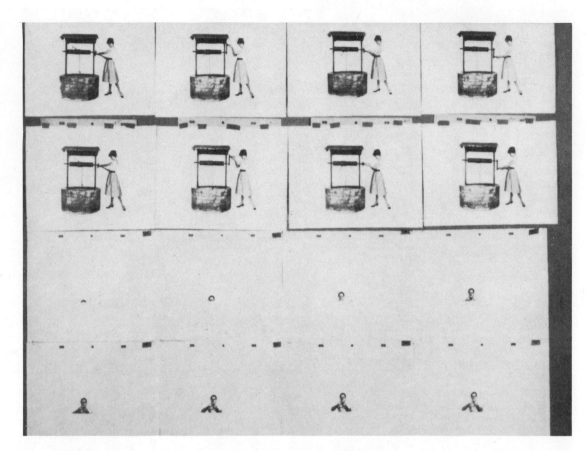

The "drawings" used in Scene 1.

uct is flashed on the screen for a fraction of a second during a televised show, is still in the experimental stage at this time. A distant relation of the visual squeeze technique, it is designed as a suggestive influence on the viewer's subconscious mind and is actually a peace-time version of the tachistoscope.

While the time required for the production of a one-minute visual squeeze television commercial is considerably less than the time needed for the production of a fully animated commercial of the same length, there is very little difference in production costs of the two techniques. The visual squeeze presentation, the fully animated film, and most of the technical animation productions all cost about the same to produce.

The Aero Shave commercial is an excellent example of the technique that uses still photographs for the subject and a great variety of camera and compound table movements for creating the illusion of motion in the stills.

The movement of cutouts, the animation of still photographs, and many other effects and techniques not usually found in cartoon animation are used freely in the visual squeeze film. Some of the more interesting sequences from the Aero Shave commercial, technically known as Production 6429, 60-second "Well," are reviewed and analyzed in this section.

In the opening scene of the commercial, a model, Pamela Curran, is shown turning a well handle, thereby causing the appearance of Stan Sherwin, another actor used in the film presentation. The entire action, achieved with still photographs, is filmed on the animation stand. Since the still photographs contain all of the props and subject matter, no background is required for this opening scene.

Scene 1 of the Aero-Shave commercial, beginning with the fade in, is shown in this film sequence.

The cutout, "background, and animation" for Scene 2.

The first 32 frames indicated on the exposure sheet consist of the ''bumper,'' or safety footage. The photographs exposed in column 1 contain a repeat action showing the turning of the well handle. A blank cel is exposed in column 2 in order to maintain the same density throughout the two-cel level scene. At frame 26, the blank cel is replaced by the cels showing Mr. Sherwin emerging from the depths of the well. The photographs containing this action are cut out and pasted in position on cels. The repeat action, exposed in column 1, continues while the lathered hero makes his entrance.

The exposure sheets for Scene 1 of the Aero-Shave commercial.

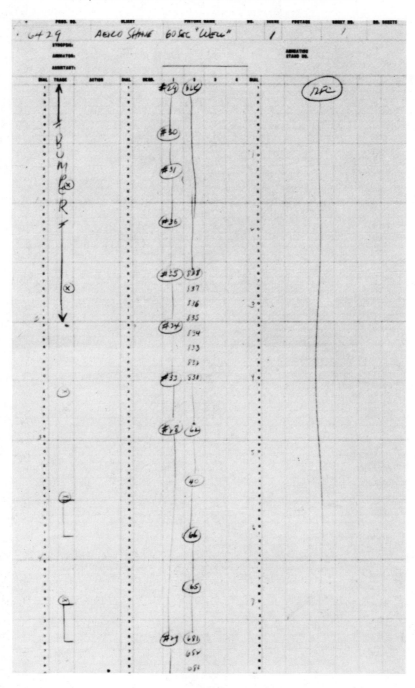

At frame 89, our hero drops back into the well and the action is replaced by a blank cel. The same cels, 688 to 681, used for dropping Mr. Sherwin into the well are exposed in reverse in order to bring him back up again at frame 103.

The action in column 1, showing Pamela Curran turning the well handle, continues to the end of the scene at frame 128. The circled X's in the track column on the exposure sheets indicate the musical beat on the accompanying sound track.

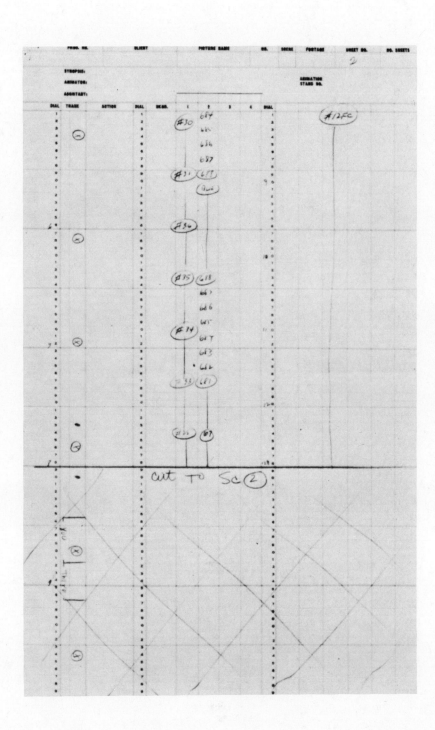

Scene 2 of the Aero Shave commercial is photographed on the 7½ field with the compound table in its center position. A continuation of the action from the preceding scene, two blank cels are exposed over the still photograph which serves as the background for this scene.

An interesting action begins at frame 189 of exposure sheet 3 (picture 4). In this sequence, a cutout made from a photograph is moved from one position to another over the still background. Unlike the photographs which were cut out and positioned on cels in Scene 1, the photograph used as a cutout in this scene

The exposure sheets used for filming Scene 2 of the Aero-Shave commercial.

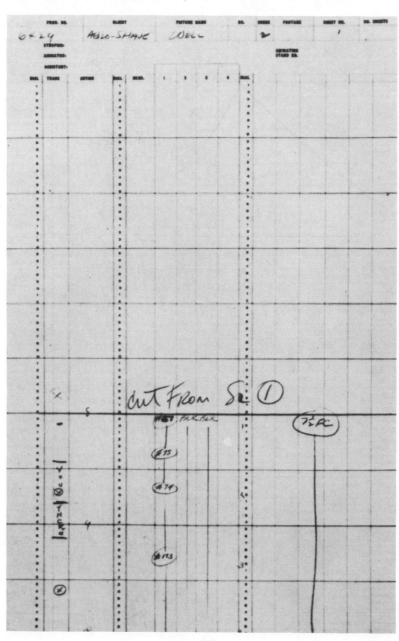

is *not* pasted on a cel. Neither is it registered to the pegs. Instead, a guide made by the animator, a pivot point on the cutout itself and a second pivot point on the background, provides the animation cameraman with the registration needed for moving the cutout dur-ing the filming process. Each of the 12 positions indicated on the guide is photographed for two frames, or a total of 24 frames for the complete action which ends at frame 211. From that frame until frame 225, the cutout remains in a static or hold position.

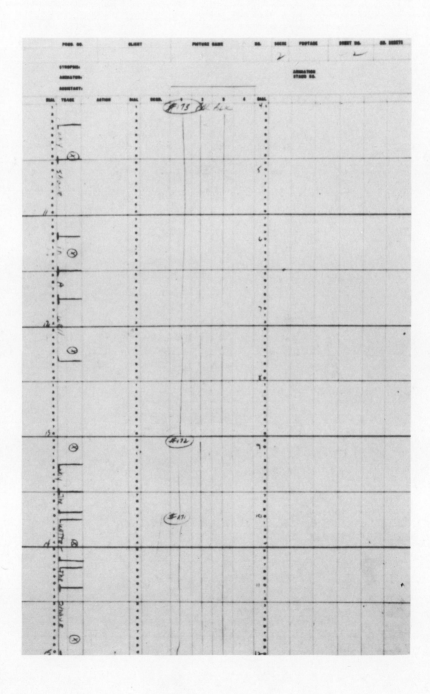

Guide X and the two pivot points, used previously for bringing the cutout to its "stop" position, are also used for moving the cutout back to its "starting" position and out of camera range. At frame 259, a zoom to a closer field is indicated on the exposure sheet. The calibrations for moving the camera from the 7½ field to the 4 field, the final position for the zoom, are indicated on the exposure sheet. A pantograph guide for moving the compound table to the 1-south position was made by the animation cameraman.

Scene 2 continued showing the moves for the cutout.

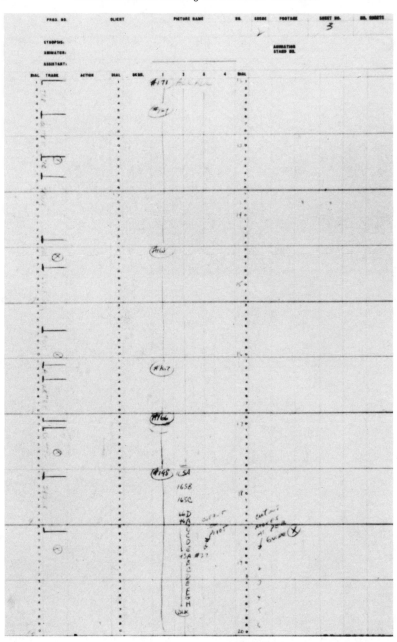

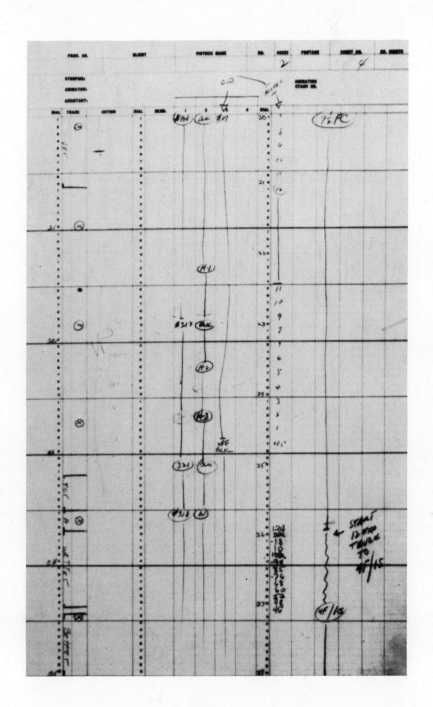

137

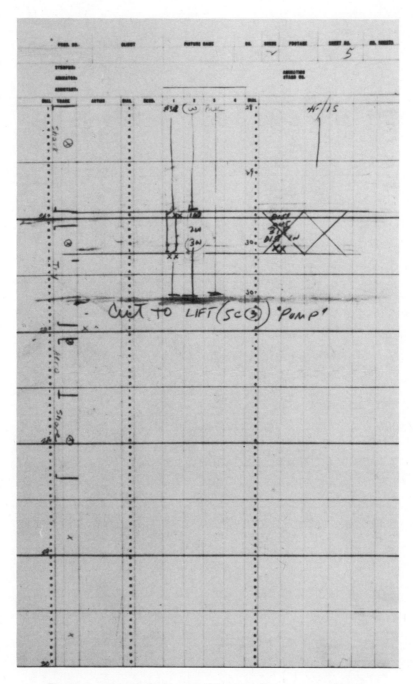

The exposure sheets for Scene 3 of the Aero-Shave commercial—
animation with lettering.

Scene 3 from the Aero Shave commercial is a complete departure from the technique used in other sections of the one-minute film presentation. Almost technical in its approach, action, and subject matter, the background for this scene shows the shaving surface of a man's face.

Cel W-1, exposed in column 1 on the exposure sheet, is a hold cel of the beard stubble. This cel is matched to cutout NA, the skin line which is pasted to the background. The blank cel in column 2 is replaced by the cels showing the animated formation of the word "Moisture." Column 3 of the three-cel level scene also begins with a blank cel. The numbers exposed in that column, beginning with B-3, are written in red pencil as an indication to the animation cameraman that the cels are also used in another scene of the commercial.

The cycle, B-3 to B-10, is a repeat action of bubbles

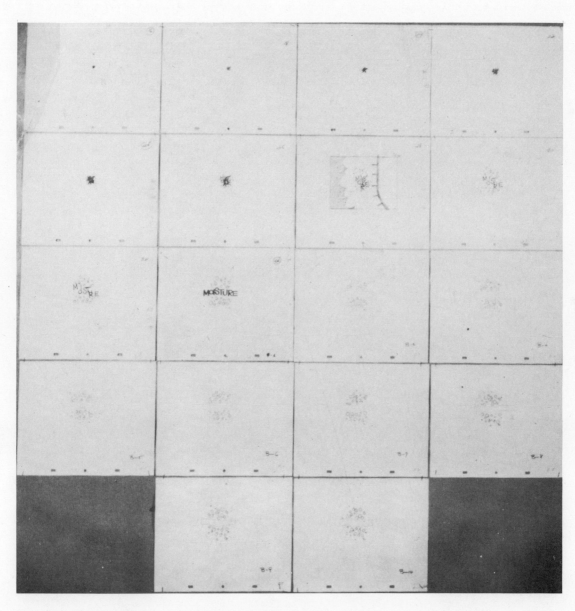

Shown here are the layouts and drawings used in Scene 3 of the Aero-Shave commercial.

animating around the word "Moisture." Cels 3-L to 10L, exposed in column 2, show the animation of the word "Moisture," another repeat cycle. Both cycles continue to frame 90 on exposure sheet 2. At that frame, the repeat action ends and an animated transition to the next action begins.

The hold cel of the beard stubble, W-1, goes into animation at frame 124 on exposure sheet 3 and is re-placed by a blank cel. The N series of cels contains the combination of the stubble and the word "Moisture." In this action, the word "Moisture" continues to animate and gradually disappears into the stubble. Cel W-2, the final hold cel of the stubble, is exposed for the balance of the scene. The second repeat cycle of the animating bubbles, B-114 to B-120, continues to the end of the scene at frame 168.

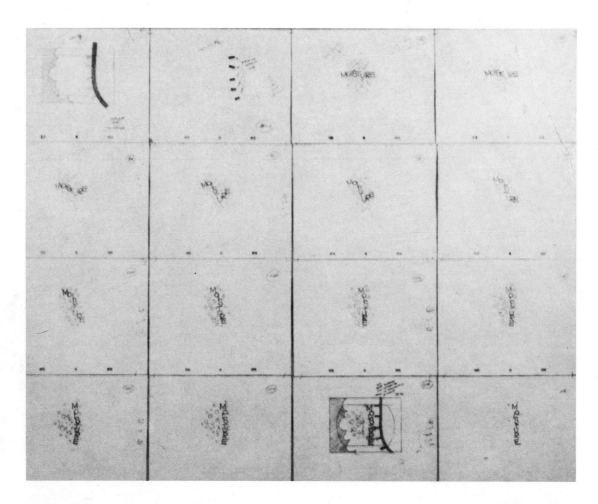

. . . Scene 3.

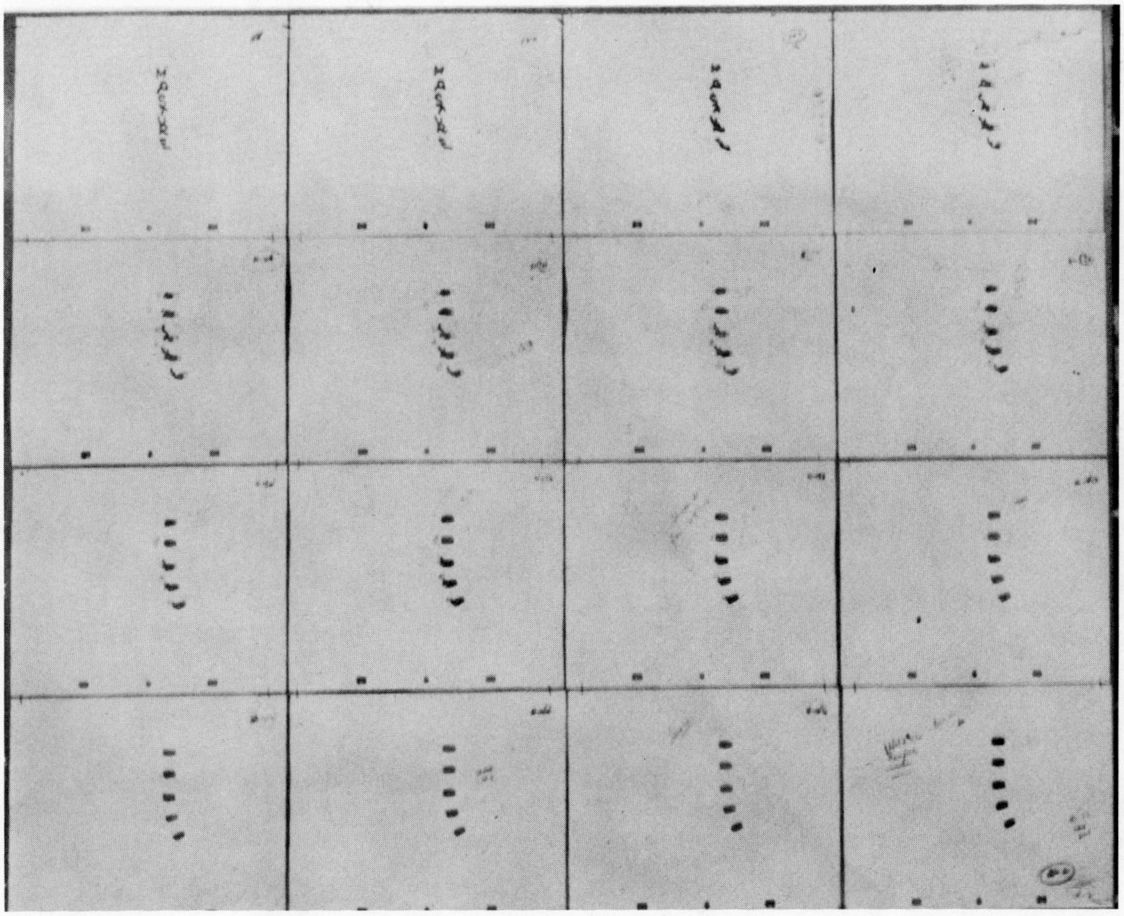

This film sequence shows the cross-dissolve to Scene 3 and the formation of the word "moisture" in the Aero-Shave commercial.

"Moisture" animating.

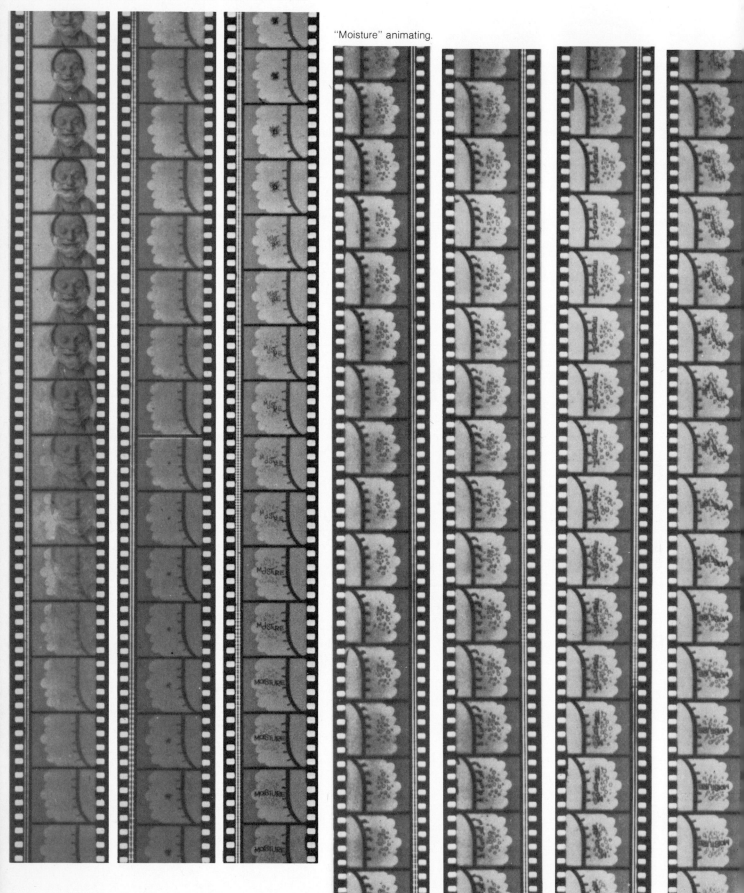

Another interesting sequence from the Aero Shave commercial illustrates the effectiveness of animation when combined with still photographs.

A pencil tracing, made from the photograph that is to be used as the background for the opening section of the scene, serves as the layout for the accurate positioning of the animated action. The field position indicated on this tracing is used as a guide for the animation cameraman as well as for the animator.

The word "Wetter" drawn on layout W cross-dissolves to the word "Better" in the scene's opening action. Each of the two words, exposed over photographs showing a model dunking a towel in a tub, was lettered on a separate cel. If each word had been lettered on the photographs used in the sequence, it would not have been possible to repeat the action with the same photos during the filming process.

Drawings B-1 to B-8 contain an animated transition from the word "Better" to "Aero Shave" and from "Aero Shave" to the line on drawing B-8. In the action

that follows, the photograph of the model, used as the background for the beginning of the scene, cross-dissolves to another photograph showing a close-up of the model's hands.

The line on drawing X in the next animation sequence is a tracing of the line on drawing B-8 in a different field position. This line animates into the shape of the Aero Shave can which matches to the hand on layout H. The position of the hand in the close-up photograph necessitated the change in field positions during the animated action.

The change from one field guide position to another while the animated action remains in the same position in relation to the film frame is made possible with the camera projection process. This previously explained process enables the animation cameraman to project a frame of film onto the compound table for the purpose of matching and accurately positioning the art work.

Another interesting sequence in the Aero-Shave commercial.

The film sequence from the Aero-Shave visual squeeze commercial shows the many possibilities of the technique and the effective combination of animation with live-action photographs.

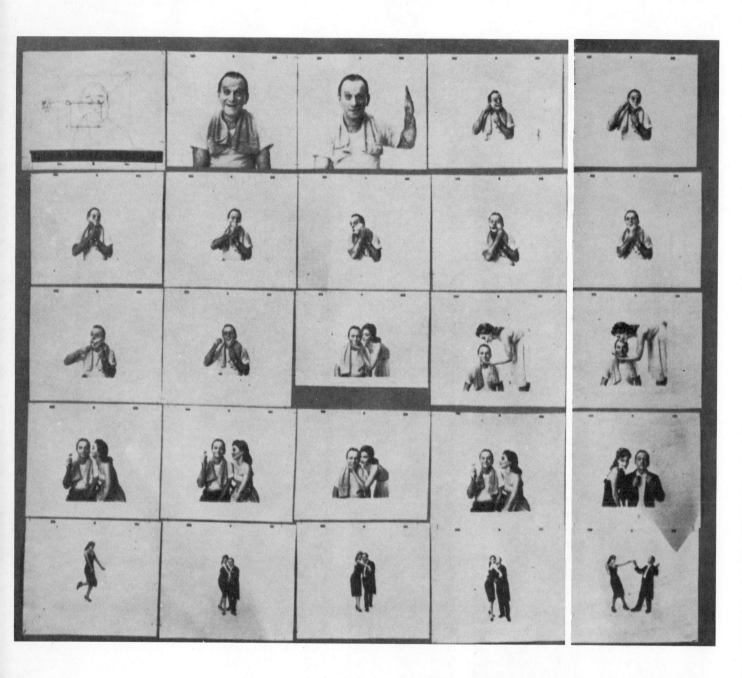

Another sequence of still photographs used in the Aero-Shave
commercial. Here again, each of the stills was photographed
for the amount of film footage needed to fit the music and dialogue
on the accompanying sound track.

Letters of the alphabet for identification purposes are used quite frequently in this type of production. Each of the three layouts used in this animated sequence is identified by a letter rather than by a number. Layout W, for instance, contains the word "Wetter." The second layout, B, has the word "Better" as a part of subject matter, while the letter H identifies the third layout, the close-up of the hands.

Each of the animated actions also uses letters of the alphabet, along with numbers, for similar reasons. The cycle of drawings containing the bubble animation was identified by the letter B, while the drawings of the animating word "Moisture" were identified by an L, obviously for "lettering."

The examples included here are representative of the techniques used in the visual squeeze film presentation. They indicate the almost unlimited variety of effects that can be achieved by combining animated actions with still photographs. The examples also help to explain the reason behind the increasing popularity of the technique.

"Coins to cans" could very well be the caption for this film sequence. Used near the end of the Aero-Shave commercial, the clever transition effectively emphasizes the comparatively low price of the product.

Technical Animation

Unlike cartoon animation, in which the primary objective is entertainment, technical animation, as the name implies, is used for entirely different purposes.

The importance of technical animation in educational and training programs has been generally recognized and acknowledged in recent years. Specialized visual aid films using technical animation have not only speeded up training programs but have proven themselves superior in many ways to other educational methods in use today.

While technical animation films teach more thoroughly and quickly than other audio-visual techniques, surveys have shown that a greater percentage of the subject matter in these films is retained by the viewer. For this reason, the technique has been eagerly accepted by advertisers as well as educators. For commercial demonstration purposes, in which animation techniques are needed to show actions that cannot be demonstrated with live-action or stop-motion processes, technical animation has no peer.

More than 70 percent of men in uniform, and those working in war plants, saw films using technical animation processes during World War II. While no comparative figures or statistics exist, it is highly improbable that any other educational method has the capacity for instructing so many people in such relatively short periods of time.

Most of the processes used in this film technique, from script and story board to the composite or final print, are similar to the processes used in standard animation production. Whereas cartoon animation uses caricatures and comic situations as subject matter, technical animation uses objects, diagrams, symbols, and other graphic material. The use of sliding cels in cartoon animation is generally limited to movement cycles and other actions when the panning of the traveling peg bars is required. In technical animation, however, it is the standard-size cel that is the rarity and not the sliding cel.

An excerpt from the script for the Amoco commercial.

THE JOSEPH KATZ COMPANY
Advertising

AMOCO BUILDING
555 FIFTH AVE., NEW YORK 17, N. Y.

Advertiser AMERICAN OIL COMPANY
AM-3086, Rev.
Product AMOCO-GAS

Station_____

Date of Telecast_____

Length of Telecast 1-Minute

Type Film

TV COMMERCIAL

COMMERCIAL "C" - Lawn Mower

VIDEO	AUDIO
6. MAN & WOMAN GLIDING ALONG HIGHWAY IN MODERN HARDTOP SEDAN.	6. can convince people to switch their buying habits!
7. ANIMATED LINE OF CARS BECOMES AMOCO OVAL SIGN (LOGO)	7. In the gasoline industry -- that product is unleaded AMOCO-GAS! Yes, in the past 12 months ...
8. LOSE LOGO & DISSOLVE IN THREE STATION MONTAGE INTO OVAL.	8. more motorists switched to AMOCO-GAS (BEAT) than to any other premium gasoline!
9. ZOOM-IN AMOCO PUMP FROM ENGINE. STATION IN BG.	9. Because only AMOCO contains no lead! That's why .. only AMOCO
10. SUPER: "MORE GAS PER GALLON!"	10. guarantees you - MORE GAS PER GALLON!
11. CUT TO ROAD SHOT & CAR TRAVELING.	11. And more gas means (BEAT) more mileage ...
*12. ZOOM-IN ON CAR'S HOOD AND DISSOLVE THROUGH TO ENGINE.	*12. Plus -- more engine protection! Because there's ..
*13. SUPER: "Contains no lead"	*13. No lead in Amoco to form lead acids that corrode your muffler. No lead to form deposits
*14. SUPER OUT ON "muffler"	
*15. ZOOM-IN PISTON ON "that"	15. that foul your valves, plugs, and pistons.
16. CUT TO GAS GAUGE FROM FUEL NEEDLE.	16. So, next time your gas gauge reads (BEAT) "LOW" -- join the switch to ..
17. NEEDLE MOVES EMPTY TO FULL. WIPE IN THE WORD: "AMOCO"	17. unleaded AMOCO ...
18. DISSOLVE MONTAGE TO HANGING AMOCO OVAL.	18. and get more gas per gallon (BEAT) at your neighborhood Amoco Dealer's!

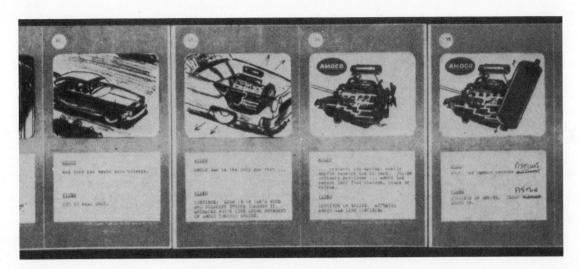

The story board for the Amoco commercial.

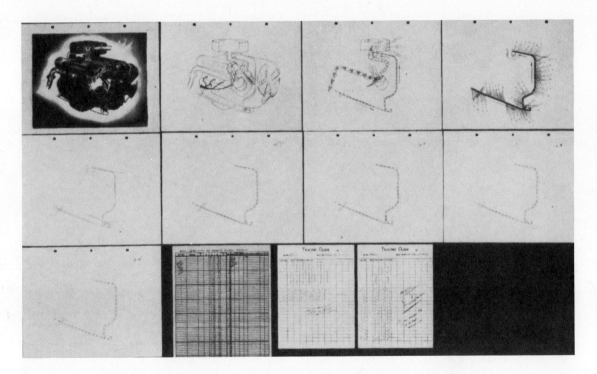

The background and layouts used in the production of the Amoco commercial.

Multiple runs, mattes, and burn-ins, or double-exposures, are other processes that are seldom used in cartoon animation. In technical animation, the multiple run, the use of mattes, and the double exposure are considered the norm and must be included as standard procedure. Cutouts of figures and objects are used freely, and relatively complicated processes such as the scratch-off are also considered routine in this type of film presentation.

In recent years, three-dimensional models of machines have been especially constructed in order to demonstrate complicated processes and mechanisms. Titles, arrows, directional lines, and other effects photographed on the animation stand are often combined optically with the live action film showing the three-dimensional models in motion.

When educational or training films using these models in combination with technical animation have been included as a part of a regular course of instruction, students have shown greater progress in proportionately less time than in courses given at schools where no film program exists. More important, however, is the fact that a greater percentage of the information imparted through this film medium is retained by the student.

Industry today is well aware of the effectiveness of this type of instruction. That awareness is reflected in the expanded training and visual aid programs sponsored by an ever increasing number of industrial organizations throughout the world.

Although the prices for technical animation films vary considerably, they cannot be included in the low budget category. The production cost for technical animation footage in many cases exceeds the footage cost of the animated cartoon film.

Production AM-3086, a one-minute commercial made for the American Oil Company, contains an effective example of technical animation. Although the animation sequence was used in order to illustrate the unleaded properties of Amoco gasoline, the same film footage might have been used for educational purposes as well.

A photograph of a four-cycle automobile engine cut away to show the moving parts served as the background for the animation. Animated repeat actions showing the four cycles in their exact relationship to each other were combined in order to demonstrate the various parts of the operating engine. Ten separate series of drawings were needed in order to explain and illustrate the engine's four cycles. In all cases, the drawings were animated as repeat actions so that the inked cels could be used repeatedly during the photographic process in order to show the continuous action of the operating engine.

Each series of drawings was combined with others to decrease the number of cel levels during the filming. (Only two cel levels were actually used during the photographic process.) For the intake, the first of the four cycles of the operating engine, a four drawing repeat showed the gasoline flow from the tank to the

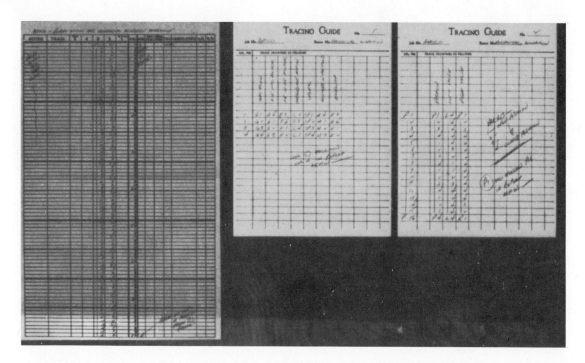

The exposure sheet and the tracing guides used for combining the various animated cycles.

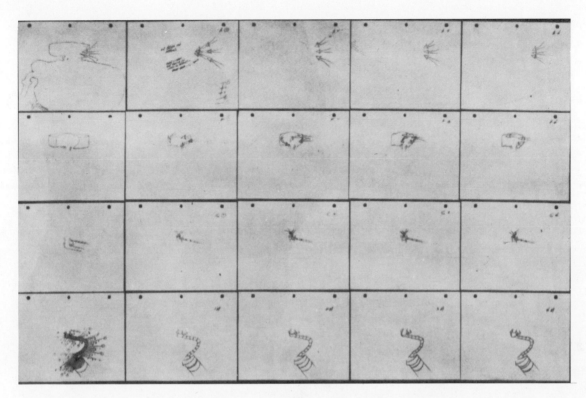

The cycles.

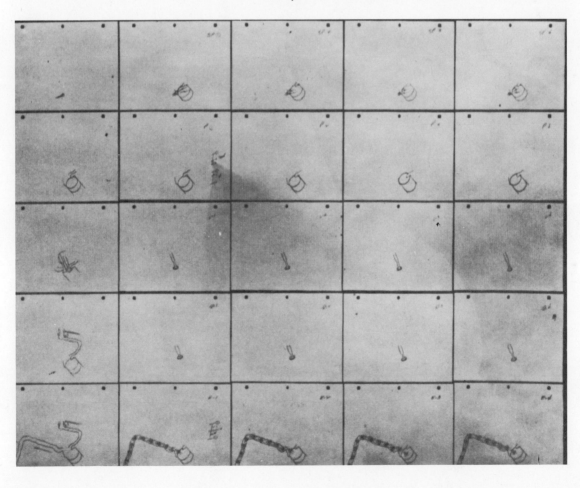

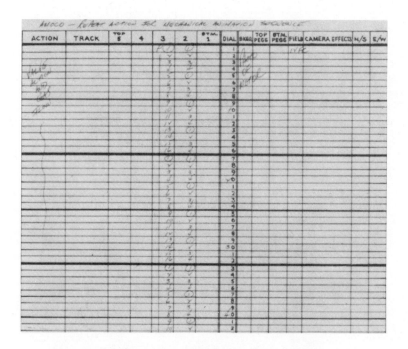

These tracing guides show how the ten sets of drawings in the mechanical animation sequence were combined during the inking process. The combination of these repeat cycles on two cel levels resulted in a great saving of time during the photographic process.

Only one exposure sheet accompanied the cels and background of the mechanical animation sequence to the camera department. Frame 1 on the exposure sheet followed frame 80 as a hook-up for the continuation of the action. The only other information needed by the animation cameraman was the actual film footage count for the entire sequence.

fuel pump and then on to the engine's carburetor. Another series of four drawings was needed to show the air being drawn into the air filter at the top of the engine.

In the second stage, or compression cycle, two other four drawing repeats illustrated the mixing of the air and gasoline in the carburetor and the flow of the mixture from the carburetor into the intake manifold on the way to the combustion chamber.

The mixture of gasoline and air in the combustion or third stage of the four-cycle process is drawn into the manifold by the vacuum created by the action of the piston in the cylinder. Four sets of drawings were needed to illustrate this action. The first of the four drawing repeats showed the mixture flowing through the intake manifold. The opening of the intake valve, permitting the mixture to flow into the cylinder, the compressing action of the piston, and the spark needed to ignite the mixture were all animated as separate repeat cycles.

For the exhaust stage, the last of the four cycles, one series of drawings showed the exhaust valve opening and allowing the mixture to enter the exhaust manifold. The dissipated mixture on its way out of the car by way of the muffler was shown as another animated repeat action.

When seen as a continuous action, the effect of the combined animation is amazingly realistic. The fact that the operation of a complicated engine could be explained by this amateur mechanic is proof of the effectiveness of this type of animation for educational purposes. Today, thousands of industrial organizations throughout the country have adopted this graphic method for teaching and training personnel in the use of complicated mechanisms and processes. While the textbook and instructor have not been replaced completely by the animated film, the motion picture technique has, nevertheless, been generally accepted as the more efficient teacher.

The film sequence.

THE SCRATCH-OFF

Although cameramen once flinched and turned pale at the mere mention of the words "scratch-off," the process has now become a routine assignment in the production of technical animation. Today, the scratch-off is respected, rather than feared, by production personnel and producer alike.

During the filming of a scene that includes a scratch-off, portions of the inked lines and/or opaqued cels are scratched off or removed, according to the instructions on the exposure sheets. Guides made by the animator indicate the exact area that is to be removed for each frame during the photographic process. The cels containing the subject matter are usually com-

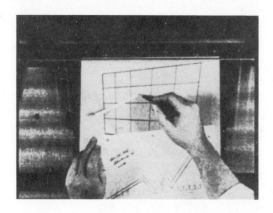 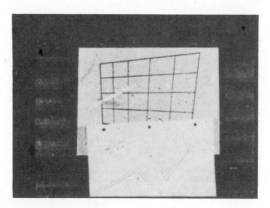

These photographs, taken with the animation camera, show the cameraman scratching away a portion of the line during the reverse filming.

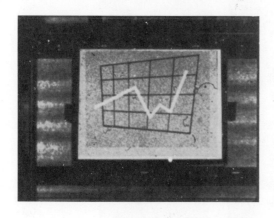 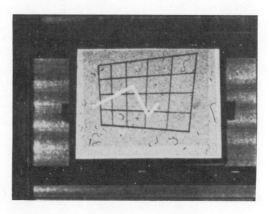

In these photographs, taken during the actual filming of the sequence, portions of the line have already been scratched away.

pletely blank after the filming has been completed. For this reason, a scene containing a scratch-off is almost always photographed in reverse, the last frame in the scene being the first one photographed. When the processed film is projected after a scene has been photographed in this manner the subject matter that had been scratched off becomes progressively more visible on each frame of film.

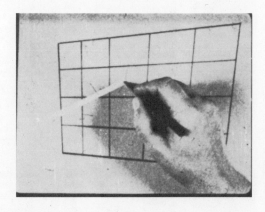

The end of a pen holder, sharpened to a fine point, is usually used for scratching away small areas.

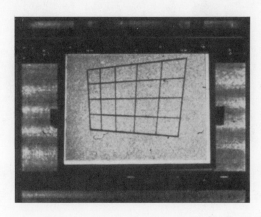

The line has been completely scratched away in this photograph. The last frame to be filmed will be the first one projected after the film has been processed. When seen on the screen, the line will animate across the frame, from left to right.

The use of a single cel for achieving a scratch-off effect, instead of the large number of cels which would have been needed in order to show a similar action with animation, not only assures the smoothness of the action but eliminates a considerable amount of retracing during the inking process. (It would be almost impossible for an inker to retrace portions of an animated action on a great number of cels and maintain accurate registry or duplicate the consistency of the inked lines throughout the retracing.)

Although similar effects can be achieved by masking the areas to be removed instead of scratching them away, the method is not always practical.

If, for example, it is necessary to show a line animating from one side of the field to the other, the complete line is inked on a cel in white and photographed over a black card. Although the inking procedure is the same for both the scratch-off and masking methods, when the masking method is used, the line must be photographed as a separate run, similar to the burn-in or double-exposure.

With the camera running in a forward direction during this separate run, a second black card is placed over the cel containing the white line and then moved progressively across the screen for each frame of the filming process in order to reveal the white line underneath. The lack of any visible relationship between art work photographed on the first run and the areas to be masked on the second run makes this type of masking impractical in most cases. If it were necessary to match the masked areas to an animated action that had been photographed on a previous run, the lack of visible relationship would make the matching process an extremely risky undertaking.

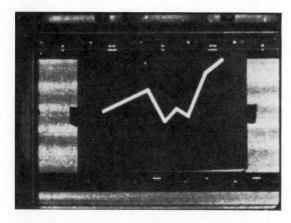

For the masking process, the white line is inked on a cel and photographed over a black card.

A second black card placed over the line cel is panned across the cel, revealing the white line underneath.

This film sequence shows the line animating across the frame via the masking process.

Where it is necessary to duplicate camera or compound table movements that had been made on the first run, the masking method would also be considered impractical.

The use of either method, depending on its practicality in a scene, makes possible the smooth flow of animated movement needed for the proper presentation of the type of subject matter usually found in technical animation. Besides being a great time and budget saver, the many and varied uses of the scratch-off in animation make possible a great variety of effects unobtainable with other methods.

The one-minute Anacin film presentation contains an effective example of the scratch-off process and its commercial application.

In order to achieve the desired effect for the split-screen shot, the X is photographed in reverse by the animation cameraman. Each of the lines forming the X is inked and opaqued on a separate cel. Pencil guides for each of the two lines indicate the exact area that is to be scratched off for each frame during the reverse filming.

If the same action had been animated, the effect would have required the inking and opaquing of ten cels. Each of these cels would have to match each of the other cels used in the formation of the X in order to avoid the undesirable jiggling effect caused by improperly traced lines.

The Anacin commercial also contains many excellent examples of the processes used in technical animation. Repeat actions, the scratch-off, and other animation short cuts for illustrating the unusual subject matter generally found in this type of film presentation are used freely and to advantage. Although some of the animated sequences in the commercial are quite lengthy, surprisingly few drawings are needed for the graphic demonstration of the subject matter.

The titles, animation, and the 2 cels for the scratch-off action are shown in position over the background.

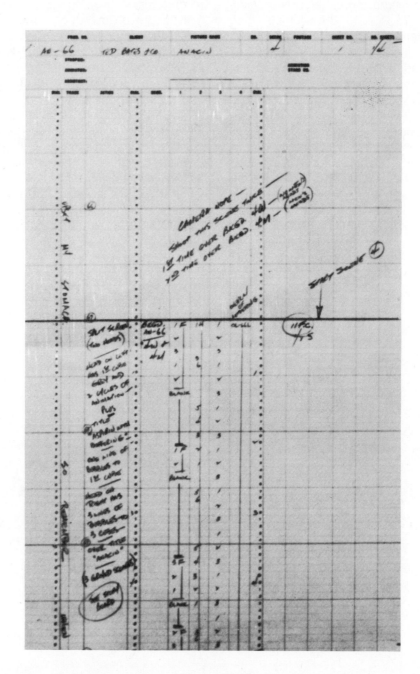

The exposure sheets used for photographing the repeat cycles in the Anacin commercial.

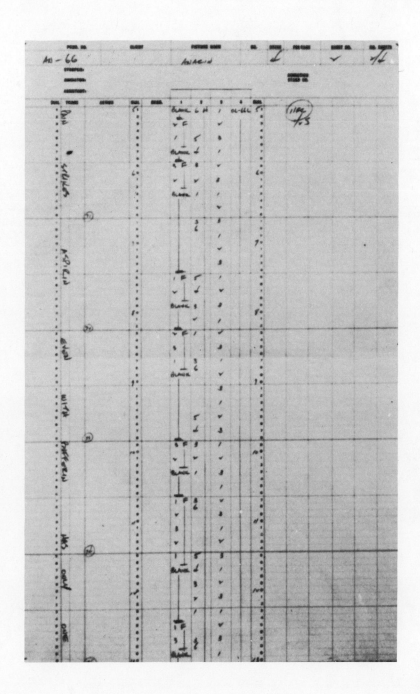

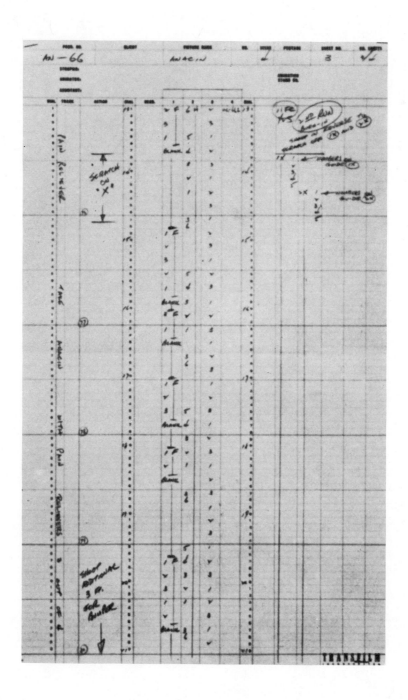

Below right:

In some scratch-off actions, a cutoff photograph of a hand is shown holding a pen, pencil, or brush. The touch of realism this adds to the scratch-off effect is well worth the additional time and effort during the photographic process. While the scratch-off process remains the same, the tip of the pen, pencil, or brush is placed at the end of each scratch-off position. The movement of the hand is, of course, consistent with the scratch-off action. The cutout of the hand is moved smoothly by registering it against a push pin set in the compound table.

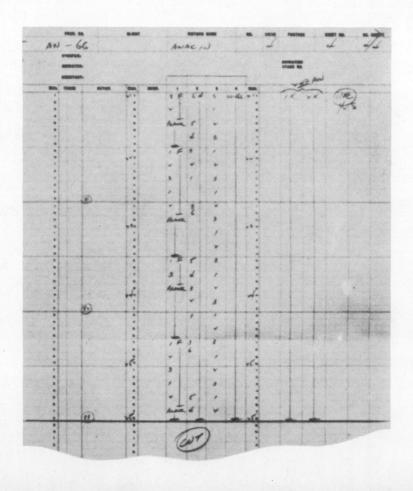

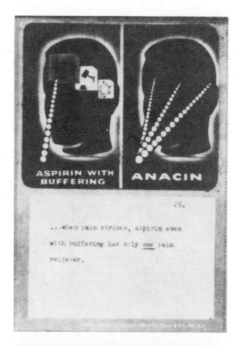

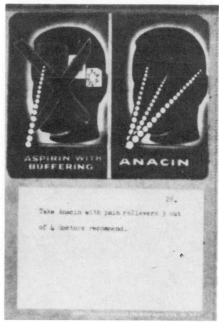

The scratch-off and the transition to the following scene.

A part of the story board used in the production of the Anacin commercial.

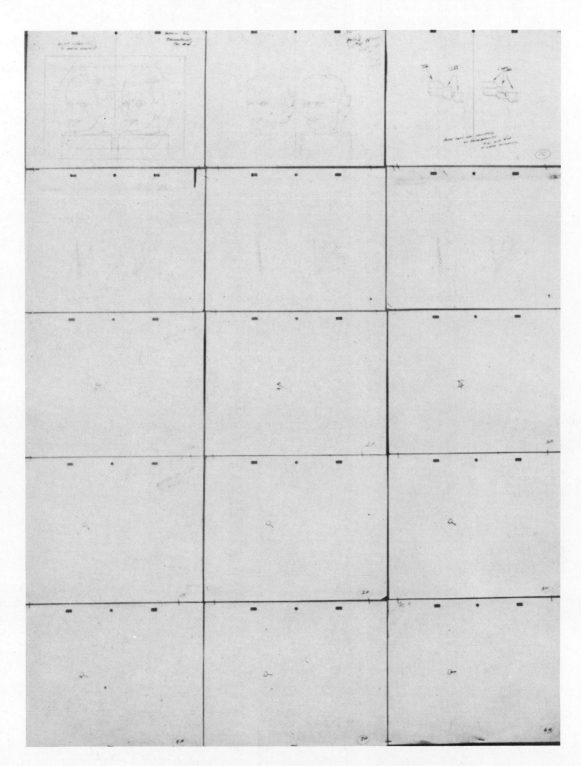

The animation cycles used in the Anacin commercial.

The wipe effect to the animated sequence in the Anacin commercial.

Titles

Since the motion picture industry's infancy, titles have been used in a wide variety of ways for as many purposes. In addition to spelling out the name of the picture being exhibited, the members of the cast, and other related credits, titles also advised ladies to please remove their hats and advertised the wares of local merchants. And, for many years before the industry found its voice, titles in the form of captions complemented the projected images and helped the viewer follow the film's story line.

The industry's voice, in the form of a sound track synchronized with the corresponding picture, has replaced the explanatory captions. Stylized or specially-designed main titles and credits, however, still follow the time-honored tradition and, in many cases, establish a mood or theme for the picture that follows. Legibility is, of course, the all important requirement. During our more than 40 years in the industry, we have seen titles lettered on a strip of sandy beach and, at the other extreme, a title spelled out by a sky-writing plane. Some of the more recent psychedelic effects achieved with computer-generated techniques are truly "out of this world." Obviously, since no specific rulings exist, title treatments will continue to be subject to the whims of imaginative art directors—and budget limitations.

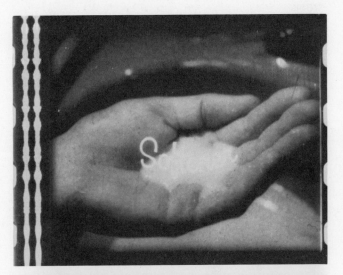

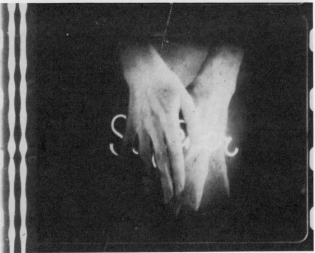

Animating titles were used in the Proctor & Gamble Thrill commercial to visually suggest the qualities of the product. Poured out of its container, the product animated to form the word "Softener" sandwiched between the woman's hands. Mattes were needed for those sections of the 290-frame sequence in which the woman's fingers covered any part of the animating word that described the qualities of the dishwashing aid.

In television-commercial production, the title is an integral part of the presentation. Complementing the accompanying picture, the title lends visual support to the corresponding sound track. Like the specially designed titles prepared for feature films, titles used in television commercials are also expected to establish a theme or visually suggest the qualities of a product. Words like "clean" or "fresh," for example, dictate the use of white lettering. (Remember, black hats are for bad guys.) The word "flavor," similarly, should be designed to whet the viewer's appetite and make him rush to the refrigerator in search of the advertised product. Words like "big" should be larger than the other words in the same message. The word "speed" should be lettered so that a maximum of movement is suggested. A word like "soft" should be designed to create the desired impression. Whatever the design, titles must appear on cue and remain in synchronization with the message on the accompanying sound track.

Animating titles have always been particularly effective. For introducing a feature film or for suggesting a product's qualities, the title is prepared using the same general procedures that are used in the production of an animation sequence involving cartoon characters. The animated title is drawn, inked, opaqued, and then photographed over a suitable background on the animation stand. If the title is to be superimposed over a live-action scene, it is positioned over a black card and photographed on high-contrast film. Titles are usually lettered on clear acetate cels—the same type used for inking and opaquing the cartoon characters—and photographed over an appropriate background on the animation stand. If the title is to be superimposed over a live-action scene, the negative and positive images on the high-contrast film that is used for photographing the title is combined optically with the live scene. White titles are merely "burned" in over the scene. If a color is to be introduced, however, the negative title—black lettering within the clear area of the film frame—is exposed with the live scene during the first camera run of the optical combination. The shutter is then closed and the film is backed up to the frame where the title was first exposed. At that point, the positive title—white lettering in the opaque black frame—is threaded on the projection side of the printer and a filter representing the desired color is exposed during the second camera run.

Double-exposure effects are achieved by varying the amount of exposure during the optical printing process. With the shutter completely open at the 180-degree reading, the title will "burn" in and be completely opaque; half-way open, the scene will be partially visible through the superimposed title; when the shutter is closed down to about 25-percent, a title would be quite transparent.

Titles may be introduced in a number of ways. A title may be zoomed up from infinity or zoomed back from beyond the limits of the film frame until it seems to disappear completely into one of the film's emulsion layers. If possible, assuming the effect would not interfere with the scene's subject matter, a title may be zoomed to its final position in the film frame from several points—simultaneously. This type of effect is spectacular and worth the planning that makes it possible. The effect is achieved by photographing the title in its final position and then reshooting the title from any of the start positions to the frame immediately preceding that final position. Obviously, if the title is to zoom from each corner of the frame to its final position, four separate zooms must be plotted. Each of the zooms requires a separate camera run to the final frame that precedes the hold position.

If desirable, a title may be panned into its hold position from a point outside the film frame, or it may be made to appear gradually by means of a fade effect. A title may also be made to materialize on successive frames of film by using the scratch-off process or through the use of any one of the large number of available wipe patterns.

Titles can be made more readable by introducing a dropped shadow. This effect seems to separate the title from the background. To achieve the effect, the optical cameraman exposes the negative title over the background scene. The negative title acts as a matte during the first optical camera run. During the second camera run, the positive title is offset. The negative title thus provides the shadow which may be slightly higher, lower, or to the right or left of the burned-in positive title.

A crawl title, also referred to as a running title, is a convenient method for dispensing information on a wholesale basis. The large, economy-size message containing credits, acknowledgments, or a scene-setting synopsis for the movie or play that is about to be presented, is lettered on long sliding cels or black cards. The title is photographed either on the animation stand or set up in a panning device and exposed to a television camera. During the panning movement, each line of the title appears at the bottom of the film frame, travels upward at an appropriate reading speed, and disappears beyond the top limits of the film frame.

In this Nabisco commercial, the name of the cracker, Premium, animates to form the package.

Montage

In montage, a number of related images are visible within the film frame simultaneously. It is used in many ways for as many different purposes. In a feature-length production the film editor may use a series of extremely short lengths of film spliced together to create an impression. There is no attempt at visual continuity: the effect is used to save time, film footage, and several pages of explanatory script. In a television commercial, montage is not only a necessity but a merchandising aid as well. In a one-minute commercial, montage is used to increase the amount of information reaching the consumer. Compare Collage and Visual Squeeze.

Collage is a montage effect. The subject matter displayed throughout the film frame may consist of a wide variety of graphic elements, including photographs, drawings, or abstract materials.

The Slide Film or Filmstrip

Narration for "TEXAS" Slide Film--73 frames

1--Musical opening continues over frames 2, 3 and 4. 5--Texas, nicknamed the Lone Star State, 6--in 1845, became 7--the 28th State to be admitted to the Union. It is by far 8--the largest with its 267,339 square miles. That figure represents almost 1/11th of the nation's total area.

9--The name Texas, is of Indian derivation and means appropriately enough -"Friends." 10--"Friendship" is the state motto. 11--Although Texas was discovered in 1519 by dePineda of Spain, it remained unsettled until 1682, when a mission was founded at Ysleta, in the extreme western part of the State. 12--There was very little American interest in Texas until after the Louisiana Purchase. Since 1836, when Texas became an independent republic, 13--its population has steadily increased until at the last census-taking, 14--the figure reached 8,397,000 and 15--6th in the national rankings.

16--The entire state of T··

··· ···creased rapidly in the reconstruction period that followed. Railroads helped push back the frontiers as 64--did the more adventurous stage coach companies 65--and the more picturesque Mississippi steamboats. 66--More and more settlements sprang up as 67--cowboys drove cattle over the Western trails and the grasslands to the North.

68--The development of wheat 69--and cotton farming increased rapidly. 70--The rich strike at Spindletop, near Beaumont, in 1901, was the first of a succession of 71--spectacular oil discoveries throughout Texas 72--which have dominated the State's economic life in the 20th Century.

73--The number one citizen of Texas, birthplace Abilene, is, of course, Ike.

* The individual frames of the Slide Film are projected and timed to fit the narration even though it is sometimes necessary to introduce and project a new frame in the middle of a sentence.

Each frame of the slide film is a separate unit with its own picture subject, title, and narration. Here is the narration and script for a slide film on Texas.

Unlike any of the other motion picture techniques, in which many frames of film are needed in order to show the simplest action, each frame of a slide film tells its own story.

Although standard motion picture film is used for the photographic process, each frame of the slide film is projected in sequence with specially designed equipment for the length of time needed for the accompanying narration. In most cases, the dialogue or narration for the slide film is recorded on discs. Similar to phonograph records, these discs are played on turntables while an operator advances each frame of film manually to coincide with the narration on the disc.

When the slide film technique was a relatively new process, the narration or dialogue for each frame of the filmstrip was separated by the sound of a bell on the recorded disc. For this reason, early slide films were often referred to as "bell" pictures.

The specially designed equipment for the projection of slide films. The turntable for the accompanying sound track is attached directly to the projector. (Courtesy Dukane Corp.)

About half of the 73 frames shown here make up the average slide
film or filmstrip.

A description of the subject matter across the lower portion of each frame of film is sometimes used in place of the recorded disc. The inclusion of such titles eliminates the need for a sound track or disc and makes that type of slide film much less expensive to produce.

Photographs, art work, cartoons, the combination of art work with photographs, and many other art techniques have all been used successfully in the production of slide films. All of these techniques are included in the accompanying example of a typical slide film.

Although most slide films are made for educational purposes and classroom use, today many of these films covering a great variety of subjects are available in public libraries. In many cases, large industrial organizations sponsor the production of these films as a gesture of good will.

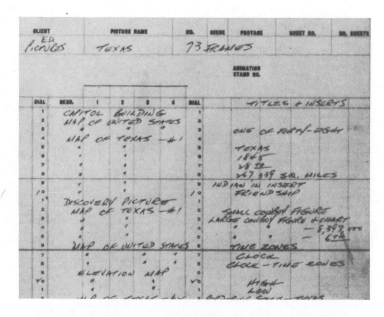

This ambitious presentation depicted the historical, geographical, and industrial development of the state of Texas in one film. The narration, pre-recorded on a disc or record, accompanied the projection of the individual frames of film. Photographs, illustrations, cartoons, maps, and charts were combined effectively in order to add interest to the slide film.

The Slide Motion Film or Filmograph

A comparative newcomer when compared with older and more established motion picture techniques, the slide motion film is sometimes referred to as a filmograph.

The subject matter or art work for both the slide film and the slide motion production is prepared in similar fashion. Unlike animation techniques, in which each movement or action is achieved by photographing a great number of cels or drawings in sequence, here the illusion of movement is usually accomplished with camera movements.

The subject matter or art work is photographed on the animation stand for the corresponding film length of the sound track. The sound track, similar to those used for other motion picture techniques, is analyzed and timed by the film editor. Frame counts, provided by the film editor, guide the animation cameraman during the photographic process.

Zooms and pans are the most frequently used camera movements in this type of film presentation. Additional effects such as fades, cross-dissolves, and wipes also help remove the static qualities found in the individual slide-film frame. The generous use of cutouts, moving about in sync with the sound track, heightens interest and adds to the over-all illusion of movement.

While each individual slide-film frame is projected on specially designed equipment for the length of time required by the narration or dialogue on the recorded disc, the slide motion film is projected at normal motion picture speed on conventional equipment.

More involved than the slide film but far less technical in the production processes than other films using animation techniques, the slide motion production solves the cost problem for the low budget producer. Although this type of presentation can be referred to as a bargain basement motion picture, large industrial organizations are finding the slide motion film a valuable aid for training personnel.

Because of the increased use and acceptance of the slide film and slide motion presentation for educational and training purposes, many organizations in recent years have set up their own departments for the production of these films.

Frames 11 through 21 from the slide film described in the preceding chapter are discussed here for the purpose of showing the relationship between the static frames in the slide film and the movement potential of the same frames in the slide motion production.

The same art work and material, beginning with the illustration showing the discovery and settlement of the territory of Texas, was also used for the slide motion presentation. Each of the photographs and cels from the individual frames of the slide film was photographed for the film footage needed to sync up with the narration on the accompanying sound track. The camera movements and effects added during the photographic process are explained in the accompanying layouts.

Although the production cost of a slide motion presentation is greater than the comparative cost of a slide film, the additional cost is certainly justified by the results.

*Wherever the term fade-in is used, except at the beginning of a scene, the same procedure for making a cross-dissolve must be followed. It is first necessary to fade-out existing subject matter before new material can be faded-in. This process keeps the color and density of the subject matter consistent during the fade-in and throughout the scene.

Population Sequence

1. Fade-in illustration showing discovery and settlement of Texas.

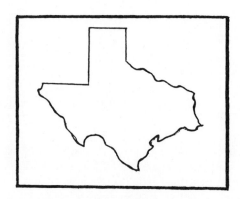

2. Cross-dissolve to map of Texas.

5. Pop on larger figure of cowboy representing the population of the state at the last census taking.

6.* Fade-in title, "8,397,000" (present population of state).

172

The same art work as it appeared in the slide film.

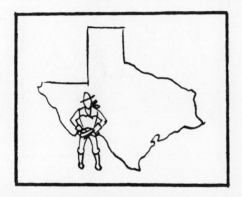

3. Pop on small figure of cowboy representing the population in the days of the early settlements.

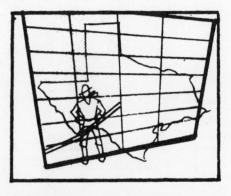

4. Superimpose graph over map of state. Scratch-on graph line, tracing population increase, on second run.

7. Fade-in second title, "6th" (ranking compared with other states). Cross-dissolve to tone card and scene showing time zones.

Where it is *not* necessary to change cels for each frame during the photographic process, abbreviated or shorthand exposure sheets are often used. These exposure sheets provide the animation cameraman with all of the information needed for photographing limited animation or slide motion sequences.

173

Time Zones

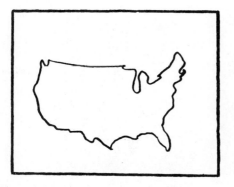

1. Scratch on white outline of map of United States (second run).

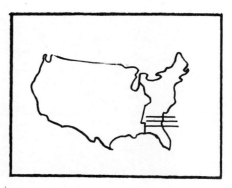

2. Fade-in first time zone within outlines of map. Pop on title, "Eastern Standard."

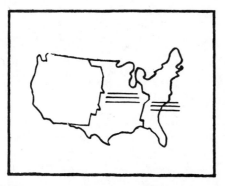

3. Fade-in second time zone within outlines of map. Pop on title, "Central Standard."

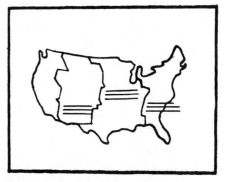

4. Fade-in third time zone within outlines of map. Pop on title, "Mountain Standard."

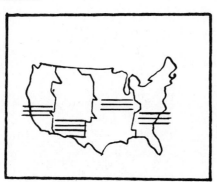

5. Pop on fourth time zone within outlines of map. Pop on title, "Pacific Standard."

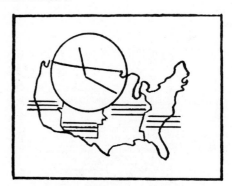

6. Fade-in cutout of a clock over state.

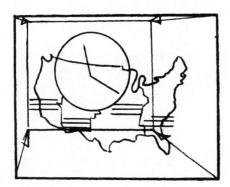

7. Zoom and pan to a close-up of the clock. Wipe to tone card and elevation sequence.

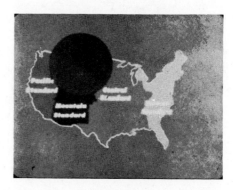

The composite frame as it appeared in the slide film.

Elevation Scene

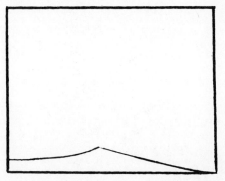

1. Fade-in first section of elevation scene over tone card.

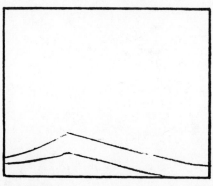

2. Immediately following the first fade-in, repeat with second section.

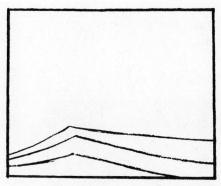

3. Fade-in third section.

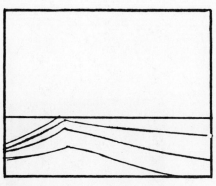

4. Fade-in fourth section and line.

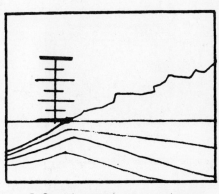

5. Scratch on scale on second run.

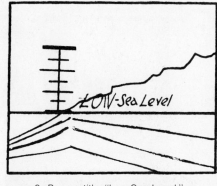

6. Pop on title, "Low-Sea Level."

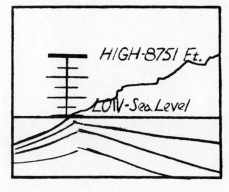

7. Pop on title, "High-8751 Feet." Fade-out scene.

The same art work as it appeared in the slide film.

175

Stop-Motion

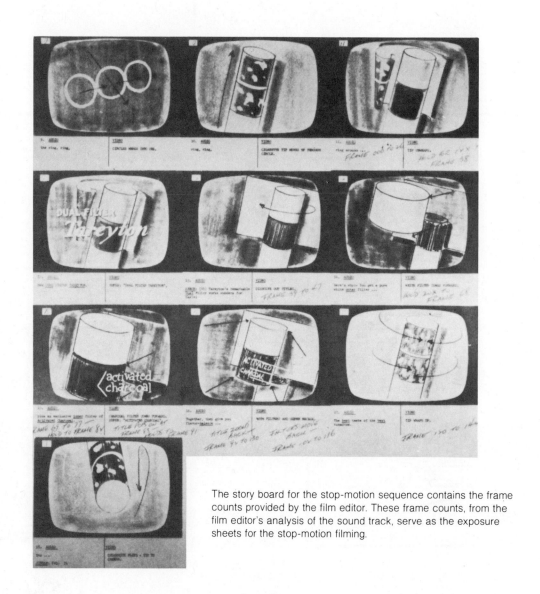

The story board for the stop-motion sequence contains the frame counts provided by the film editor. These frame counts, from the film editor's analysis of the sound track, serve as the exposure sheets for the stop-motion filming.

All animation techniques are basically stop-motion processes. The stop-motion mechanism, attached to the camera, makes possible single-frame photography on standard motion picture film.

The single-frame filming of subject matter, other than animation, is also made possible with the stop-motion mechanism. The "marching cigarette" commercials, in the early days of television, contained excellent examples of the stop-motion technique. More recently, commercial films using stop-motion processes have shown wrappers folding themselves neatly around products and bottles or glasses being filled, or emptied, without visible assistance. Other commercial films using this technique have, at different times, impressed and amazed the television viewer. To the advertiser, however, the impressive fact is that product identification for commercials using stop-motion techniques is considerably greater than the identification percentages of many other commercial techniques.

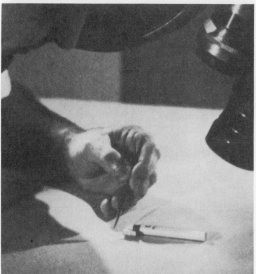

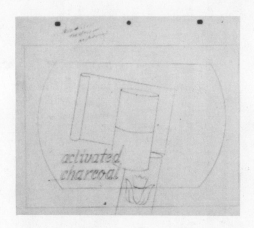

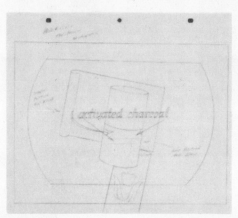

Instructions for the animation cameraman for the stop-motion sequence. Compare this drawing with the film clips of the same sequence.

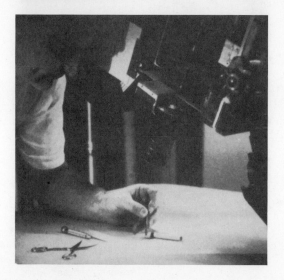

In these close-up photographs of the stop-motion action, the wrapper is being moved away from the cigarette in order to show the dual filters. The wrapper, for each frame of film, is moved approximately 1/32nd of an inch with the patience, precision, and skill of a surgeon performing a delicate operation.

The lengths of film show the entire sequence of action as it appears on the home television screen. For each frame of the stop-motion action, skilled technicians with animation experience carefully make the moves needed to show the action of the filter-tip wrapper.

The stop-motion mechanism attached to the camera and frame counter.

For the photographic process, miniature backgrounds or sets similar to those used for live action shooting must be especially constructed. Technicians with experience in both live action filming methods and animation processes arrange the lighting for the set, handle the cameras, and move or manipulate the subject matter for each frame of the action.

The stop-motion photographic process is usually slow and painstaking. For this reason, the costs vary considerably, depending on the subject matter. The average production cost for each foot of film is slightly higher than the cost of cartoon animation.

To meet today's demand for increased animated film production and lower costs, a variable, high-speed, stop-motion motor is necessary in order to handle the tremendous shocks that shutter mechanisms must withstand. The stop-motion motor is attached to the animation camera, either directly or through an adaptor.

The speeds usually range from 60 rpm or ½-second exposure to 240 rpm or ⅛-second exposure. This range provides latitude for slow or fast film stock and for variations in lighting systems.

A fast rewind speed operates at 720 rpm or the equivalent of 1/24-second exposure. The four forward speeds permit a greater choice of lens stops and the 180 and 240 speeds save time on long, continuous camera runs for titles and similar work.

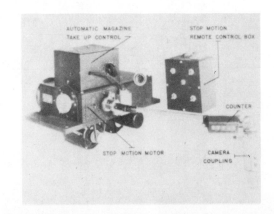

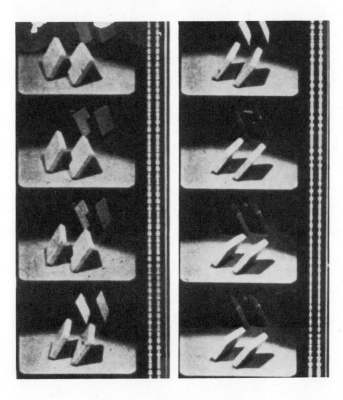

Stop-motion. These pats of margarine never attended dancing classes but, in synchronization with the pre-recorded sound track, they did their own version of the "twist" for a Kraft television commercial. For each frame of the stop-motion sequence, the pats were carefully moved to new positions by skilled technicians who carried out their assignments in compliance with the choreographer's instructions.

Time-Lapse Photography

This is the process of exposing subject matter at predetermined time intervals. The process is of particular importance in those filming situations where the subject matter moves too slowly to be detected as continuous movement by the eye. The filming technique requires the use of timing devices that control the camera, studio set lights, and other related equipment. Exposure can be made at one-minute or one-hour intervals, day and night, for long periods of time. The technique is extremely valuable for scientific observation as well as for industrial and commercial purposes.

When the film is run at normal projection rates (24-frames-per-second), chemical processes that would normally require long periods of constant observation can be viewed conveniently in minutes and the action can be studied on large screens. Flowers have magically progressed from bud to full bloom in seconds and lumpy pieces of dough have been transformed into mouth-watering delicacies in less time than it takes to flip the switch on the viewer's microwave oven.

Time-lapse photography. This mouth-watering effect was produced for the General Foods Corporation. Using time-lapse techniques, a lumpy mound of dough becomes a golden, luscious roll in just a few seconds of projection time.

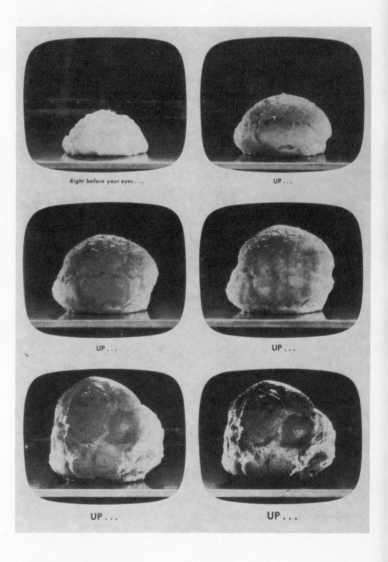

Right before your eyes . . .

UP . . .

UP . . .

UP . . .

UP . . .

UP . . .

Techniques Combined

The first frame of the story board.

Several motion picture techniques are very effectively combined in the 1440 frames of film used in the production of the Dual Filter Tareyton commercial made for The American Tobacco Company.

Noted simply as production 618 on the Gumbinner Advertising Agency's schedule, the one-minute film presentation also includes a variety of animated effects that are combined optically with live action and stop-motion sequences. The transition effects used in the commercial are cleverly introduced and well integrated with the script's subject matter. A good sound track that includes a catchy jingle provides the background for the well-paced visual portion of the commercial.

The production of the animation that is used in conjunction with the live action and stop-motion sequences is, in itself, a most interesting process. References to the film clips and storyboard accompany the detailed explanation of the production, filming and optical processes needed for combining the animation and titles with the live action and stop-motion sequences.

The live action scene that introduces the Tareyton cigarette commercial shows a young couple fishing from a motor boat. A camera pan from the boat to the ripples in the water precedes the cross-dissolve to the animated "rings" shown in panel 6 of the story board.

More of the story board used in the production
of the Tareyton commercial.

2. AUDIO

(MUSICAL VAMP)

VIDEO

CAMERA PANS IN TO SHOT OF
MAN SHOWING WOMAN HOW TO
USE FISHING ROD.

3. AUDIO

(MUSICAL VAMP)

VIDEO

WOMAN CASTS FISHING ROD
WITH MAN ASSISTING.

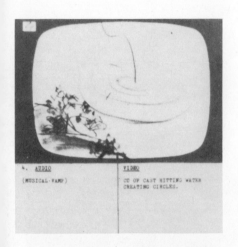

4. AUDIO

(MUSICAL VAMP)

VIDEO

CU OF CAST HITTING WATER
CREATING CIRCLES.

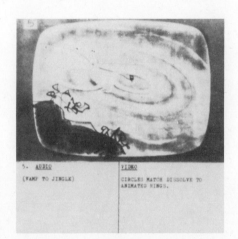

5. AUDIO

(VAMP TO JINGLE)

VIDEO

CIRCLES MATCH DISSOLVE TO
ANIMATED RINGS.

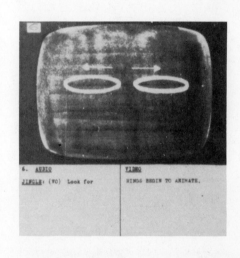

6. AUDIO

JINGLE: (VO) Look for

VIDEO

RINGS BEGIN TO ANIMATE.

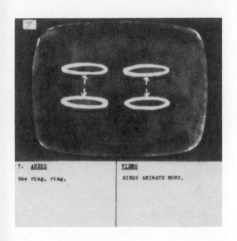

7. AUDIO

the ring, ring,

VIDEO

RINGS ANIMATE MORE.

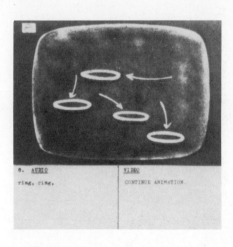

8. AUDIO

ring, ring.

VIDEO

CONTINUE ANIMATION.

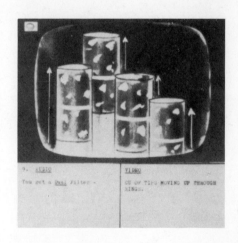

9. AUDIO

You get a Dual filter -

VIDEO

CU OF TIPS MOVING UP THROUGH
RINGS.

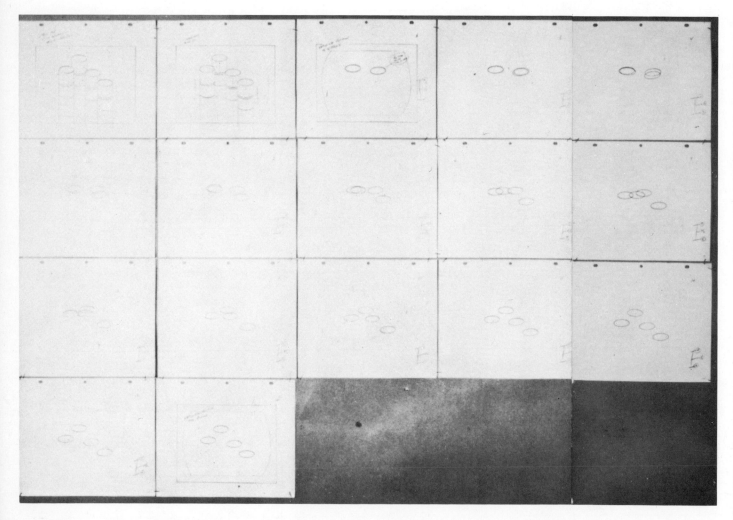

The drawings used for the ring animation.

For the positioning and matching of these animated rings to the ripples in the live action scene, one of the frames of the live action scene is projected onto the compound table. A tracing of the ripples in the projected frame of film is used as a layout for the ring action by the animator. This process assures a perfect match and the smoothness of the transition from the live action ripples to the animated rings during the cross-dissolve from the live action scene.

The same projection process used for determining the matching position at the beginning of the animated action is also used for matching the ring animation to the stop-motion sequence that follows. The rings on the completed drawings are inked in white and the cels are photographed over a black card on the animation stand. A high contrast film is used for the photographic process.

This film sequence contains a portion of the animation showing the rings matching to the cigarettes in the stop-motion film.

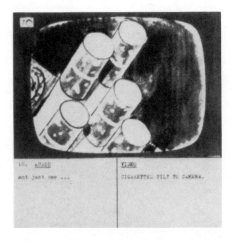

10. AUDIO
not just one ...

VIDEO
CIGARETTES TILT TO CAMERA.

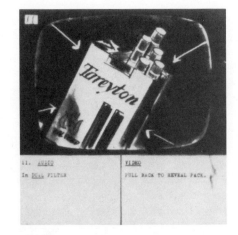

11. AUDIO
In DUAL FILTER

VIDEO
PULL BACK TO REVEAL PACK.

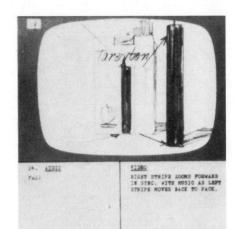

14. AUDIO
full

VIDEO
RIGHT STRIPE ZOOMS FORWARD IN SYNC. WITH MUSIC AS LEFT STRIPE MOVES BACK TO PACK.

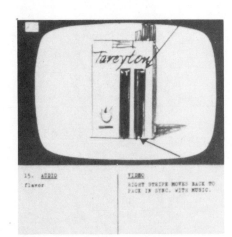

15. AUDIO
flavor

VIDEO
RIGHT STRIPE MOVES BACK TO PACK IN SYNC. WITH MUSIC.

18. AUDIO
as no single filter can.

VIDEO
LEFT STRIPE MOVES ACROSS SCREEN LEFT & BACK WIPING IN SUPER: "AS NO SINGLE FILTER CAN."

19. AUDIO
DUAL FILTER .

VIDEO
TITLE "DUAL FILTER" ZOOMS TO FRONT OF SCREEN .   WIPE

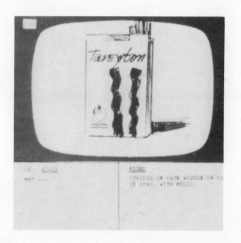

Don't touch that dial . . .

In the first step of the optical combination, the opening live action scene of the commercial is photographed, or copied, according to the instructions on the optical layout sheets. At the frame indicated for the start of the cross-dissolve to the stop-motion film, the live action scene is faded *out*. The film in the optical camera is then returned to the same frame in which the fade out began. The shutter remains closed during the run-back of the film.

To complete the cross-dissolve, the stop-motion film is faded *in* over the same frames in which the live action scene was faded out. The animated rings on the high contrast film are photographed on a second run over the previously exposed film in the optical camera until each of the four rings is in its matching position in relation to the cigarettes. The stop-motion film serves as the background for the rings on the high contrast film.

The layouts for the stripe animation used in the film sequence that follows.

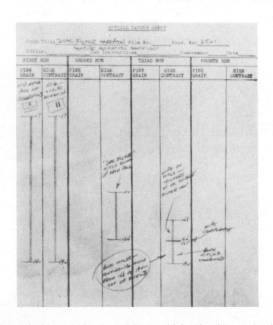

The optical layout sheet used for combining the titles and stripe animation with the stop-motion film in the Dual Filter Tareyton commercial.

The accompanying film clips show the entire animated action as it appears in the composite print. Panels 6, 7, 8, and 9 of the story board show the various stages of the animated transition between the live action scene and the stop-motion sequence.

For the production of the "stripe" animation and its subsequent superimposure over the cigarette package in the stop-motion film, the camera projection process is again used for layout purposes. A single frame from the stop-motion film is projected onto the compound table and a tracing of the cigarette package is used by the animator for the positioning of the stripes.

Synchronized with the musical jingle on the sound track, the stripes animate off the face of the cigarette package to different positions in the frame. During the animated action, a stripe pans across the screen and wipes on one of the titles used in the commercial. In the concluding action of the sequence, both stripes animate back to their original positions on the face of the package in the stop-motion film.

These 29 frames of film show the continuing zoom of the combined titles from the middle of the frame to a point beyond the limits of the field.

An effective action because of the timing involved, the stripes, after the drawings have been completed, are inked and opaqued on cels in white and photographed over a black card on the animation stand. Here, too, a high contrast film, such as 5362, is used for photographing the animated action.

To achieve the wipe effect shown in panel 18 of the story board, one of the stripes is inked and opaqued on a sliding cel. Registered on the bottom peg bar, the sliding cel is panned to the left side of the frame and then back to its original position. The second stripe, registered to the top pegs, remains in a hold position during the panning of the sliding cel.

In order to make the matte needed for the optical combination of the wipe with the stop-motion film, the title cel containing the white lettering, "Filters as no single filter can," is played over a black card. Another black card is placed over the cel so that none of the lettering is visible. The black card, covering the white title, is panned across the screen revealing the title underneath. The pan moves used for this wipe action are identical to the pan moves used for panning the stripe across the screen during the filming of the animation. When the animated stripes, title, and matte are combined optically with the pack of cigarettes in the stop-motion film, the stripe will seem to be wiping on the lettering as it moves across the screen. The tracing of the projected stop-motion frame of film that was used as a layout for the stripe animation is also used by the animation cameraman for positioning the titles used in the commercial. The same procedure used for plotting and calibrating zoom and compound table movements is used for moving the titles from one field guide position to another.

Hand lettered on cels in white, the titles are photographed over a black card on high contrast film. To simplify the photographic process, two of the titles, "Dual Filter" and "Filters as no single filter can," were lettered on the same cel. During the zoom of the "Dual Filter" title to the upper part of the frame the second title, "Filters as no single filter can," was covered with a black card. The "Dual Filter" title was similarly masked during the wipe that revealed the second title, "Filters as no single filter can." Since both titles zoom past the limits of the field at the end of the action, the combination of the two titles on one cel eliminates the need for plotting, calibrating, and photographing each title separately.

For the optical combination of the stop-motion film with the animated stripes, titles, and mattes, the high contrast *negative* containing the stripe animation is first photographed with the stop-motion film. Mattes are not needed for this combination as the stripes are black in the clear area of the frame.

In the next step of the optical process, each of the titles is photographed on separate runs over the previously exposed film according to the frame count on the optical layout sheets. On the frame following the completion of the wipe, the film containing the combined titles is photographed until the titles move past the lower part of the frame and out of the field in a continuing zoom.

This completes the optical process for this portion of the commercial. The exposed film in the optical camera, ready for processing, contains the opening live-action scene, the stop-motion sequence, the animation, and the titles.

In the next action, the pack of cigarettes in the stop-motion film moves forward to the extreme close-up position shown in panels 20 and 21 of the story board. In sync with the musical jingle, the title, "Tareyton," is superimposed over the close-up of the cigarette. The unwrapping action of the filter tip is discussed in detail in the stop-motion chapter.

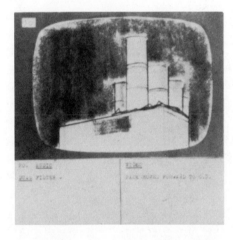

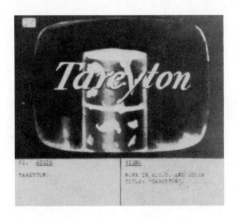

OPTICAL CUE SHEET

PRODUCTION _DUAL FILTER TAREYTON_   SHEET NO. _____

SPOT NO. _×5×1 — STRIPE ANIMATION SECTION_   PAGE NO. _1_

FRAME #	ACTION	REMARKS	FIRST RUN	SECOND RUN
17/3×	HOLD STRIPES ON PACK			
33/48	LEFT STRIPE ZOOMS UP TO LEFT —	DRAWINGS 1 TO 16		
49/5×	HOLD			
53/68	RIGHT STRIPE ZOOMS TO RIGHT — LEFT STRIPE ZOOMS BACK TO PACK —	DNGS. 17 TO 3× " 16 TO 1		
69/7×	HOLD			
73/88	RIGHT STRIPE MOVES BACK TO PACK	DRAWINGS 3× TO 17		WHITE TITLES OVER BLACK CARD
89/9×	HOLD			
93/108	STRIPES ON PACK JIGGLE	DRAWINGS 1A TO 9A		
109/11×	HOLD			
P	ZOOM UP			

The optical cue sheet shown here serves a twofold purpose.
Originally designed as a guide in addition to the optical layout
sheet, the cue sheet is sometimes used in place of the regular
exposure sheet by the animation cameraman during the photographic process.

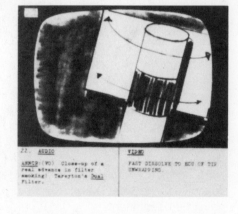

22. AUDIO
ANNCR (VO) Close-up of a
real advance in filter
smoking! Tareyton's Dual
Filter.

VIDEO
FAST DISSOLVE TO ECU OF TIP
UNWRAPPING.

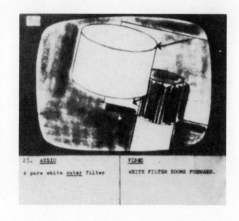

23. AUDIO
A pure white outer filter

VIDEO
WHITE FILTER ZOOMS FORWARD.

Another live action scene showing an announcer holding a package of cigarettes, panels 24 through 27 of the story board, precedes the final stop-motion sequence. In the last scene of the commercial, the package of cigarettes tilts forward towards the camera as the title, "Dual Filter Tareyton," is superimposed optically for the remaining film footage.

So ends the production of 618 on the Gumbinner Advertising Agency's schedule. For those readers interested in statistics, three studios participated in the production of the live action, stop-motion, and animation sequences. One studio photographed the live action, another handled the stop-motion filming, and a third studio produced the animation, titles, and mattes needed for the optical combination of the three motion picture techniques. Each of the studios can take a bow for a job well done and for helping to make the Dual Filter Tareyton cigarette commercial an outstanding film presentation.

Story board for Ballantine commercial. This is essentially the same as for animation except that action is performed by puppets rather than characters drawn by an artist.

Puppets

The increasing use of puppets in commercial television is due in no small measure to the acceptance of the three-dimensional characters as effective salesmen. Their popularity with viewers is in evidence at sales counters wherever products represented by these miniature messengers are sold. The percentage of audience product identification where puppets are used is among the highest, in comparison with other techniques used for the same purpose.

Practically all of the processes used in the production of motion pictures are also used in the making of films involving puppets. The script and story board are prepared along generally accepted lines and the sound track is recorded as for the animated cartoon production.

A star in the Ballantine commercial.

Mr. Koos Schadee, art director, and Wim Hannaart, scenic painter, prepare a portion of the Old West for the Ballantine commercial.

The art director and scenic painter work on a miniature set for the production. One of the puppets is approximately eight inches tall, shown in relation to the "background."

The stage—and the actors.

The film editor's analysis of the sound track and the story board are both used as the shooting guide in place of the exposure sheets used in cartoon production.

The composite print is the result of months of preparation and effort by highly skilled technicians in an entertainment medium older than the motion picture itself.

"The Gold Miner," or 51-28-60, is the commercial used here as an example of the puppet technique at its very best. Made for P. Ballantine and Sons, brewers of Ballantine beer and ale, the commercial shows the three-dimensional characters in a delightful film presentation.

Following the completion and approval of the script and story board, the cartoon characters that are to be used in the commercial are designed by a layout man. Unlike the flat or single dimensional characters used in animated cartoon production, the layout man must visualize and design the characters in relation to the miniature sets or stages that are to be used by the three-dimensional figures.

The sketches of the proposed characters are turned over to the puppet maker, who follows the drawings in preparing the three-dimensional models. After being assembled, these models are painted and made ready for the photographic process.

Since the actions of the puppets are synchronized with the music and dialogue on the sound track, the movements for each scene of the commercial are governed by this timing. Following the story board carefully, "puppeteers" move all of the characters in the scene to new positions and poses for each frame during the filming process. Generally accepted animation principles are used for these movements and actions.

Three-dimensional backgrounds are built and painted by set designers after the preliminary sketches and layouts have been approved. Since the backgrounds are built to scale, great attention is given to the most minute details. The miniature, three-dimensional models of the product featured in the commercial are also designed and built to scale. These models are proportionately identical to the actual product in every detail.

Standard motion picture cameras with stop-motion mechanisms are used for the filming process. For some scenes, two cameras are used to photograph the same action. One camera is fitted with a special lens for close-up shots, while the second camera, some distance away from the first, photographs the same scene for a medium or long shot.

The film clips shown here are from scenes in the Ballantine Beer "puppet" commercial, *The Gold Miner*.

The use of footage from two cameras enables the film editor to intercut different shots for a more dramatic presentation. The double-filming method also eliminates the necessity of photographing the same scene at different times in order to obtain various close-up, medium, and long shots of similar actions.

Certain effects, not possible in the original filming, are photographed separately on the animation stand or with live action methods and combined optically with the film containing the puppet action. The actual pouring of the beer in the commercial is photographed as a live sequence while the glow around the neck of the bottle in another scene is photographed on the animation stand. Both of these actions are shown on page two of the story board.

For positioning and matching the animated glow to the bottle, a frame of film is projected by the animation cameraman. The pencil tracing of the bottle serves as the layout for the animation process of the glow. This camera projection process is again used for making the layouts needed for filming the three-ring trademark in the final action of the commercial. The trademark (or logo) and the matte, needed for the subsequent optical combination, are both photographed on the animation stand.

Upon completion of the three photographic processes, the puppet action, the live pouring of the beer, and the animation effects, the film editor prepares the frame counts for the optical combination. The composite print is the result of months of preparation and effort by a small army of skilled technicians. This old technique, modernized by its commercial adaptation, is always a welcome visitor to the home television viewer, even when disguised as a salesman.

The I D or Station Identification

A portion of an I D, including the television station's call letters, is shown in these film clips.

The I D or station identification is the spot commercial that is used during the station break between regularly scheduled television programs. Although the I D remains on the screen for only ten seconds, it requires the same careful planning and preparation needed for the production of commercial films of greater length.

For the few precious seconds that are needed to announce a station's call letters to the viewer, scripts and story boards must be prepared, a sound track recorded, and all other production processes used for lengthier films duplicated. Almost every animation and live action motion picture technique may be used in the production of this type of commercial.

The I D could very well be called a three-quarter production. The upper right hand corner of the picture area in the shared time spot must remain clear for the standard video identification of the station. This is a requirement in the production of all shared I D commercials.

Background and call letters used for the typical I D.

The visual portion of the I D must not be more than ten seconds in length. This is exactly 240 frames, 15 feet in 35mm. film or six feet in 16mm. film. The picture must continue on a "freeze" frame for five seconds and must contain the TV Station's standard video identification in the upper right hand quarter of the picture area.

The sound track in the shared commercial must not be more than seven seconds in length. The remaining three seconds of audio time are devoted to the station identification made by live announcement.

The seven-second sound track is equal to eight frames, ten feet, in 35mm. film. The diagram shows the physical film, sound track, and other specifications in the one-minute, 20-second, and 10-second commercials.

SLIDES AND TELOPS

Slides and telops are used in the same way and for the same purpose as the filmed I D commercial.

The commercial message in the slide or telop, however, is limited to a single picture which is projected for the entire ten seconds. A live announcement usually accompanies the projected picture. Sometimes referred to as "bargain basement" commercials, the two inch by two inch slide is mounted between two pieces of glass for projection purposes. The opaque telops, by comparison, must appear on double-weight photographic paper with a matte or semi-matte finish. The over-all size of the telop is usually four inches by five inches.

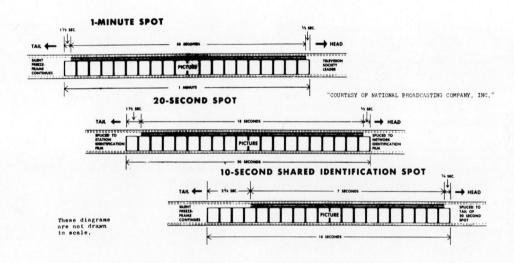

Commercial film standards.

A slide

and a telop.

Computer-Generated Animation Techniques

This section is as up-to-the-minute as any treatise can be of a field that is still in its infancy. New hardware and new methods are constantly being devised and revised. Electronic imaging has been called dynamic display, motion graphics, computer kinetics, etc. Computer-generated and computer-controlled techniques for producing and recording sequences of motion have actually made it necessary to redefine the generic term.

Commercial production studios and advertising agencies will soon make room and provide special titles for the computer oriented artist whose training includes higher-level courses in computer programming. At the present time approximately 25,000 students are receiving this training for degrees in motion-picture production, television, and related areas from more than 3,500 faculty members and instructors at more than 800 colleges and universities in the United States.

The potential for the new electronic techniques is great. How great? That question cannot be answered with any degree of authority at this time. Commercial acceptance on a professional level has actually preceded the developmental and experimental stages—an amazing fact in itself. This section of the book, intended primarily for the talented and imaginative people already in animation and commercial-film production, will open the door to more interesting presentations, new techniques, and a variety of unusual illusory effects.

GT40

The GT40 system, based upon the PDP 11/10 minicomputer and an interactive graphics scope, lends itself to real-time animation displayed on a CRT. Because of its small size, programs tend to be written in assembly language. An interesting feature of the system is its graphical processor, which can access the computer's memory directly. It permits variations in line intensity, italicization, line blink and the like without interfering with the operation of the standard central processor. A larger XVM medium-scale computer, used for interactive graphical design, can be adapted to the generation of animation artwork.

KEY-FRAME COMPUTER-GENERATED ANIMATION

Key-frame computer-generated animation techniques are analogous to conventional processes used by an animator to prepare key drawings in an action sequence. The animator's drawings (extremes) are used by his assistant (inbetweener) as a guide for the intermediate drawings needed to complete the action. Except for the hardware involved in electronic-imaging processes, the generation of key frames by computer follows the same general pattern. The system does not require the animator to become a computer programmer: in fact, any contact or communication between the animator and the computer-controlled system is through the artwork, which is displayed directly on the CRT (cathode-ray tube).

Although most computer-generated imaging techniques are language-driven, the key-frame system for animation sequences is picture-driven. The key drawings created by the animator from either the script or the storyboard are used to program the required action. The animator generally prepares the artwork for exposure at key intervals. During the playback the flow of action is previewed on the CRT display, and the intermediate positions computed by interpolating between the key frames are included in the display. Timing information indicating the number of frames needed

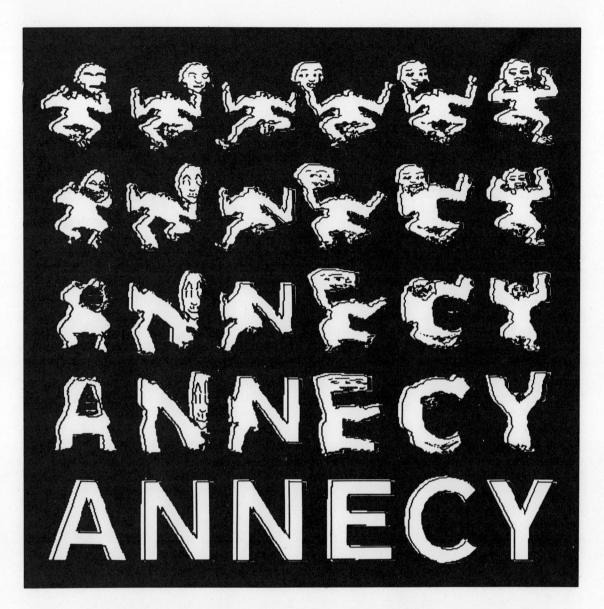

9ᴱᴹᴱ JOURNÉES INTERNATIONALES DU CINÉMA D'ANIMATION

13-17 JUIN 1973

COMPOSITION DE PETER FOLDES SUR L'ORDINATEUR DU CONSEIL NATIONAL DE RECHERCHES DU CANADA

A reproduction of the computer-generated poster prepared for the
1973 Annecy Festival. (Courtesy of the National Research Council,
Ottawa, Canada.)

to develop a smooth flow of movement is fed into the computer at the same time as the key drawings are exposed. After the entire sequence of action is developed, it can be monitored or previewed at real-time rates. As in the conventional pencil test, changes may be made, reprogrammed, before the sequence is subsequently photographed on film or recorded on videotape.

The same techniques developed for conventional cel-animation production are the basis for key-frame animation. In place of the punched sheets of drawing paper mounted on the registration pegs of the underlit animation board the animator's key drawings, or extreme positions, are displayed directly on the CRT. The type of computer-generated figure best suited for this technique is a line drawing. The figures produced by electronic means reflect the animator's style and talents just as the more conventional production processes do.

The lines on the image-forming key drawings may be subdivided into groups of lines on a number of cels if necessary in order to facilitate programming and storage. The component cels, each with its own group of lines, are programmed in their precise positions in relation to the other cels needed to form any of the key-frame composite images. Individual instructions regarding the required motion of each of the component cels are programmed separately. Similarly, specific interpolation laws may be assigned to each of the cels making up the composite drawings. These interpolation laws can be compared with the guides on an animator's extreme drawing that indicate how the inbetween drawings are to be spaced in order to produce the timing and action specified by the animator. The inbetween frames computed by interpolating between key frames are displayed during the playback at the cine rate. The entire sequence of action displayed on the monitor can be previewed, and any necessary changes reprogrammed immediately.

The hardware for the process consists of a high-speed digital computer and the cathode-ray tube used to display the sequence of action. The memory capacity of the processor is adequate for the most complex types of animation. The software consists of a number of interactive graphics programs that are used to create, modify, and manipulate the graphics fed into the computer.

Each of the lines in any of the component cels forming the composite key frame is made up of a number of small, interconnected lines. Each of these small lines, as seen in the reproduced display, is connected to x- and y-coordinates, coded with regard to intensity, and assigned separate interpolation laws that control its movement throughout the programmed sequence of action.

Communication between the animator or graphic artist and the computer is initiated with the artwork. Using industry terminology, the animator is able to manipulate the picture components and combine them with geometrical shapes generated by the computer. Preprogrammed routines and distortion functions are available in a menu from the computer's storage bank, which also includes a library of effects from previous productions. Access to such lists in this type of filing or retrieval system provides the animator with a great time and budget saver.

Since each of the lines in the interpolated images is produced in its entirety, lines that would normally be hidden behind some part of a solid, dimensional figure or object are clearly visible—one of the disadvantages of the technique. Similarly, lines that would be invisible behind an opaque or solid shape are clearly defined behind or through the interpolated transparent images. It is visually confusing, for example, to see part of the background through a figure. The obvious way to eliminate the undesirable see-through effect is to use some form of opaquing. Introducing or generating areas of color in specific locations is one way of solving the problem. Without departing from the basic technique of animating line drawings, conversion to a raster-scan format can be applied on a frame-by-frame basis to the computed image sequence. In this way any area that is completely bounded by an outline is filled in by adjacent horizontal lines. The filled-in areas obtained as a result of the scanning process serve as mattes and are used in the final display to eliminate transparency. An alternative method for removing transparency from computer-generated outline images is to use the low-resolution TV-data format for producing mattes. The random-line data is compared on a frame-by-frame basis with its corresponding blocking matte. Transparency is removed by controlling visibility with the low-resolution matte as each of the component cels is merged in turn to produce the composite image.

At the present time the cartoon characters used in the Alka-Seltzer commercials are excellent examples of the type of animation figures available with this technique. The computer is not yet a match for the artist capable of producing Disney-type animation.

Computer-generated animation from *La Faim*, a film by Peter Foldes. (Courtesy of the National Research Council, Ottawa, Canada.)

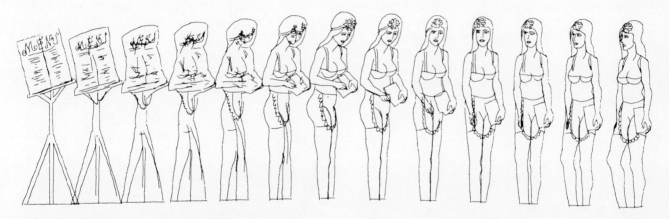

This sequence of images was extracted from *La Faim*. Produced by René Jodoin of the National Film Board, Canada, the interpolated images reflect the same artistic style as the extremes, or key frames, drawn by the animator. The film received the Prix du Jury at Cannes in 1974, the Golden Hugo in Chicago, and a special prize at the Barcelona Film Festival. The film was also nominated for an Academy Award in the animated-shorts category. Unfortunately, the film's producers couldn't find a computer capable of making an acceptance speech! (Courtesy of the National Research Council, Ottawa, Canada.)

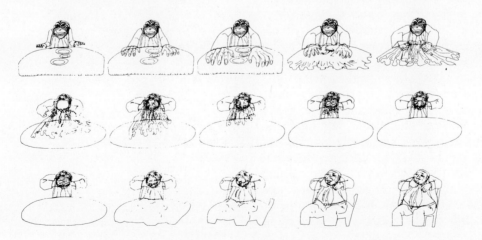

Key Frames from an animated sequence in *La Faim*. (Courtesy of the National Research Council, Ottawa, Canada.)

TELEMATION

Telemation is an electronic titling generator that prepares printed graphic material almost instantaneously. Since the titling generator itself is the video source, no TV camera is required to pick up the prepared information.

Designed by Telemation, Inc., of Salt Lake City, the titling generator's characters may be mixed, supered, keyed, or wiped in the same manner as any other video source. In this way the titling-generator output can supplant the use of superimposed slides or cards as well as provide newsflashes, credits, titles, and other support information.

The TCG-225 produces one or two lines of 25 characters each. Character-generator electronics are activated by a keyboard similar to that of a typewriter. Besides containing alphameric symbols the keyboard controls every function of the system, including a unique hop-left and hop-right centering adjustment.

VIDEO CHARACTER GENERATOR

The Aston video character generator and multipage message store, developed by the Denlen Electronics Corporation, is a system that can compose alphameric messages, store them in the computer's memory system, and superimpose them on programmed video signals—either internally within the unit or externally in a suitably keyed vision mixer.

VIDEO SYNTHESIZER

The video synthesizer is an analog-scan-conversion system that can convert the component part of an image into electric signals, modify the signals in compliance with the computer programmer's instructions, and display the continuously changing image on a monitor. The subject matter or input information for video-synthesizer systems may be either flat art, Kodaliths viewed by a TV vidicon camera, or the output from previously recorded videotape or processed motion-picture film. These images may be black-and-white or color, continuous-tone or high-contrast.

In addition to previously prepared artwork an infinite variety of abstract shapes, lines, and patterns can be generated within the synthesizer. The shape of these input images, whether previously prepared or newly generated, can be altered in part or in their entirety. Turning a dial or flipping a switch can change the height, width, shape, and position of the picture information visible on the display. The images may be rotated or zoomed from one position in the frame to another to create the feeling of depth.

The video synthesizer consists of units for controlling the graphic display along with modules for generating and controlling the animation. The display unit includes the height, width, depth, vertical, and horizontal positioning and centering controls and the intensity settings that regulate the brightness of the displayed image. The height control is capable of shrinking an image to a fine horizontal line, inverting it, and restoring it to its original position. Conversely, the width control can reduce an image to a thin vertical line or expand it until it fills the entire screen. The depth control causes the image to advance or recede, creating two- and three-dimensional effects. The vertical and horizontal positioning controls move the image up or down, to the right or left, and on or off the screen. The horizontal and vertical centering modes can move an image through a preset pattern and also make adjustments in either the horizontal or vertical axis.

The Chromaton 14 video synthesizer. Designed to produce animated video graphics in motion and color, the synthesizer accepts one or two monochrome TV signals. It can colorize black-and-white scenes in five discrete colors. Four invisible levels, similar to the animator's acetates and solid background, are simulated. Segments of the display obtained from the camera and internal generators can be placed on any or all of the four levels. Each level and the background are assigned a color by the programmer. The level concept together with other features provides an electronic-animation capability: the unit can connect to any existing studio system using studio sync, or it can operate as a separate unit by connecting it to a color monitor through an accessory built-in digital color-sync generator. (Courtesy of B.J.A. Systems, Inc.)

The synthesizer's animation-control modules include a summing amplifier, diode module, ramp generator, audio interface, and wave-form generators. The summing amplifier is used to combine functions if programmed instructions call for a number of routines to be performed simultaneously. The diode module divides the generated wave forms and timing ramps that automatically control the preset speed and length of an animation sequence. The audio interface drives the animation by using audio signals. The wave-form generators, in addition to producing the graphics for display or for subsequent animation, control sync, frequency, wave form, and amplitude and frequency modulation.

Programmed movement may be rehearsed, and, if changes are considered necessary, the entire picture or any of its component parts can be retimed or re-animated. The subsequent real-time preview, or dry run, is precisely repeatable. Unusual illusory effects can also be produced by assigning specific synthesizer-controlling frequencies to certain sounds such as the notes of a musical instrument or the resonances of human speech. The sequences of motion, displayed on a high-resolution monitor, can be picked up by a TV plumbicon camera for immediate broadcast, photographed by a motion-picture camera, or fed to a video-tape-recording system for use at a later date.

VIDIFONT

Vidifont is a TV-display system that can produce word messages from a number of different fonts and sizes in real time. The Vidifont enables the user to produce more creative and informative video displays for television broadcasting, advertising, and film production. Developed by CBS Laboratories, the type-font characters have high resolution and maximum viewer readability. Language symbols and characters in Japanese, Hebrew, Greek, or Russian can also be used with this display system. Proportional character spacing is a key feature, and character-display color control is provided on a word-by-word basis.

Part II

COMMERCIAL FILM PRODUCTION

Animation and the Camera

In all motion pictures, the subject "moves." In live action, the movement is done by the subject and photographed by the cameraman. In animation, however, the movement is achieved through a series of drawings or photographs, carefully prepared to show progressive stages of an action and photographed by an animation cameraman in a given sequence.

To attain the required precision in movement and camera calibration, the cameras and the drawings are mounted on animation stands. Briefly, these are little more than devices which permit both the camera and the subject matter to move in carefully controlled steps forward or backward, or side to side, or both. Animation stands are simple in concept but they must be extremely rigid (to hold camera and drawings steady), yet extremely flexible (to provide the various effects). To get this combination costs money: animation stands can cost from around $2000 to over $40,000.

All of them provide the essentials: a support for the camera and a place for the drawings. However, they vary in capability, convenience, and design.

THE OLD

During the industry's infancy, animation was photographed by cameras mounted on machine lathe beds. During the photographic process, "still" backgrounds and cels were registered to the single set of pegs on the movable table attached to the lathe bed. The glass platen, for each exposure, was locked in position over the frame around the table and then raised to the vertical shooting position.

Subsequent changes in design made it possible to achieve simple zooms. Although further modification allowed the single set of pegs to be moved, backgrounds were panned against the pegs by hand. Start and stop positions for panning were indicated along the top edge of the background. Moves for the intermediate positions were calibrated by the animation cameraman. Although these relatively crude camera set-ups have turned out countless miles of animation footage, they are rapidly fading from the scene. Like the horse and buggy of another era, they are being replaced—in this case by animation stands of modern design with electronic controls. This author sheds only a very small tear over their departure, but a much larger one for the many memories that go with them.

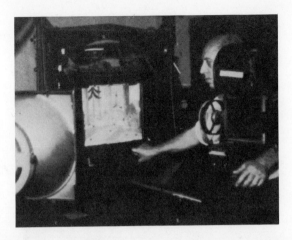

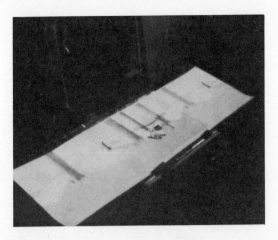

Cameras like these turned out miles of animation footage during the industry's infancy. Fades and cross-dissolves were made manually. Focus, during zooms, was maintained by precalibrating each of the positions in the zoom and adjusting the entire lens mounting for each frame.

Pan backgrounds were moved by hand against the pegs. The cels containing the animation were placed on the pegs and the platen locked in position. The frame was then raised to the vertical position and photographed.

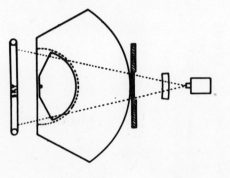

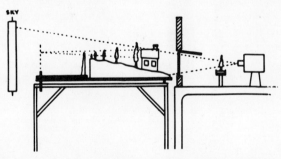

Multiplane Photograph. Although the dimensional backgrounds are built to scale in this photograph of an early multiplane set-up, the animated characters are inked and opaqued on standard cels. These cels, during the photographic process, are registered on pegs that are enclosed in a glass frame. The backgrounds used in the multiplane set-up and the frame containing the opaqued cels are lit separately. Each section of the background can be moved independently at different speeds. Because of the distance between the cartoon characters in the glass frame and the multiplane background, it was possible to achieve a great amount of perspective and realism.

Multiplane Diagrams. The diagrams, top and side views, show the relationship between the backgrounds, the cels containing the cartoon animation and the camera.

Animation stands are complex, must be precise and are not small, all of which adds up to an expensive piece of equipment. The Oxberry is shown here as typical, though not the only animation stand available. Check any good supply house for details.

The camera motor, zoom control, and automatic dissolve mechanism are all controlled from the panel board shown in this photograph.

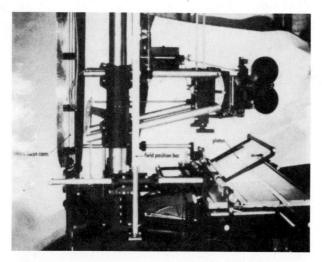

This side view of the animation stand shows the follow focus cams, the field position bar and the platen in a raised position.

The camera mounted on the machine lathe bed and the present day models have very little in common. One of the few things the modern animation stand and control panel shown in this photograph cannot do electronically is read exposure sheets.

THE FIELD GUIDE

The animator's stage is the field guide, a pattern made to conform to the proportions of the 35mm. frame which indicates what will be on the film and what will be outside the field of view of the camera.

The field guide shown here is less than actual size, but all dimensions are in proportion to the film frame. Each field size is indicated by a number which corresponds to the actual width of the field in inches. Thus, the 11 field is 11 inches wide and its proportionate height is 8¼ inches. The 4 field is 4 inches wide by 3 inches high.

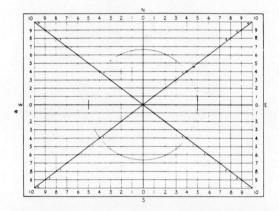

Field guide, reduced in size. This is placed on the compound table to guide the animation cameraman in positioning the camera in relation to the subject matter being photographed.

The field guide, used for positioning art work, is as important to the animation cameraman as is the pencil to the animator. Most cameramen have two guides. One is in position on the pantograph table and the other is on the compound table for lining up art work.

A field guide has holes punched, similar to the ones on drawings, cels, and backgrounds. This enables the guide to be positioned on the peg bars over the art work. These peg bars, on the compound table, position all material in relation to the table and the animation camera. This positioning, which insures that all material is aligned within the film frame, is extremely important in animation work.

ZOOMS, PANS, AND SPINS

Zooms, or trucks (moving the camera toward or away from the subject), are the most frequently used effects in both animation and live-action motion picture production.

In live motion pictures, the zoom is used most effectively as an establishing shot, or one in which a long shot of a general area precedes the camera's movement to a relatively closer shooting position and a smaller, more specific part of the larger area. The camera zooms to an extreme close-up of eyes, lips, or even hands, from the establishing full figure shot of an actor or actress, increases the dramatic qualities of the ordinary scene.

The camera zoom is also used effectively for other than dramatic purposes. In the educational film, for example, a zoom to a closer shot of a machine in operation gives the employee in a training program a closer look at the moving parts. The bottle, box, jar, or tube held by the announcer in the commercial film is emphasized and accented when the camera moves in from a full shot of the narrator to an extreme close-up of the product. Regardless of the purpose for which the zoom is intended, the effect must be plotted and calibrated before the actual shooting process begins.

For the live action shot, tracks are laid on the floor of the set, and the "crab dolly," the movable carriage on which the camera is mounted, is rolled forward or backward according to instructions in the shooting script while the camera runs continuously. Calibrated tapes are laid on the floor alongside the tracks and a technician moves the crab dolly, from the start to the stopping position of the zoom, with measured strides. Several "takes" are usually made of the same action or scene in order to insure the smoothness of the effect.

This view of the animation stand and compound table shows the field guide used for lining up and composition purposes registered to the floating pegs.

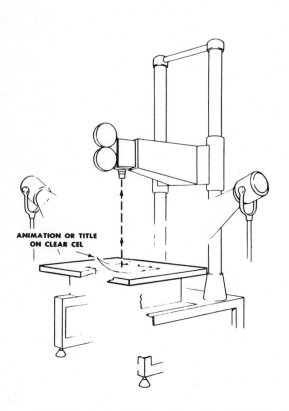

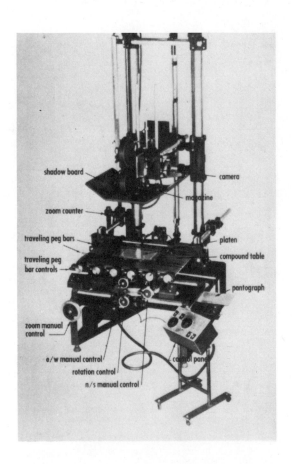

shadow board

camera

zoom counter

magazine

traveling peg bars

platen

traveling peg
bar controls

compound table

pantograph

zoom manual
control

e/w manual control

rotation control

control panel

n/s manual control

ANIMATION OR TITLE
ON CLEAR CEL

The compound table is shown in its center position in this diagram.

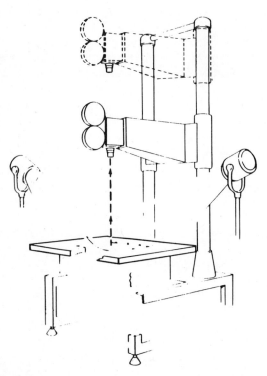

The superimposed broken lines show the camera at its extreme top position in relation to the compound table.

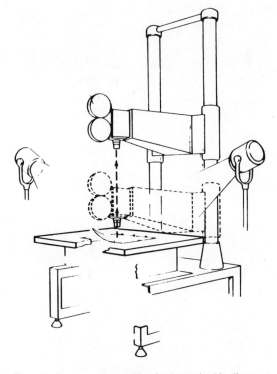

The close-up camera position is shown in this diagram.

This view from the back of the animation stand is a rarity. The automatic follow focus cams, 35mm. and 16mm., are directly in front of the left supporting column.

The mechanism for rotating the compound table is shown in this photograph. The rotation counter and the manual control can be seen below the giant circular gear.

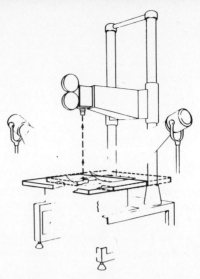

The superimposed broken lines show the extreme north position of the compound table.

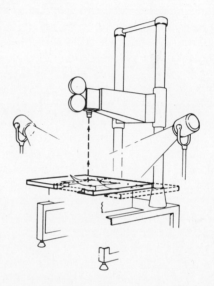

The superimposed broken lines show the extreme east position of the compound table.

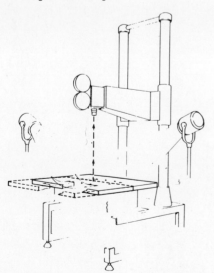

The extreme south position of the compound table is shown by the superimposed broken lines.

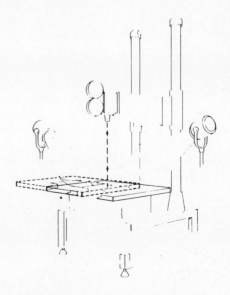

The extreme west position of the compound table is shown by the superimposed broken lines.

Calibrating or plotting a zoom on the animation stand, however, is a much more involved process. The camera on the animation stand is mounted in a fixed position and can only move vertically. All horizontal movements are accomplished with the compound table upon which the art work or subject matter is placed. These horizontal movements must be calibrated and plotted in relation to the camera.

Four separate and distinct camera and compound table movements enable the animation cameraman to center the table and art work in any predetermined position. The first of these movements, the zoom mechanism, allows the camera to be positioned on any field called for by the animator. The position bar on the animation stand indicates the exact field size or shooting area of the camera in relation to the art work. Thus, if the art work is to be photographed on a 12 field, that is, a shooting area 12 inches wide, the camera is moved to the 12 field setting indicated on the position bar. A counter synchronized with the zoom mechanism permits even greater accuracy in the positioning of the camera. Follow focus cams automatically adjust focus as the camera is positioned on other fields or intermediate positions.

The second and third movements make possible an off-center positioning of the art work in relation to the camera. The compound table can be moved to north-south and east-west positions either mechanically or manually. Here, again, counters for each movement help the cameraman position the art work with amazing accuracy. If necessary (and in technical animation it very often is) these north-south and east-west movements can be calibrated to the thousandth of an inch.

The fourth movement is the spin or rotating mechanism. This movement allows the compound table to be spun or revolved independently, regardless of the other movements. A counter, synchronized with this spin mechanism, enables the cameraman to position art work at any angle during the photographic process.

The combination of these four camera and compound table movements gives the animation cameraman a great deal of latitude and an amazing amount of control in positioning art work and attaining various zoom, pan, and spin effects. The pantograph, which is attached to the animation stand, makes it possible to plot straight line or complicated curved pan movements and gives the cameraman a visual check on the position of the art work on the compound table in its relation to the camera. However, the counters, synchronized with the four compound movements described in previous paragraphs, insure an even greater degree of accuracy than the indicator attached to the pantograph.

When all the movement counters are at the 0000 reading, the compound table is at the exact center po-

sition in relation to the camera. On most animation stands where the field guide or chart shown here is used as the standard, each movement from one field to another, in an east-west direction, totals 50 numbers on the east-west counter. These 50 numbers are equal to and indicate one-half inch of movement.

Each full field in the north-south movement totals 36 numbers. The difference of 14 numbers between the north-south and east-west movements is in direct proportion to the dimensions of the motion picture frame.

The counter, synchronized with the spin movement, has a ratio of 10 numbers for each degree of rotation. One complete table turn in either direction would, therefore, total 3600 numbers on the counter.

While the figures for each of the table movements are reasonably standardized, numerical differences in other animation stands would involve no changes in the method used for calibrating and plotting movements from one designated position to another. Although the counter numbers might differ greatly, the general plotting procedure would remain the same. The calibrating and plotting of camera and compound table movements, from one position to another, is done by the animation cameraman. The most frequently used movement, and the easiest to plot and calibrate, is the straight center zoom. Since only one movement, the zoom mechanism, is involved, the plotting of the straight center zoom is a relatively simple procedure.

Field	Size	Counter Reading
2	Field	000
3	"	250
4	"	500
5	"	750
6	"	1000
7	"	1250
8	"	1500
9	"	1750
10	"	2000
11	"	2250
12	"	2500

These field positions and numbers are not alike on all animation stands. Any differences would not affect the plotting of a zoom or the photographic procedure described here.

When plotting a straight center camera zoom from one field position to another, the animation cameraman merely takes readings of the numbers on the zoom counter for both the starting and stopping positions of the zoom. No plotting or counter readings are necessary for the compound table, since it remains in its normal center position, in relation to the field guide, during the camera zoom.

A

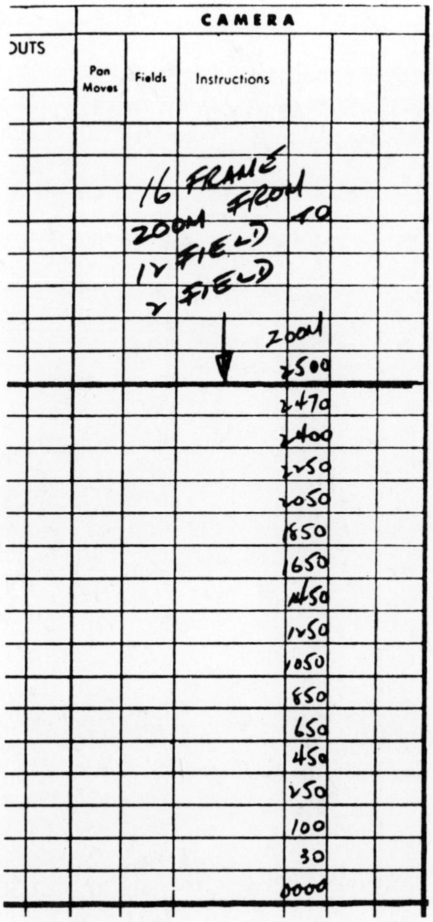

		CAMERA		
OUTS	Pan Moves	Fields	Instructions	

16 FRAME
ZOOM FROM
1" FIELD TO
2" FIELD

ZOOM
2500
2470
2400
2350
2050
850
650
2450
1250
1050
850
650
450
250
100
30
0000

B

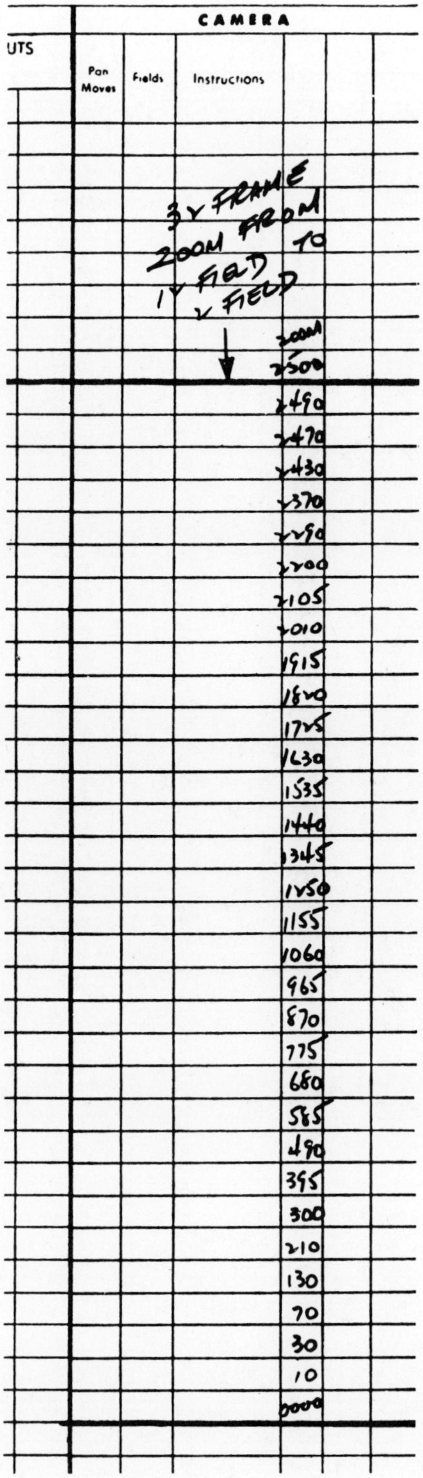

		CAMERA		
UTS	Pan Moves	Fields	Instructions	

32 FRAME
ZOOM FROM
1" FIELD TO
2" FIELD

ZOOM
2500
2490
2470
2430
2370
2290
2200
2105
2010
1915
1820
1725
1630
1535
1440
1345
1250
1155
1060
965
870
775
680
585
490
395
300
210
130
70
30
10
0000

Typical instructions for the animation cameraman. The notations refer to calibrations on the compound table.

C

OUTS	Pan Moves	Fields	Instructions	ZOOM	N/S	E/W
			16 FRAME ZOOM AND PAN FROM 1X FIELD CENTER TO 2X FIELD — 2 SOUTH 3 WEST			
				2500	0000	0000
				2470	2	2
				2400	6	7
				2350	11	16
				2050	16	27
				1850	21	39
				1650	26	51
				1450	31	63
				1250	36	75
				1050	41	87
				850	46	99
				650	51	111
				450	56	123
				250	61	134
				100	66	143
				30	70	148
				0000	072	0150

The 2-field, 2-south, 3-west position is indicated on the field guide below.

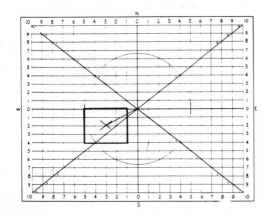

D

Pan Moves	Fields	Instructions	ZOOM	N/S	E/W
		32 FRAME ZOOM AND PAN FROM 1X FIELD CENTER TO 2X FIELD — 2 SOUTH 3 WEST			
			2500	0000	0000
			2490	1	1
			2470	2½	2½
			2430	4	4½
			2370	6	8
			2290	8½	12
			2200	11	16½
			2105	13½	21½
			2010	16	27
			1915	18½	33
			1820	21	39
			1725	23½	45
			1630	26	51
			1535	28½	57
			1440	31	63
			1345	33½	69
			1250	36	75
			1155	38½	81
			1060	41	87
			965	43½	93
			870	46	99
			775	48½	105
			680	51	111
			585	53½	117
			490	56	123
			395	58½	128½
			300	61	133½
			210	63½	138
			130	66	142
			70	68	145
			30	70	147½
			10	71	149
			0000	072	0150

E

	Pan Moves	Fields	Instructions	ZOOM	N/S	E/W
			16 FRAME ZOOM, PAN AND SPIN FROM 1X FIELD CENTER TO 2X FIELD — 2 SOUTH 3 WEST			
	SPIN 0000		(↓)	ZOOM 2500	0000	0000
	50			2470	2	2
	150			2400	6	7
	300			2250	11	16
	500			2050	16	27
	800			1850	21	39
	1130			1650	26	51
	1465			1450	31	63
	1800			1250	36	75
	2135			1050	41	87
	2470			850	46	99
	2800			650	51	111
	3100			450	56	123
	3300			250	61	134
	3450			100	66	143
	3550			30	70	148
	3600			0000	0072	0150

F

	Pan Moves	Fields	Instructions	ZOOM	N/S	E/W
			3X FRAME ZOOM, PAN AND SPIN FROM 1X FIELD CENTER TO 2X FIELD — 2 SOUTH 3 WEST			
	SPIN 0000		(↓)	ZOOM 2500	0000	0000
	20			2490	1	1
	60			2470	2½	2½
	120			2430	4	4½
	200			2370	6	8
	300			2290	8½	12
	425			2200	11	16½
	550			2105	13½	21½
	675			2010	16	27
	800			1915	18½	33
	925			1820	21	39
	1050			1725	23½	45
	1200			1630	26	51
	1350			1535	28½	57
	1500			1440	31	63
	1650			1345	33½	69
	1800			1250	36	75
	1950			1155	38½	81
	2100			1060	41	87
	2250			965	43½	93
	2400			870	46	99
	2550			775	48½	105
	2675			680	51	111
	2800			585	53½	117
	2925			490	56	123
	3050			395	58½	128½
	3175			300	61	133½
	3300			210	63½	138
	3400			130	66	142
	3480			70	68	145
	3540			30	70	147½
	3580			10	71	149
	3600			0000	0072	0150

In a zoom from the 12 field to the 2 field, for example, the numbers on the zoom counter would read 2500 at the 12 field position and 0000 at the 2 field. When the camera is at the 12 field—the starting position for the zoom—it is photographing an area 12 inches wide and 8¾ inches high, proportionately the same as the motion picture frame of film. At the 2 field level—the final position for the zoom—the camera is photographing an area 2 inches wide and 1-7/16 inches high.

If a one-foot zoom is indicated on the exposure sheets, the animation cameraman divides 2500, the numerical difference between the 12 field and 2 field counter readings, by 16, the number of frames in the zoom. Simple division would show a total of 156¼ numbers for each of the 16 frames or moves.

It is advisable to begin the zoom slowly and increase the numerical difference, or spacing, gradually. This progressive increase at the beginning of a zoom is known as an "ease in." The gradual numerical decrease at the end of the zoom is known as an "ease out." The intermediate moves, between the ease in and ease out, should be kept at a constant speed.

Example A shows a well-calibrated 16-frame zoom with an ease in and ease out. If the length of the zoom is 2 feet instead of one, the same 2500 numbers must be divided by 32. Example B shows the calibrations for the 32-frame zoom with the ease in and out at the beginning and end of the zoom.

It is possible, of course, to plan combinations of camera and compound table movements in order to achieve pans and off-center positioning of art work. The word "pan" is introduced here in order to explain the difference between camera and compound table movements. Basically, any camera movement, towards or away from stationary art work, can be described as a zoom. Any movement of the art work or compound table, while the camera remains in a still position, is referred to as a pan.

The method used for calibrating the straight center zoom is also used for calibrating the off-center zoom. The north-south and east-west compound table movements in off-center zooms, however, make it necessary for the animation cameraman to calibrate two additional columns of numbers on the exposure sheets. When plotting and calibrating the off-center zoom and pan, the animation cameraman must take readings of the zoom counter as well as the north-south and east-west counters at the starting and stopping positions.

On these extremes, if the exposure sheets indicate a 16-frame zoom and pan from the 12 field, centered on the field guide, to the 2 field, at the 2 south, 3 west position on the field guide, the following counter readings would be used for calibrating the zoom and pan.

The method for calibrating the zoom has already been discussed and is shown in examples A and B. For the north-south calibrations, the animation cameraman divides 72, the difference between the counter reading at the center position on the field guide and the counter reading at the 2 south position, by 16, the number of frames in the zoom.

The east-west pan movement is calibrated by dividing 150 by 16. The number 150 represents the difference between the center position on the field guide and the counter reading at the 3 west position. An ease in and ease out are included in the calibrations for the 16- and 32-frame zoom and pan in examples C and D.

Where a spin or compound table rotation is indicated on the exposure sheets, the method used for plotting and calibrating that movement is the same as for a zoom or pan movement. One complete turn of the compound table is equal to 3600 numbers on the counter, or 10 numbers for each degree of rotation. The one-foot spin is calibrated by dividing 3600, the counter reading for one complete compound table turn, by 16. Since one degree of movement on a 2 field would be more noticeable than a one degree movement on a 12 field, the ease in and ease out is especially important when calibrating a spin. The four columns of numbers in example E show the calibrations for a one-foot spin combined with the zoom and pan movements. Example F shows the four movements calibrated for a length of 2 feet or 32 frames.

In technical animation, these four movements are sometimes complicated by the additional movement of the top and bottom traveling peg bars upon which the art work is positioned. Fortunately for the cameraman, this is not a normal occurrence. But, with or without the additional movement made possible through the use of the traveling peg bars, the four movements enable the animation cameraman to achieve almost any kind of zoom, pan and spin effect.

	Zoom Counter	North-South Counter	East-West Counter
Readings at the 12 field centered on the field guide	2500	0000	0000
Readings at the 2 field 2 south and 3 west position on the field guide	0000	0072	0150

The Zoom and Spin

The zoom and spin are both used very effectively in the 10-second Martinson's coffee commercial.

A newspaper spins as it zooms up from infinity against an abstract background. The newspaper headline duplicates the message on the accompanying sound track during the zoom.

In the final position of the zoom, the can of Martinson's coffee bursts through the front page of the newspaper in synchronization with the sound effect of a cash register drawer opening. The accompanying sound effect gives additional impact to the brief sales message contained in the commercial.

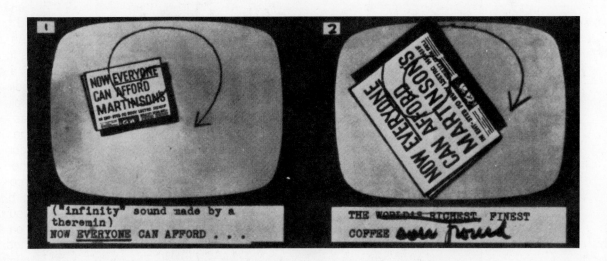

Story board for Martinson commercial. Both picture and sound are plotted. Compare story board notation with same sequence as it is recorded on film.

217

The film sequence shown here is from an actual television commercial and shows a practical, commercial application of the camera zoom and spin, and the effects made possible through their use.

Types of Zooms

The straight center zoom, as described earlier, is a direct camera movement, from one specific position to another, in relation to the art work or subject matter. In the off-center zoom, a panning action is added to the camera movement. Where no cel changing is involved and a zoom is indicated on the exposure sheets, zooms can be made in a continuous "run" by setting the automatic controls for the camera and compound table movements at a predetermined speed. A much faster method than the single frame "move and shoot" process, the camera photographs continuously during the run.

In the continuing zoom, the subject matter, usually a title, moves past the limits of the field. Since this type of zoom has a definite starting point but no definite stopping position, it is referred to as a continuing zoom.

The animated zoom does not require any camera or compound table movement since the zoom effect is achieved with the art work. The animated zoom is explained in greater detail in the next chapter.

The Animated Zoom

Although similar effects can be achieved with either method, the animated zoom and the camera zoom are used for entirely different purposes and have very little in common. Some zooms are easily achieved by plotting and calibrating the camera movement from one position, in relation to the art work, to another. Other zooms are accomplished more easily by using animation processes and principles.

The camera zoom, explained in detail under "Zooms, Pans, and Spins," is achieved by the movement of the camera from one position to another. The movements, for each frame of the zoom, must be plotted and calibrated. The art work, in relation to the camera movement, remains in a stationary position on the compound table.

In an animated zoom, however, the camera remains in a stationary position during the entire zoom. The zoom effect is achieved by moving the art work in relation to the camera. This method, of course, eliminates the necessity for plotting and calibrating camera and compound table movements. The art work or subject matter, for the animated zoom, usually consists of photographs or photostats which are cut out and positioned on cels. The positioning of these cutouts, each progressively larger in size, must be extremely accurate since their arrangement determines the smoothness of the zoom effect. The animated zoom is not used where it is possible to make a camera zoom. It is used only on those occasions when the camera zoom is considered impractical.

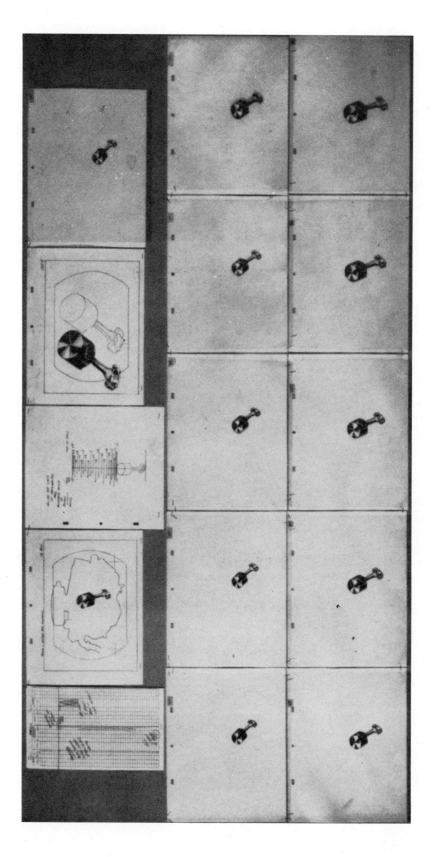

Shown here are the layouts, exposure sheets, and the 25 cels used in the animated zoom.

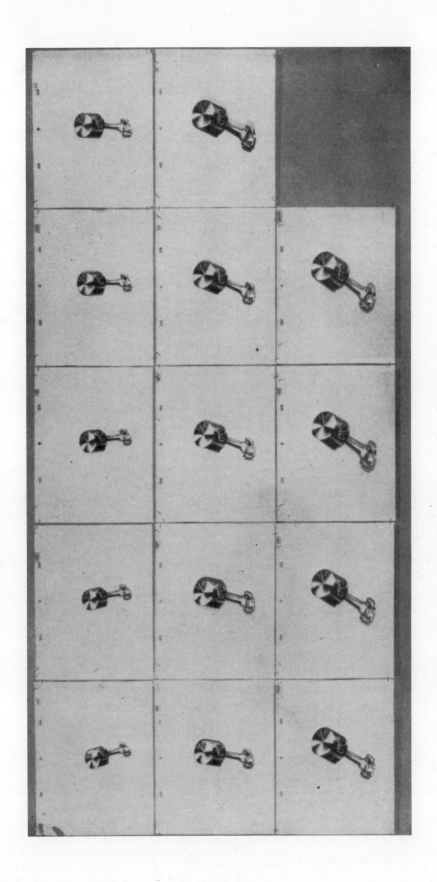

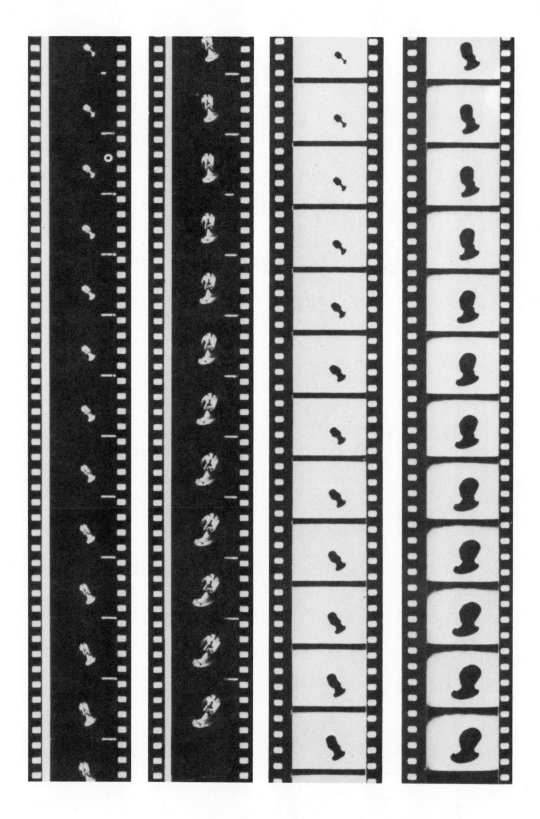

The animated zoom also makes possible a progressive build-up
and the simultaneous showing of each of the zoom positions.
The piston, used in the Amoco commercial animated zoom, is
shown as a build-up in columns 1 and 2. The high contrast mattes
for the zoom are shown in columns 3, 4, 5, and 6.

A camera zoom might be considered impractical (if not impossible) for any one of several reasons. If, for example, the cameraman is required to make a zoom or compound table movement to a specific area in a scene, the effect is easily achieved with a camera zoom. Where a zoom is indicated for only a *part* of the subject matter in a scene, while the background and other art work remain in a stationary position, the camera zoom would be considered impractical. (In order to achieve a camera zoom, mattes would have to be specially prepared and very carefully matched to the stationary art work during the zoom. The positive and negative mattes, for masking the art work during the camera zoom, would necessitate two runs. The zoom and compound table movements would also have to be duplicated in each run.)

The animated zoom, by comparison, would merely require an arrangement of the subject matter on cels, in relation to the camera and stationary background. The camera zoom would also be considered impractical where more than one zoom or pan movement is needed over the same film footage. If neither one of the zooms can be achieved by photographing the subject matter as a double exposure, on a second run, the animated zoom would be used in place of the camera zoom. (If the subject matter for the second zoom consists of a white title, however, the animated zoom would not be used. The title, in such cases, can be "burned in" and the camera zoom accomplished on a second run.)

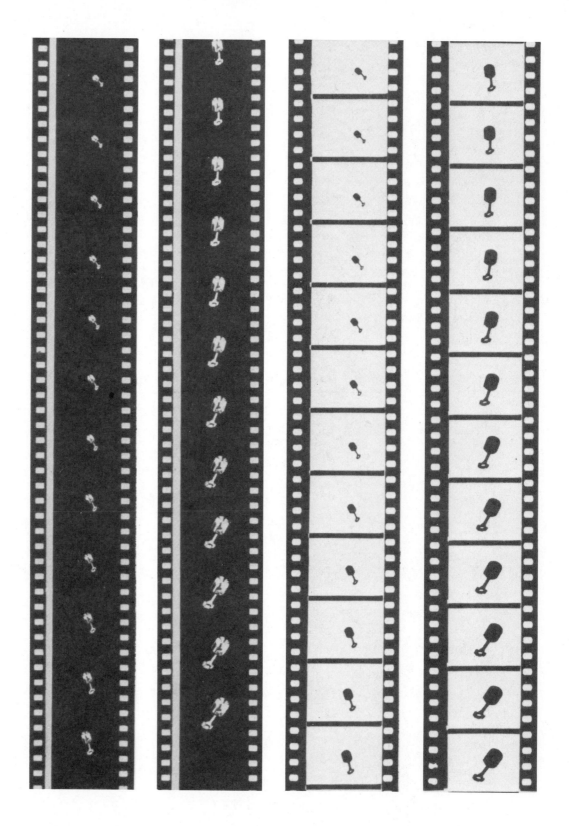

The 25 positions of the animated zoom in the Amoco commercial are shown in columns 1 and 2. The high contrast mattes for combining the animated zoom with the motor animation in the Amoco commercial are shown in columns 3, 4, 5, and 6.

If each of the cels used during an animated zoom were photographed in sequence without removing any of the previously exposed cels, it would be possible to see the subject matter in all of the zoom positions simultaneously. After photographing the first cel, for example, the second cel is added and both cels are photographed together. The third cel, for the next frame of the zoom, is then added to the first two cels. This process is continued until each of the cels used in the zoom has been added to the ones preceding it.

Although the background would be darkened considerably because of the simultaneous use of the many cels in the zoom, the problem is solved by combining the subject matter as shown on the accompanying exposure sheet. If, for example, 4 cel levels are to be exposed over the background throughout the zoom, cels 1, 2, 3, and 4 are photographed in sequence. Cels 5, 6, and 7 are then photographed over 1, 2, 3, and 4, all combined on one cel. In this way, no more than 4 cel levels are used over the background during any part of the scene or zoom. Although this effect is used quite often for product "shots" in television commercials, it is impossible to achieve similar effects with the camera zoom, since only one cel contains the art work for the entire zoom.

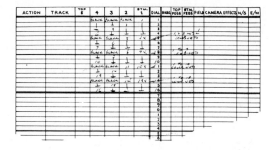

The Animated Zoom. Shown here is the method used for combining the subject matter in order to maintain 4-cel levels and a uniform density over the background throughout the animated zoom.

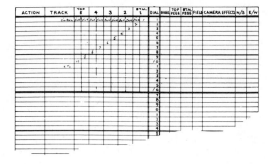

The Animated Zoom. In theory, the exposure of 16 cels, including blanks, would be necessary for the simultaneous showing of all the subject matter as a build-up in a one-foot animated zoom.

Production AM-3086, a one-minute commercial made for the American Oil Company, includes an excellent example of the animated zoom.

Photographs of an automobile piston, ranging in size from 2-11/16 inches to 6-7/8 inches, were cut out and positioned on the 25 cels used in the zoom. These cels, showing the piston zooming up from the motor, were photographed on the animation stand and then superimposed optically over an animated sequence on another strip of film. The animated sequence, showing the flow of gas through an automobile motor, served as the background for the animated zoom.

The accomplishment of such a zoom with camera and compound table movements, although possible, would have involved a great deal of complicated plotting and calibrating of the pan and table rotation movements by the animation cameraman. Each of the camera and compound table movements would also have to be duplicated when photographing the mattes needed for the optical combination of the zoom with the film containing the motor animation. The time-consuming process involved in photographing the zoom with camera and compound table movements was considered impractical in this case and the less complicated animated zoom was used to achieve the desired effect.

The 25 cels used in the animated zoom were photographed on the animation stand over a black card with normal top lighting. These same 25 cels were then re-photographed on high contrast film with underneath lighting to achieve the matte needed for the optical combination. The camera and compound table remained in the same field position for both filmings.

The high contrast print, after processing, showed the animated zoom of the piston in silhouette on the clear frame of film. The piston animation, on the high contrast negative, showed the piston zoom as the clear film area on the completely black frame.

For the optical combination, the high contrast print was exposed with the film containing the motor animation. On a second run, the film containing the animated zoom was combined with the high contrast negative and photographed over the previously exposed film in the optical camera.

Not only was the possibility of a double exposure completely eliminated with these mattes but the great saving of time during the original filming process completely justified the use of the animated zoom over the camera zoom.

Animated Zoom. Superimposed over the mechanical animation in the Amoco commercial, the 25 positions of the piston in the animated zoom are shown in this film sequence.

The Pantograph

History books tell us that the first sustained free flight was made at Kitty Hawk, December 17, 1903, by Orville Wright. Orville, who won the toss from his brother, Wilbur, stayed aloft twelve seconds and traveled approximately 100 feet in a straight line.

Several years ago, through the magic of animation and the maneuverability of the camera compound table, the plane was made to stay aloft on film for a considerably longer period of time.

Although the compound table is at a 90-degree angle in relation to its normal position, the Pantograph pointer indicates the exact center of the photographic field.

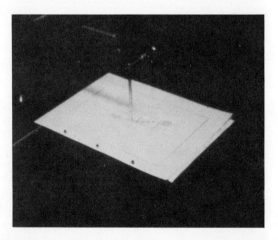

In some cases, the panning action during a zoom is achieved by using a Pantograph guide.

Where the constant changing of cels is not required, shorthand or abbreviated exposure sheets such as these are used as a guide by the animation cameraman during the photographic process.

During this flight, the animation cameraman was able to pilot the plane through inside and outside loops, force the plane into a spin and successfully accomplish a barrel roll before the aircraft was panned out of camera range. He was able to do this with the pantograph guide.

This item, the pantograph unit, is attached to the animation stand and makes possible the convenient panning of the compound table from one position to another.

Plotting straight line movements or complicated curved pans are both done in the same manner. The panning path is drawn on animation paper and registered to the pegs on the pantograph unit. The spacing for each move is calibrated on the panning path by dividing the number of moves indicated on the exposure sheets by the length of the path. By using north-south and east-west compound table controls, the animation cameraman can move the pantograph pointer along the projected panning path easily and quickly.

In order to allow the compound table to be panned to any position indicated on the pantograph guide, the Wrights' plane was inked and opaqued on a cel approximately four times larger than those used in cartoon animation (36 × 30 inches compared to the usual 13 × 10½-inch cel). The cel was then placed over a blue tone card which served as background. The pegs on both traveling peg bars were removed so that the large cel and tone card could lie flat on the surface of the compound table.

Zooms and table spins were combined with the panning action in order to give added realism to the over-all effect. Projection time for the 465 frames of the flight was 19-1/3 seconds, slightly more than seven seconds longer than the original flight time.

Many other effects can be achieved with the pantograph. Its main use, however, is as a guide attached to the animation stand in planning movements from one field position to another without the need for complicated plotting and calibrating.

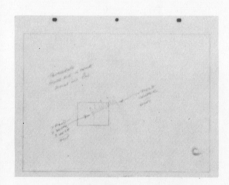

This type of guide during short zooms or zooms with widely-spaced moves saves a great deal of time and eliminates the need for calibrating the north-south and east-west panning movements.

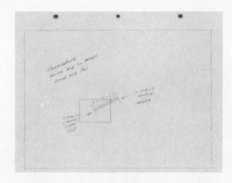

The photograph shows a Pantograph guide made for the panning movement of the zoom described under Zooms, Pans, and Spins.

The plane.

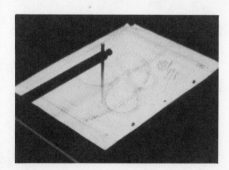

The guide, positioned on the Pantograph, is used for the panning movement of the airplane. The pointer indicates the exact center of the shooting field for every frame during the photographic process.

Pantograph guide tells the animation cameraman the moves and the number of frames for this sequence. Frame 1 is at the far left and frame 465 at the far right.

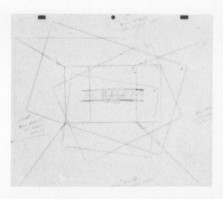

Compound table movements and field guides for the famous flight. Note the various angles and the areas covered by the animation camera during this sequence.

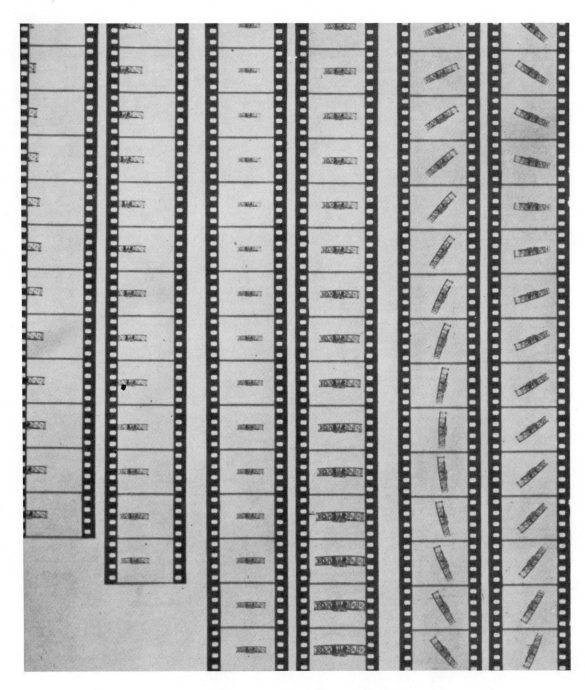

The film clips show the unusual amount of movement that can
be achieved without plotting or calibrations by using the Pantograph attached to the compound table of the animation stand.

Under Lighting

Under lighting, or back lighting, has many uses. A series of photographic exposure tests help determine the best and most efficient lighting system in relation to shutter openings on different cameras and animation stands.

An opal glass is used for diffusion and even light distribution over the light source. The glass is inserted in the opening in the center of the compound table.

Under lighting makes possible the photographing and subsequent review of the animator's pencil drawings before the drawings are finally inked and opaqued. Mattes needed for combining animation with live action scenes, the copying of transparencies and other special effects are all made possible through back lighting or under lighting.

Animation equipment manufacturers have designed special containers for under lighting purposes. An ingenious cameraman, however, can quickly and easily make his own under lighting set-up by wiring several lamp sockets together and inserting them in a flat piece of wood. Proper exposure, regardless of the lighting system, can be determined by photographing the art work, pencil drawings in this case, with different lens settings. DuPont 928B or DuPont 805B motion picture films are especially good for pencil test purposes.

The camerman should photograph four drawings or pieces of paper at ½-stop intervals (f/4, f/4.5, f/5.6, f/6.3, for example). A few frames photographed at each lens opening is sufficient to give the cameraman the exact exposure for the lighting system in use.

The animation cameraman placing the drawings over the glass insert in the compound table.

The platen is shown here in a raised position. Directly under the platen, the opal glass used for underneath lighting is in position in the center of the compound table.

The opal glass used for under lighting is shown in position in the center of the compound table.

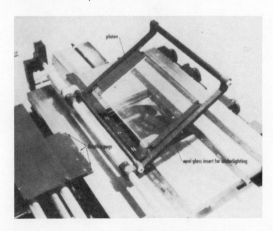

231

The Pencil Test

After all of the animator's and inbetweener's drawings for a scene have been completed, these drawings are photographed on the animation stand. The photography of the drawings, before they are traced on cels and opaqued, is called the "pencil test" or "pencil testing."

The film negative of these drawings is then viewed by the animation director and animator. If the animation is smooth and the drawings satisfy story-board require-ments, the drawings are given to the inking and opaqu-ing departments for the next step in production.

Pencil testing, which is done using under lighting, is well worth the extra time and effort. Changes in the animation are much easier and cheaper to make at this stage than after the drawings have been inked and opaqued and photographed for the final production.

These film clips show some frames from a pencil test after pro-cessing. The lines of the background and the drawings are white on the developed negative.

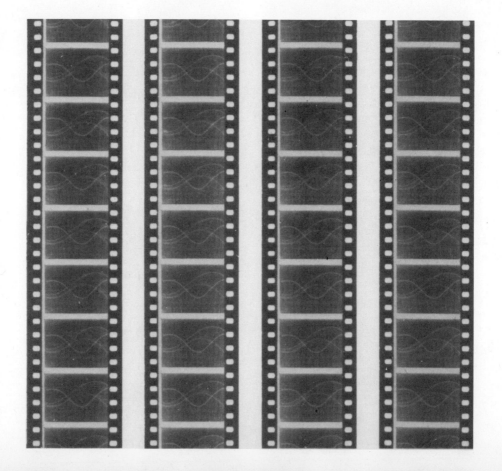

Fades and Dissolves

Two of the most frequently used effects in motion pictures are the fade and the dissolve.

The fade, as the name implies, refers to the appearance or disappearance of a scene or image from the screen. The fade *out* is used at the end of a scene or sequence and has a note of finality about it. The fade *in*, by comparison, has a completely opposite effect and is used to introduce a scene or sequence.

The fade effect is achieved by the gradual opening or closing of the camera shutter for each frame of the effect. Most motion picture cameras, including those adapted for animation work, have 170-degree shutters. When the shutter is fully open, the position for photographing, the shutter indicator is at the 170-degree position. At the closed position, the shutter reading is zero.

In order to fade *out* a scene or sequence, the cameraman divides the 170 degrees by the number of frames indicated on the shooting script or exposure sheet. If a one-foot fade *out* is indicated, the cameraman divides the 170 degrees by 16, the number of frames in one foot of film. If a two-foot fade *out* is indicated, the 170 degrees are divided by 32, the number of frames in two feet of film.

An example of a 16-frame fade in beginning with a completely black frame.

The 16-frame fade out used at the end of the Dual Filter Tareyton commercial.

233

A

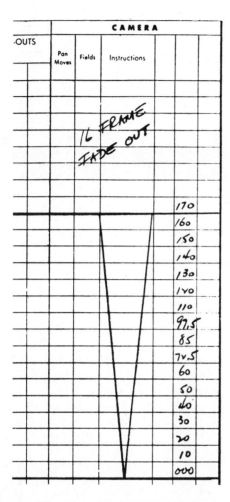

B

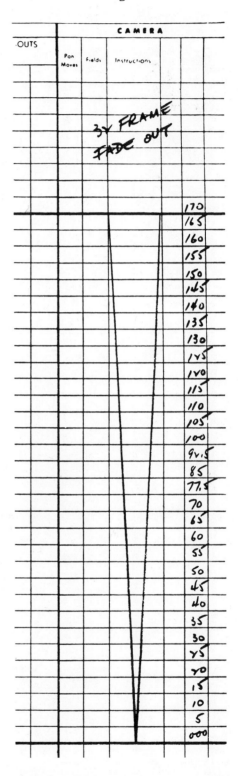

Example A shows the calibrations for a one-foot fade *out* with evenly spaced shutter moves. The calibrations for the two-foot fade *out* are shown in Example B.

The fade *in* is achieved by reversing the process used for making a fade *out*. The frame of film preceding the fade *in* is completely black and the picture or image is made to appear by opening the shutter gradually. At the 170-degree position, the fade *in* effect is complete and the picture is fully exposed. The same method used for calibrating the fade *out* is also used for calibrating the fade *in*.

Unlike the calibrations for zooms or compound table movements, it is *not* necessary to include an ease in or ease out for the fade effect. The gradual dimming or brightening of the picture and the progressive increase or decrease in light between frames is so slight when looking at the actual film that, in most cases, the changes are discernible only through the use of a light-measuring device known as a Densitometer.

When a fade *out* and a fade *in* are superimposed over the same frames of film, an effect known as a cross-dissolve results. Also referred to as a lap dissolve

The exposure sheets show symbols and shutter markings used for a 16-frame and 32-frame fade in and fade out. The numbers refer to shutter openings in degrees, from completely closed (zero degrees) to completely open (170 degrees), plus frames at which changes in shutter settings are made. Note that changes are more gradual in 32-frame series than for 16-frame series.

234

CAMERA

OUTS | | Pan Moves | Fields | Instructions | | |

16 FRAME FADE IN.

000
10
20
30
40
50
60
72.5
85
97.5
110
120
130
140
150
160
170

because of the overlapping fades, the effect is used frequently for transition purposes in motion picture production.

The cross-dissolve, almost self-explanatory, is used to fade or blend one scene or picture into another. Also used as a transition effect in order to show a time lapse or a change in location, the dissolve is never used as a substitute for the fade. Neither is the fade ever used in place of a dissolve. Each effect has its own distinct role in motion picture production.

Although the cross-dissolve is achieved by following the same basic procedure used in making the fade, one additional step is required. After a scene or action has been faded *out*, the film in the camera must be returned to the exact frame where the fade *out* was begun. The runback of the film is made with the shutter in the closed position. At the same frame in which the fade *out* was begun, the new scene is faded *in* and the effect is completed. Illustration C shows the calibrations for a one-foot cross-dissolve. The calibrations for a two-foot cross-dissolve are shown in example D.

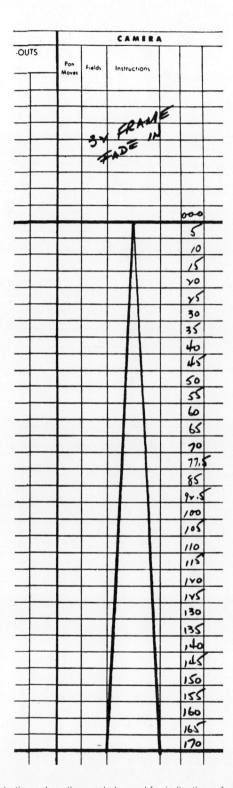

The illustrations show the symbols used for indicating a fade in on the exposure sheets. Also shown are the shutter calibrations for a 16- and 32-frame fade in.

Compare the incremental breakdown of a 16-frame fade out for a camera with a 180-degree shutter, with that of a camera that has a 170-degree shutter (left). Also, compare the breakdown of a 32-frame cross-dissolve using a camera with an 180-degree shutter, with the calibrations needed for a cross dissolve of similar length using a camera with a 170-degree shutter (right).

An example of a 16-frame cross dissolve is shown in this strip of film from the Dual Filter Tareyton commercial.

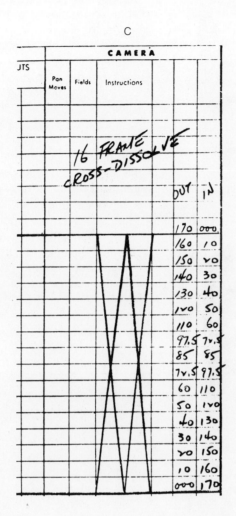

C — CAMERA

JTS	Pan Moves	Fields	Instructions		OUT	IN
			16 FRAME CROSS-DISSOLVE		170	000
					160	10
					150	20
					140	30
					130	40
					120	50
					110	60
					97.5	72.5
					85	85
					72.5	97.5
					60	110
					50	120
					40	130
					30	140
					20	150
					10	160
					000	170

D — CAMERA

	Pan Moves	Fields	Instructions		OUT	IN
			32 FRAME CROSS-DISSOLVE		170	000
					165	5
					160	10
					155	15
					150	20
					145	25
					140	30
					135	35
					130	40
					125	45
					120	50
					115	55
					110	60
					105	65
					100	70
					92.5	77.5
					85	85
					77.5	92.5
					70	100
					65	105
					60	110
					55	115
					50	120
					45	125
					40	130
					35	135
					30	140
					25	145
					20	150
					15	155
					10	160
					5	165
					000	170

The calibrations and symbol used for indicating a 16- and 32-frame cross dissolve are shown in these illustrations.

The shutter indicator is shown in its completely open position (170 degrees).

THE CAMERA SHUTTER AND THE DOUBLE-EXPOSURE

Varying degrees of transparency, for double-exposure effects, are achieved with the camera shutter. At 170 degrees, the shutter is open and in position for photographing. At the zero reading, the shutter is completely closed and the film in the camera cannot be exposed. Between these two positions, however, almost any degree of transparency may be achieved. In the open position, or 170-degree shutter reading, the exposed picture or image is completely normal. The lower the shutter reading, the more transparent and ghost-like the image becomes. The film clips, from a Paramount Pictures animated cartoon, were especially prepared to illustrate the double exposure effect made possible with the camera shutter.

The "burn in," another double-exposure effect that is used frequently in commercial film production, has made the multiple run a routine assignment for the animation cameraman.

In many instances, for example, it is inadvisable to photograph a title on the same run with the art work or subject matter. Very often, when complicated compound table movements during the first run prevent the photographing of a title in a hold or still position on the same run, the title is burned in on a second run in order to simplify the photographic process.

At other times, zoom and compound table movements for the art work may conflict with zoom and compound table movements for a title that is to be used in the same scene. Obviously, the conflicting movements

The automatic dissolve mechanism is shown in this photograph. The larger dial beneath the frame counter is in the open or shooting position. The length of the cross dissolve is controlled by presetting the smaller dial on the right to the number of frames needed for the effect.

Varying degrees of transparency achieved with the camera shutter. In column 1, shutter opening was 25 percent of normal. In column 2, opening was 50 percent or 85 degrees. Column 3 was made at 75 percent, while the last column was photographed with a completely open (170-degree) shutter. The greater the transparency, the lower the shutter setting.

make it impossible to photograph both the art work and the title on the same run. Here, again, the burn in process is used on a second run in order to achieve the required effect.

During the photographic process, the cameraman, after filming the subject matter in the first run, closes the shutter and runs the film back to the first frame in which the title is to be exposed. At that frame, the shutter is opened and the white title, registered on pegs, is photographed over a black card. The black card, used as the background for the burn-in effect, eliminates the possibility of exposing anything but the title over the subject matter photographed during the first run.

Any reduction of the shutter opening, on any run following the original photography, affects the density of the burn in. With the shutter at the 170-degree position, the white title will burn through the previously exposed film. At the 85-degree position, however, the subject matter photographed during the first run would be visible through the burned-in title. An even greater reduction of the shutter opening would cause the title to lose most of its whiteness and become quite transparent and ghost-like.

CROSS FADE

Cross-fade is an optical effect in which the subject matter in the outgoing scene cross-dissolves to a selected color or shade of gray instead of to the incoming scene. The color or shade of gray is then cross-dissolved to the incoming scene to complete the effect. Mathematically, two cross-dissolves equal one cross-fade.

These film clips from a Paramount Pictures animated cartoon show the double-exposure effect made possible with the camera shutter.

In the first step of the filming process, the background for the animation is photographed with the shutter in the open position at 170 degrees. The cels containing the animation are not used in this filming. After the background has been photographed for the entire length of the scene, the film in the camera is returned to the scene's starting frame with the shutter in the closed position.

The cels containing the animation are then photographed over a black card. On this second run, the shutter remains halfway open at the 85-degree setting on the shutter indicator. The amount of transparency can be controlled by setting the shutter indicator at different positions. The greater the amount of transparency desired, the lower the degree or setting on the shutter indicator.

Slit-Scan Photography

This photographic process is also referred to as "smear" or "streak" photography. Exposure takes place through a masking slit that is moved in a horizontal plane over the subject matter. Each successive frame of film photographed in this manner provides a time reference relating to a movement, condition, or phenomenon. The technique was originally designed to obtain data pertaining to stress-and-strain conditions, explosive phenomena, and movement patterns normally exposed with high-speed photographic processes. Variations of this masking technique are currently used to achieve unusual abstract-lighting effects in commercial productions. This adaptation re-

quires a motion-picture camera driven by a stop-motion motor. The camera is mounted so that each frame in the sequence of movement—the panning of subject matter behind the slit and the movement of the camera itself—is precisely repeatable. Animation stands with underlighting are ideally suited for this purpose. During the photographic process a light source directed on the portion of the subject matter that is visible through a slit is moved across one plane of the film frame. During each of the multiple runs needed to achieve the effect, the position of the slit in relation to the subject matter is changed incrementally to allow exposure on different planes. The abstract-light patterns in the composite effect create the illusion that the camera is moving through the subject matter along a rainbow-lined route. The technique was developed by Trumbull Film Effects and used in the Stanley Kubrick production *2001: A Space Odyssey*.

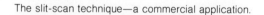

The slit-scan technique—a commercial application.

Two frames from a Lufthansa commercial using the slit-scan technique.

240

The Superimposure

The superimposure is similar to the double-exposure or burn-in in many ways. In recent years, the superimposure process has been used for other purposes and is now generally regarded as a technique in itself.

Where it is used as a commercial technique, the film is projected or superimposed over a regularly scheduled television program. The superimposure, as it is used by advertisers sponsoring sports events, makes possible the projection of the commercial message without disturbing the program's continuity for the television viewer. Because of this, the technique has become extremely popular.

The superimposed material often consists of a title only. At other times, the subject matter may be fully animated. In either case, the subject matter is prepared by using conventional production methods.

In the layout and animation stages of the production, the cartoon characters are first designed and the animated action is drawn and timed to the film editor's analysis of the sound track. The completed drawings are traced on cels with *white* ink instead of the black or colored inks used in standard animation production.

These cels are then photographed over a black card, on the animation stand, according to the exposure sheets prepared by the animator. The inked cels are *not* opaqued and art backgrounds, except in special cases, are not necessary, since the picture on the television screen serves as the background for the animation.

The high contrast film used for photographing the animation or titles, Eastman 5362, is processed by the film laboratory in a high contrast positive bath. The print, after processing, is completely black except for the white lines of the animated action. Only these white lines are seen when the film is projected over the picture on the TV screen.

This process makes it possible for the viewer to continue watching the action and sideline color during time-out at a football game, or a fighter, back in his corner after an exciting round, without the continuity of the sports event being interrupted by a message about the sponsor's product. Appreciation of this gesture by the sponsor is reflected by the viewer's support and patronage at sales counters.

If any commercial technique can be singled out as an example of good will by an advertiser, the superimposure would be the overwhelming choice of a large, appreciative following. Gadgets designed to tune out the audio or visual portion of a commercial are rendered superfluous by the superimposure technique.

Several examples of the superimposure are shown as they would appear on the home television screen during the telecast of a sports event.

Positioning by Camera Projection

When preparing animation that is to be used in conjunction with a live action scene, it is often necessary to position the art work in relation to the live film. This matching or positioning process is accomplished by projecting one of the frames from the live action film onto the working surface of the compound table.

The following technical information and explanation of the actual projection process is included for those readers who are particularly interested in motion picture cameras and the photographic processes: The pressure plate of the camera shuttle with its removable cutout accommodates special projection work. After removing the shuttle mechanism from the camera, the live action frame of film is positioned on the locating pins. The back pressure plate is then removed from the shuttle and an accessory light is mounted on the open camera door. When the camera is racked over, the image on the live film is projected onto the table for accurate positioning.

The pencil tracing of the projected frame of film enables the cameraman to position a product, title, matte, or animated action with an amazing degree of accuracy. The same tracing of the projected frame of film is also used as a layout for the preparation of the art work.

The projection process is *not* used for the simple positioning of a title or similar subject matter. The superimposure viewing device, which facilitates composing and focusing, is used in place of the projection method.

The camera door is open showing the sprocket assembly and the shuttle. The lens and bellows are directly below the camera shuttle. The vertical cylinder mounted in front of the open camera door contains the lamp used for projection. The take-up control, when the film magazine is mounted in shooting position, is shown on the left side of the photograph.

The rack-over viewfinder with ground glass focusing is mounted on the camera door. A reticle gauge is located at the bottom of the viewing device and consists of a plate, registration pins, and reticle. The superfine ground glass is precisely mounted and aligned to match the film registration pins in the shuttle. This arrangement permits a previously exposed and devel-

In this photograph, a strip of film is in position on the registration pins at the bottom of the viewing device. When the camera is in the racked-over position, the animation cameraman is able to view the film in its relation to the field by looking directly into the eyepiece located at the top of the viewing device.

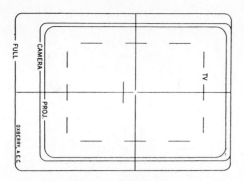

These reticle markings indicate proper composition for the animation cameraman.

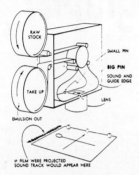

Unlike the usual movie camera in which the film travels emulsion-side-in, the film is loaded emulsion-side-out in the animation camera.

oped frame of film to be placed on the top side of the ground glass, on the fixed registration pins, so that the cameraman views through the film first and then the ground glass which shows the rectangular field markings. The eye piece faces the cameraman when the camera is on the animation stand. An optical system rectifies the subject so the image is right side up and permits copy to be read from left to right. The viewfinder has a special control for magnifying the position of the markings on the ground glass in the viewfinder for extremely accurate positioning.

Many commercial films include live action scenes showing an announcer holding the product featured in the commercial. The product, in most cases, zooms out of the announcer's hand to a close-up position in the frame. In order to achieve this type of zoom effect, the cameraman must project a frame of the live action film in order to determine the starting and stopping positions for the product. The method used for the subsequent plotting and calibrating of the zoom, from the starting to the stopping position, is discussed under "Zooms, Pans, and Spins."

The cross-dissolve, as a transition effect, is used frequently with this type of scene. During the animated zoom of the product to the close-up position, the live action film of the announcer is faded *out*. An art background is faded *in* behind the product to complete the cross-dissolve and the transition from the live action film to the "glamour" shot of the product.

ROTOSCOPE

This is one of the first techniques for duplicating human motion graphically. To produce the effect, live actors, made up and costumed to resemble animated-cartoon characters, are photographed in front of neutral backgrounds. The processed film, positioned in the animation-camera shuttle and projected onto the compound table, is traced by the animator. The outline and detail of each figure on the successive frames of film are traced on separate sheets of drawing paper registered to the pegs in the compound table. These drawings are, in turn, inked on transparent cels and opaqued or hand-colored. In the final stage of production the cels are photographed over appropriate backgrounds prepared by the studio's art department. The processed film is synchronized with the corresponding sound track by the film editor. The projection process is also used to produce mattes for subsequent optical work: areas within the film frame in which new material is to be inserted are carefully traced by the graphics department, and the mattes are photographed on high-contrast film for optical combination.

The frames of film in column 1 show an announcer holding the product featured in the commercial. During the animated zoom that follows, the product appears to zoom up from the announcer's hand to a close-up position in the film frame. The live action film of the announcer is faded out during the animated zoom and an art background (on film) is faded in to complete the effect shown in column 2.

The layout for the above zoom.

Aerial Image Photography

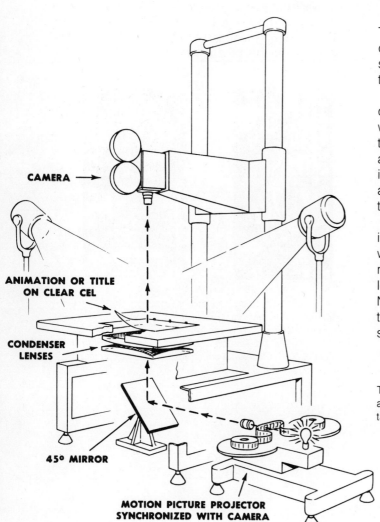

CAMERA →

ANIMATION OR TITLE ON CLEAR CEL

CONDENSER LENSES

45° MIRROR

MOTION PICTURE PROJECTOR SYNCHRONIZED WITH CAMERA

The aerial image underneath projection unit is a self-contained background projector that is electrically synchronized with the stop-motion motor that drives the animation camera.

The unit makes it possible to combine top-lighted cels with previously photographed live action scenes without using mattes. With the aerial image system, the live action film is projected from underneath the animation stand, in stop motion, on a ground glass set in the opening of the compound table. Top-lighted cels are positioned on the pegs over the projected live action film and photographed simultaneously.

In a commercial film produced recently, the aerial image system was used to achieve the following award-winning effect: The live action scene used in the commercial was a stock shot showing a group of people looking up at a billboard in the Times Square area in New York. The advertising matter on the billboard in the stock shot had to be changed in order to correspond with the message shown in the story board.

This diagram shows the relationship between the top-lighted cel and the live action film projected from underneath the compound table of the animation stand.

In order to achieve the desired effect with aerial image photography, the live action scene was projected on the ground glass in the compound table. A cel containing the new billboard advertisement was then placed on the pegs over the projected live action film and photographed with normal top-lighting. The opaque section of the cel matted out the old advertising matter on the billboard.

The area surrounding the billboard in the projected frames of the live action scene was unaffected during the photographic process. The people continued to move, look up at the billboard and, we suspect, wonder how one advertising message could dissolve out while a second message dissolved in and animated.

The aerial image process not only makes possible a great variety of effects but enables the film producer to achieve them at a great saving in time and production costs.

The aerial image unit, in position beneath the compound table, is shown in this photograph.

THE BIPACK

Some animation studios use the bipack method for achieving the simpler optical effects. With this method, it is possible to combine processed film with art work or other subject matter positioned on the compound table of the animation stand.

The special bipack film magazines used in this process have four sections or compartments. The first section contains the unexposed film, or raw stock. The second section is used as the take-up after the film has passed through the camera. Previously exposed and processed film is loaded in the third section of the bipack magazine. This processed film passes through the camera along with the unexposed film loaded in the first section of the bipack magazine.

Since both the processed film and the unexposed film pass through the camera shuttle together, the art work positioned on the compound table of the animation stand is photographed with the processed film and exposed on the raw stock, or unexposed film. In this way, the camera acts as a contact printer. The fourth section of the bipack magazine is used as the take-up for the processed film after it has passed through the camera.

Because of the limited variety of effects that can be achieved with the bipack method, it is sometimes referred to as the "poor man's optical camera."

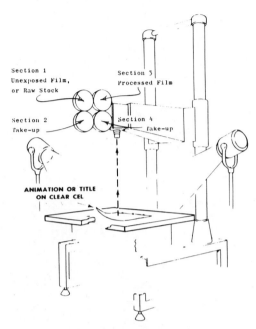

The diagram shows the bipack magazine mounted on the animation stand in relation to the art work.

The bipack magazine.

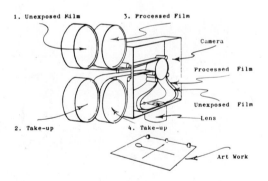

This diagram shows how both the processed film and the unexposed film are loaded in the bipack magazine. Also shown in the diagram is the relationship between the film and art work positioned on the compound table.

246

Off-Line Computerized Animation Recording

The computer has eliminated practically all of the time-consuming tedium that characterizes the operation of the conventional animation stand. Before computers the animation cameraman, in addition to following cel-change instructions on the animator's sometimes indecipherable exposure sheets, plotted zoom and pan movements, fades, and dissolves (manually, of course) and consumed many cups of coffee in an attempt to meet impossible deadlines. Before the first frame of film could be exposed, the hapless cameraman checked and rechecked start and stop positions,

took the veeder-counter readings needed for calibrating stop-motion zooms and pans, and racked the camera over to its nonfilming position for a final look through the viewfinder. The ever-present possibility of human error and the resulting inevitable retake hung over the cameraman's head like Damocles' sword. Computer electronics has removed the drudgery from animation-filming procedures and restored the smile to the cameraman's face. Through the magic of this modern miracle the animator or animation cameraman types filming instructions, using industry terminology, to the

Off-line computer-controlled animation recording: (1) teletype, (2) PDP-8 computer, (3) control-tape console, (4) adjustment panel, (5) animation camera, (6) compound table. This system is particularly useful for studios in which one computer is expected to service a number of animation stands. The intermediate medium between the computer and the animation stand is the perforated-paper control tapes that carry the filming instructions programmed through the teletype.

computer via a teletype—and all systems are go.

The computerized animation-recording system consists of a teletype, an automatic tape punch, a digital computer with a vocabulary of approximately 8,000 words, a camera control console, and the animation stand itself. The filming process actually begins when the computer's memory bank translates the teletyped instructions into binary-coded decimals (BCD). A high-speed tape perforator produces the tape, with the BCD numerical equivalents, that is fed into the console that controls the animation stand's camera and compound-table movements and functions. In addition to providing precisely repeatable incremental movements as small as 1/1000" the computer-controlled animation stand has an automatic lens iris, an automatic platen lift, and specially built pulse-action motors that control all north/south, east/west, and zoom movements.

The lengthy exposure sheets that contain the animator's filming instructions are no longer necessary. Plotting times for programming complex camera moves are greatly reduced, and dry runs for previewing movement are accomplished quickly and easily. If changes or revisions are needed, only those sequences of action that are involved have to be reprogrammed.

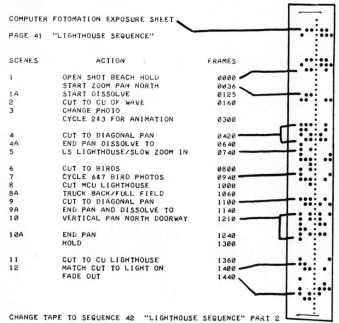

CLIENT: CBS SHOW "LOOK UP AND LIVE"
SUBJECT: "POETRY AND PHOTOGRAPHY"
PRODUCER: CHALMERS DALE
CONCEIVED BY: DOUGLAS STERLING PADDOCK
ANIMATION AND PROGRAMMING: AL STAHL/ANIMATED PRODUCTIONS, INC.

COMPUTER FOTOMATION EXPOSURE SHEET

PAGE 41 "LIGHTHOUSE SEQUENCE"

SCENES	ACTION	FRAMES
1	OPEN SHOT BEACH HOLD	0000
	START ZOOM PAN NORTH	0036
1A	START DISSOLVE	0125
2	CUT TO CU OF WAVE	0160
3	CHANGE PHOTO	
	CYCLE 2&3 FOR ANIMATION	0300
4	CUT TO DIAGONAL PAN	0420
4A	END PAN DISSOLVE TO	0640
5	LS LIGHTHOUSE/SLOW ZOOM IN	0740
6	CUT TO BIRDS	0800
7	CYCLE 6&7 BIRD PHOTOS	0940
8	CUT MCU LIGHTHOUSE	1000
8A	TRUCK BACK/FULL FIELD	1060
9	CUT TO DIAGONAL PAN	1100
9A	END PAN AND DISSOLVE TO	1140
10	VERTICAL PAN NORTH DOORWAY	1210
10A	END PAN	1240
	HOLD	1300
11	CUT TO CU LIGHTHOUSE	1360
12	MATCH CUT TO LIGHT ON	1400
	FADE OUT	1440

CHANGE TAPE TO SEQUENCE 42 "LIGHTHOUSE SEQUENCE" PART 2

Control tape for an animation stand.

In indirect, or off-line, computerized animation recording the tapes are fed to a control console, which is connected to the animation stand. Since the computer is not connected directly to the animation stand, it is free to produce the perforated-paper control tapes for other filming projects—an obvious advantage and an important consideration for studios in which several animation stands are in constant use. With this system for recording animation the animator is able to plan complicated sequences of action that would be impossible or highly impractical without the precise control provided by the computer. Exceedingly troublesome moves, such as superimpositions combined with multiple runs or zoom and pan movements programmed over a skip-frame action, can be achieved easily.

Built-in warning systems ensure error-free operation. Even the programmer's instructions are checked as the information is teletyped, and prompt warnings urging the animator to review his instructions are not uncommon. Checks against panning rates that would produce a strobe effect, for example, are built in: the computer sends back a request to change speed and reprogram. Similarly, zoom movements that extend beyond the designated length of a scene are rejected, and the programmer is asked to review his instructions. The system also warns the cameraman if the shutter is closed or if the camera is set for a reverse rather than a forward mode.

The artwork mounted on the registration pegs in the animation stand's compound table may be given a dry run in order to check the flow of action. For this type of preview the positioning controls are reset to their start positions, the camera is racked over to the nonfilming mode, and the movement is monitored through the viewfinder. If the programmed action is satisfactory, the camera is returned to its filming position, the control tape is activated, and filming begins.

Since the filming process is no longer a tedious, time-consuming race against a deadline, both the animator and the animation cameraman are free to combine their skills to produce a more imaginative and creative film. At any time during the actual filming process the animator can make revisions to improve the total effect by reprogramming portions of the film. This capability is extremely important if a client is standing behind the cameraman and second-guessing every phase of the process. The animator or animation cameraman takes the last-minute suggestions in stride, reprograms that part of the sequence to satisfy the client, and filming continues.

Motion-picture and television production, whether a 2-hour feature film or a 1-minute commercial, generally begins with a concept and (subsequently) an approved script. The computer-controlled filming process follows the same pattern. In addition to the script or storyboard animation production is preceded by the soundtrack recording and its analysis by the film editor. Using a sound reader and synchronizer, the editor literally measures the prerecorded sound track that will accompany and complement the animation. The resulting frame counts are used by the animator in preparing the bar, or lead, sheets that account for every frame of film in a scene. These sheets are basically a synopsis that indicates where specific actions take place within a scene, the number of frames allotted for the particular action, the timing for synchronizing a cartoon character's mouth movements or lip sync with the prerecorded sound track, the frames in which camera effects such as zooms and/or pans occur, and the frame in which the scene cuts, fades, or dissolves into the next.

In order to increase the efficiency of computer-controlled filming, the sound track can be mixed on ¼″ tape instead of magnetic film, thereby eliminating transfer costs. Since each scene in the animated production is usually photographed in sequence using exact frame counts, the entire editing process is greatly simplified. Splices are few and far between and in many cases work prints in any form are completely unnecessary. The control tape is threaded into the control console, and the numerical equivalents are decoded by a tape-reading device. The digital-coded instructions (the frame counts provided by the film editor) are converted into electrical signals, which motivate the mechanisms that regulate the animation stand's camera and compound-table movements and functions—the north-south, east-west, and zoom positioning motors.

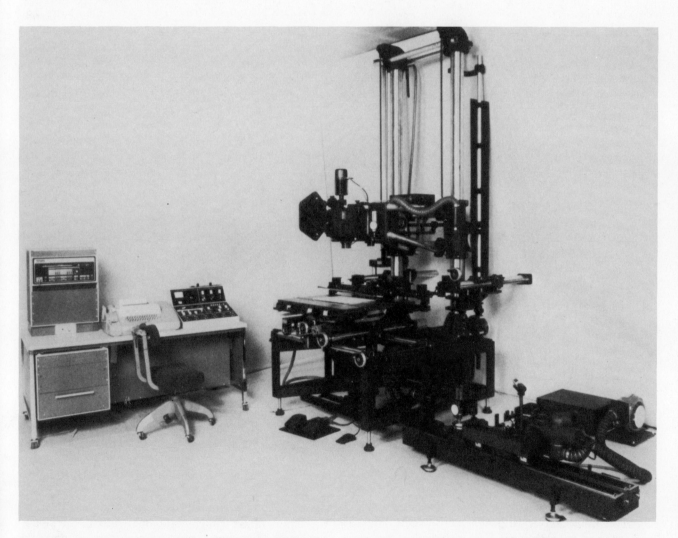

Model 5442-C animation stand. (Courtesy of Oxberry—division of Richmark Camera Service.) This stand is an on-line computer-controlled animation system. It permits direct, precise computer control over the entire operation of the stand. The operator can direct the computer to execute complex sequences of animation photography with simple, compact instructions in animation photography with simple compact instructions in animation language.

In practice, the animator or computer programmer and the animation cameraman discuss the scene's requirements. The general flow of action in relation to the static artwork is planned in terms of camera movement, and the instructions are fed to the computer via the teletype. Coordinates needed for plotting camera movement are obtained by sighting through the viewfinder and noting the corresponding numerical positions of the north-south, east-west, and zoom veeder counters which operate in conjunction with the respective positioning motors. After the coordinates for both the start and stop positions are determined, the computer makes the necessary calculations, based on the input information, and plots the movement from one position to another. The number of frames allotted for the movement is used as the guide for determining the speed and spacing between each of the individual stop-motion moves. Abrupt starts and stops at the beginning and end of zoom and pan movements are eliminated by programming acceleration and deceleration moves for the first and last frames of the effect. The ease-in and ease-out add a professional touch to any zoom or pan movement.

This type of programming eliminates the need to plot the positions and moves for each piece of artwork in a sequence in turn. With computer techniques as many as 50 separate pieces of artwork can be arranged as a unit. Any type of graphic information or a combination of artwork and overlay cels containing lip-sync or cyclic action can be included at any point in the display. During the filming process the camera is guided from one piece of artwork to the next by the punched control tape. The positioning motors locate each of the preprogrammed field positions quickly and precisely. This type of error-free filming can be accomplished in a fraction of the time required for conventional methods and equipment.

The camera shutter, also activated by the control tape, is used to produce precisely metered fades and dissolves in any specified number of frames. Information fed to the computer with regard to any film's characteristic curve allows it to make the necessary compensations that assure constant, total screen brightness even if the dissolving scenes range from one extreme to another during the transition. Similarly, a fadeout can be programmed to eliminate the rapid drop-off that usually occurs over the last few frames of the effect.

The shutter can also be used to eliminate one of the most monotonous, time-consuming assignments in animation photography—the filming of cyclic action. The constant repetition involved in filming even the simplest cyclic action is tedious and fatiguing, and costly retakes are quite common. An 8-frame animation cycle (the first frame is drawn so that it hooks up with or follows the eighth frame in a continuing action), repeated for a 3-second sequence, would normally involve a minimum of 72 cel changes—and background moves if a panning action is required. Computer technology virtually eliminates this frustrating process by providing a skip-frame capability through controlled shutter movement. During the filming process the first cel in the repeat cycle is positioned on the compound table's registration pegs over the scene's background. The control tape is programmed to expose cel 1 at frames 1, 9, 17, 25, 33, 41, 49, 57, and 65. The shutter closes automatically after each of these frames is photographed, and the film is advanced for the next exposure. The shutter is closed after cel 1 is exposed for the last time at frame 65, and the film is returned to frame 2. Cel 1 is replaced by cel 2 on the registration pegs, and the skip-frame process is repeated, with cel 2 photographed on frames 2, 10, 18, 26, 34, 42, 50, 58, and 66. The shutter is again closed, and the film is returned to frame 3 to film the cycle with cel 3. The process is repeated until each of the cels in the cycle is photographed at the appropriate frames. Filming the entire action for all 72 frames requires only 8 cel changes. If the background is panned during the cycle, the platen is automatically lifted between exposures, and the background advanced to its next programmed position. The entire filming process is completed in a fraction of the time that would be needed for conventional procedures.

The filming of cartoon animation, static artwork, photographs, and even three-dimensional objects for television commercials has always been considered routine for animation-stand photography. With the development of new techniques—the filmograph (limited animation) and the visual squeeze, for example—the use of 35mm transparencies increased greatly, but even the better-equipped animation stands were unable to photograph an area larger than 1" field. Within the last decade, however, new lens systems have been developed that are not only capable of photographing a slide but can zoom into an area within the slide. Attached to the camera carriage, newly installed Nikkor macrolenses that follow focus automatically during zoom movements are able to achieve an 8:1 zoom ratio. A 1:1 zoom ratio indicates the exposure of an area equivalent to the gauge film stock used for shooting. Since the subject matter requires proportionately more light as the lens is moved closer, the animation camera was redesigned so that the aperture opens automatically to compensate for the closer distances between the macrolenses and the transparencies.

Indirect computer-controlled animation-recording

systems have a number of advantages compared to both conventional and direct, on-line systems. In addition to their speed and error-free operation the programmed instructions are precisely repeatable: the control tape can be filed under its proper classification and retrieved for use at a later date. Similarly, complicated motion sequences may be cataloged and cross-filed to build a library of effects that can be used for other productions. With off-line systems tapes can be prepared while the animation stand is in use for other productions, a distinct advantage for busy studios in which a number of stands are in constant operation. The animator can discuss a scene with a computer programmer or animation cameraman and return to his underlit drawing board to plan his next move. Chances are better than good that the scene or sequence will be photographed before he finishes sharpening his pencil. Compare on-line computerized animation recording.

point-to-point area and line mode—used for convenient interactive creation of areas and lines using cursor-established vertex locations		
right control stick	1	x/y cursor positioning for vertex or line location
select	3	operator-to-processor signal for vertex or line creation
release	3	operator-to-processor signal for release of last vertex or line selection
keyboard mode—keyboard creation of image components (in directing data input), font selection, and artwork-record management		
key groups	type†	function
keyboard		standard typewriter keyboard with a complete set of alphamerics (upper- and lower-case letters, numbers, and special characters); special keys for individual character of full line editing
font select keys	5	rapid selection of or changeover to either of three preselected software-controlled font styles
transfer functions	5	read—artwork retrieval for display on console monitor write—storage of displayed artwork add—artwork retrieval for addition to image displayed on monitor prc—automatic film recording of artwork
peripheral selection	5	temp—temporary artwork storage area a—tape deck a b—tape deck b lib—library of artwork on disc file cr—card reader
file function	5	id—identify source by tape/tape deck designation inv—keyboard display of tape directory copy—hard-copy printout of tape directory del—deletes artwork records from tape

On-Line Computerized Animation Recording

On-line or direct, computer-controlled animation recording is basically the same as the off-line system. The main difference between the two lies in the relation of the computer to the animation stand. Unlike the off-line system, in which the control tape programmed by the computer is fed to a control console that is connected to the animation stand, the computer in the on-line system is connected directly to the animation stand via the control interface. This direct communication eliminates the need for an intermediate medium such as the punched control tape. Although the direct communication between the computer and the animation stand can be an advantage during the filming of long, complex sequences, the computer is tied up until the entire recording process is completed. In studios in which the computer is kept busy programming control tapes for a number of animation stands a great deal of waiting time may be involved. Compare off-line computerized animation recording.

Film and the Editor

THE FILM EDITOR

The unsung hero of motion picture production, the film editor, assumes a major part of the responsibility for the completed film presentation. In many cases, the success or failure of a motion picture depends upon the editor's judgment, experience, and his ability with the splicer and the sharp scissors he wields.

The picture reel and the sound track are shown passing through the synchronizer. The top counter records the number of 'frames passing through the synchronizer. The bottom counter records the frames and converts the total into film footages. For every 16 frames recorded on the top counter, one film foot registers on the bottom counter.

Assembling, sorting, and splicing the film used in a one-minute commercial is, in itself, a Herculean job. It is not unusual for a film editor to handle, sort, and discard approximately five to ten times the amount of film actually used in a production. The greater amount of this unused film footage consists of live action "out takes," miscellaneous titles, mattes and wipes required for optical combination purposes only.

Synchronization of the picture reel with the sound track is another of the film editor's responsibilities. Preparing the many sound tracks used in the "mix" is an important part of the film editor's over-all assign-

ment. The mix is a process wherein all of the previously recorded dialogue, sound effects, and musical background tracks are combined onto one master tape. The sound track accompanying the picture on the composite or release print is the result of this combination.

Analyzing the sound track for the timing of animated actions and lip sync has become a routine task for the editor engaged in the production of commercial films.

Each sentence in the sound track containing the dialogue is broken up into words and the words into syllables by running the track through a "sound reader." From the reader, the sound track passes over a film measuring device, the "synchronizer." Each syllable is measured in frames of film and the information is transferred to "bar" or "lead" sheets by the animation director.

For the optical process, guides known as "layout" sheets are used by the optical cameraman for combining the many pieces of film. Similar in many ways to the exposure sheets used by the animation cameraman, these layout sheets are prepared by the film editor.

Every frame of film in the entire production is accounted for in these layout sheets. The proper photographic sequence and frame count for every scene, animation and live action, is indicated on these sheets along with titles, mattes, wipes, and other effects needed to complete the production.

The sound reader for analyzing sound tracks, the synchronizer for measuring frames, the splicer for joining separate lengths of film, the scissors for cutting them apart, and the Moviola for synchronizing the picture with the sound track are the tools used by the film editor. Ever mindful of the old adage, "A soft answer turneth away wrath," the film editor, after a screening, must be a good actor and diplomat and, even more importantly, have a good sense of humor.

Four separate sound tracks can be run with the picture reel on the Moviola. Thus it is possible to synchronize dialogue, music, and effects with the picture at the same time.

PRINTS

The process whereby the picture reel and the sound track are run and projected at the same time is called the interlock. The rough-cut print, which consists of the good takes of the live action and animation spliced together by the film editor in their proper order but not necessarily to the exact length, is used for this projection.

During the course of production, many other prints are used. They are as follows:

The work print is the print used during production. Both the visual portion and the sound track are cut to the actual lengths to be used in the completed production.

The optical print is the first combination of animation and live sequences with special effects. It is used to check the continuity of the filmed picture against the story board as well as to check the temporary synchronization of the picture and the sound track.

The composite print (also known as the release print) contains both the picture portion and the sound track on the same piece of film. It is the finished print that is released to television stations or theatres for showing to their audiences.

FILM CONVERSION TABLE

Film travels through a projector at the rate of 24 frames each second. This is true of both 35mm. and 16mm. film even though they differ in film size. For example, although a strip of 35mm. film containing 1,440 frames is 90 feet long and a strip of 16mm. film containing the same number of frames is only 36 feet long, either strip would be projected in the same length of time, one minute, because the film-projection rate is based on frames, not on footage.

The table below shows: 1) the number of frames per foot for each film size and the comparable footage projected in one minute; 2) comparable footage projected for each film during periods ranging from one second to 10 minutes.

Film	35mm.	16mm.	8mm.
No. of frames per foot of film	16	40	80
Film footage projected in one minute	90	36	18
No. of frames projected in one minute	1,440	1,440	1,440

FILM CONVERSION TABLE

TIME	FRAMES	8mm Ft.	16mm Ft.	35mm Ft.	WORDS
1s.	24	.3	.6	1.5	2
2s.	48	.6	1.2	3.0	4
3s.	72	.9	1.8	4.5	7
4s.	96	1.2	2.4	6.0	9
5s.	120	1.5	3.0	7.5	11
6s.	144	1.8	3.6	9.0	13
7s.	168	2.1	4.2	10.5	16
8s.	192	2.4	4.8	12.0	18
9s.	216	2.7	5.4	13.5	20
10s.	240	3.0	6.0	15.0	22
11s.	264	3.3	6.6	16.5	24
12s.	288	3.6	7.2	18.0	26
13s.	312	3.9	7.8	19.5	28
14s.	336	4.2	8.4	21.0	30
15s.	360	4.5	9.0	22.5	33
16s.	384	4.8	9.6	24.0	35
17s.	408	5.1	10.2	25.5	37
18s.	432	5.4	10.8	27.0	39
19s.	456	5.7	11.4	28.5	41
20s.	480	6.0	12.0	30.0	44
21s.	504	6.3	12.6	31.5	46
22s.	528	6.6	13.2	33.0	48
23s.	552	6.9	13.8	34.5	50
24s.	576	7.2	14.4	36.0	52
25s.	600	7.5	15.0	37.5	54
26s.	624	7.8	15.6	39.0	56
27s.	648	8.1	16.2	40.5	59
28s.	672	8.4	16.8	42.0	61
29s.	696	8.7	17.4	43.5	63
30s.	720	9.0	18.0	45.0	65
31s.	744	9.3	18.6	46.5	67
32s.	768	9.6	19.2	48.0	70
33s.	792	9.9	19.8	49.5	72
34s.	816	10.2	20.4	51.0	74
35s.	840	10.5	21.0	52.5	76
36s.	864	10.8	21.6	54.0	78
37s.	888	11.1	22.2	55.5	80
38s.	912	11.4	22.8	57.0	82
39s.	936	11.7	23.4	58.5	85
40s.	960	12.0	24.0	60.0	87
41s.	984	12.3	24.6	61.5	89
42s.	1008	12.6	25.2	63.0	92
43s.	1032	12.9	25.8	64.5	94
44s.	1056	13.2	26.4	66.0	96
45s.	1080	13.5	27.0	67.5	98
46s.	1104	13.8	27.6	69.0	100
47s.	1128	14.1	28.2	70.5	102
48s.	1152	14.4	28.8	72.0	104
49s.	1176	14.7	29.4	73.5	106
50s.	1200	15.0	30.0	75.0	108
51s.	1224	15.3	30.6	76.5	110
52s.	1248	15.6	31.2	78.0	112
53s.	1272	15.9	31.8	79.5	115
54s.	1296	16.2	32.4	81.0	117
55s.	1320	16.5	33.0	82.5	119
56s.	1344	16.8	33.6	84.0	122
57s.	1368	17.1	34.2	85.5	124
58s.	1392	17.4	34.8	87.0	126
59s.	1416	17.7	35.4	88.5	128
60s.	1440	18.0	36.0	90.0	130
2m.	2880	36.0	72.0	180.0	260
3m.	4320	54.0	108.0	270.0	390
4m.	5760	72.0	144.0	360.0	520
5m.	7200	90.0	180.0	450.0	650
10m.	14400	180.0	360.0	900.0	1300
20m.	28800	360.0	720.0	1800.0	2600
30m.	43200	540.0	1080.0	2700.0	3900
60m.	86400	1080.0	2160.0	5400.0	7800

The recording unit used for transferring the original recording on ¼-inch tape to either 35mm. full base or 35mm. magnastripe film. This transfer process to film enables the editor to run the sound track on the Moviola along with the picture reel for synchronization purposes. The transfer of the track to film also makes it possible for the editor to analyze the sound track and provide the animator with the exact time for animated actions and lip movements.

The original recorded tape can be seen on the two narrow reels in the center of the photograph. This tape is transferred to the 35mm. width tape-on-film on the two larger reels.

SOUND TRACK TO PICTURE ADVANCE

This is the number of frames between any specified point in the sound track and the corresponding picture. In a composite 35mm. motion-picture print the sound track precedes the corresponding picture by 20 frames; in a 16mm. print, by 26 frames. The position of the gate in the motion-picture projector, through which the picture passes while the sound-track area is scanned by the projector's exciter lamp, places the picture 20 frames ahead of the corresponding sound. Advancing the sound track in relation to the picture places each element in its proper projection position simultaneously.

SOUND AND EFFECTS

The importance of the sound track to the feature motion picture production or the one-minute television commercial cannot be overemphasized. In the animated film presentation, the sound track is especially important since many visual effects depend upon the accompanying track and sound effects for added realism.

Musical backgrounds in both live and animated productions help establish the mood for entire scenes or actions. Very often, several bars of theme music set the pace or tempo and can accomplish as much as several pages of dialogue.

The musical "jingles" that are used as the background for film commercials are, in many cases, as important as the video portion of the presentation. An album entitled "The Madison Avenue Beat" contains many familiar jingles that have been specially arranged and recorded for dancing. From a commercial point of view, the album shows signs of reaching the best seller lists. When added to the visual portion of a film presentation, these jingles add to the effectiveness of the commercial.

The additional recording time made possible by the dual tracks on 35mm. full base tape in column 2 is, of course, a distinct advantage over the 35mm. magnastripe one-track tape shown in column 1. That advantage, however, can become a disadvantage if it becomes necessary to make changes and splices in either one of the two sound tracks. Since a splice is made across the entire width of the tape-on-film, it is not possible to make a splice on either track without affecting the recording on the other track.

The film length in column 3 shows the variable area sound track as it appears on the composite print. Column 4 shows a variable density sound track as it appears on a composite print.

Surveys have definitely established the desirability of good picture and sound combinations. For this reason, the sound track in the better commercials almost always repeats the visual title being projected on the screen. This repetition enables the viewer more easily to absorb and retain the sales "pitch" in the commercial.

The relationship between the sound effect and the visual portion of the film is of particular importance in both the live action film and the commercial production. Sound effects, ranging from a lion's roar to the gentle pitter-patter of raindrops against a window pane, are catalogued and readily available for the film editor's use. Some sound effects libraries contain thousands of these sound effects on both tape and film.

In cartoon animation, sound tracks are sometimes recorded after the drawings have been completed and subsequently inked, opaqued, and photographed. This is known as the post-sync method. For commercial films, however, the recording is usually made before the production begins. The animator, in such cases, times the animated actions of an analyzed sound track and definite frame count. This is known as the pre-sync system.

Following the recording of the sound track to be used in a production, the original tape is transferred to 35mm. magnastripe or 35mm. magnetic full base film by the sound technician. In this form, the track can be analyzed and run on a Moviola for synchronization purposes.

When all of the sound tracks, dialogue, music, and effects have been combined in the "mix," the tape is transferred to film by means of a galvanometer, a device used for recording optical tracks. Two types of optical tracks are used in the composite or release print. The first of these is known as the variable density track. The second type is known as the variable area track. All of the film clips used throughout this book show the variable area track.

WORDS-PER-MINUTE CHART

Surveys have shown that dialogue spoken during a television commercial must be considerably slower than dialogue spoken in a radio broadcast. In television viewing, both the eye and ear work at the same time, so the efficiency of one or the other may be considerably lessened.

For this reason, the table given here should be followed diligently when timing unrecorded dialogue. The right-hand column gives the maximum number of words that should be used in the time period shown in the left-hand column.

Maximum Words in a Given Time Period			
Time	Maximum Words	Time	Maximum Words
½ second	1	40 seconds	88
1 second	2	45 seconds	99
2 seconds	4	50 seconds	110
3 seconds	7	55 seconds	120
4 seconds	9	1 minute	130
5 seconds	11	1½ minutes	195
6 seconds	13	2 minutes	260
7 seconds	16	3 minutes	390
8 seconds	18	4 minutes	520
9 seconds	20	5 minutes	650
10 seconds	22	10 minutes	1,300
15 seconds	33	20 minutes	2,600
20 seconds	44	30 minutes	3,900
25 seconds	55	40 minutes	5,200
30 seconds	65	50 minutes	6,500
35 seconds	77		

Sound effects are catalogued and grouped together in the same general classification. Under "train effects," for instance, the film editor has at his fingertips the clatter of an elevated train, the power-packed shriek of a Diesel streamliner, the choo-choo of a locomotive, the roar of a subway train, the rattle of an old-time trolley car and many other train sounds too numerous to mention here.

INTERLOCK SYSTEM

Interlock is the synchronous projection of separate picture and sound elements, either on film or on videotape.

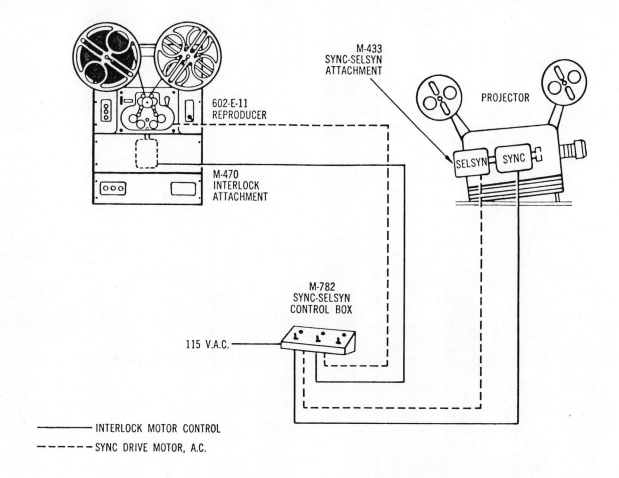

Typical Sync-Selsyn Electrical Interlock System. (Courtesy Magnasync/Moviola Corp.)

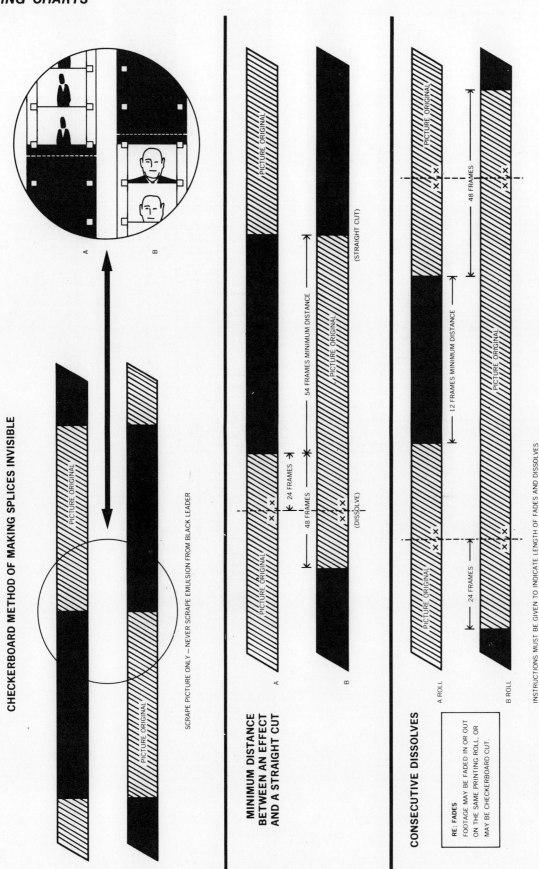

CHECKERBOARD METHOD OF MAKING SPLICES INVISIBLE

PICTURE ORIGINAL

PICTURE ORIGINAL

A

B

SCRAPE PICTURE ONLY — NEVER SCRAPE EMULSION FROM BLACK LEADER

**MINIMUM DISTANCE
BETWEEN AN EFFECT
AND A STRAIGHT CUT**

PICTURE ORIGINAL

PICTURE ORIGINAL

A

24 FRAMES

48 FRAMES

(DISSOLVE)

54 FRAMES MINIMUM DISTANCE

PICTURE ORIGINAL

B

(STRAIGHT CUT)

CONSECUTIVE DISSOLVES

PICTURE ORIGINAL

A ROLL

24 FRAMES

12 FRAMES MINIMUM DISTANCE

PICTURE ORIGINAL

PICTURE ORIGINAL

48 FRAMES

PICTURE ORIGINAL

B ROLL

RE: FADES
FOOTAGE MAY BE FADED IN OR OUT
ON THE SAME PRINTING ROLL, OR
MAY BE CHECKERBOARD CUT.

INSTRUCTIONS MUST BE GIVEN TO INDICATE LENGTH OF FADES AND DISSOLVES

Preparation of 16mm. original reversal A & B rolls. (Courtesy of
General Film Laboratories.)

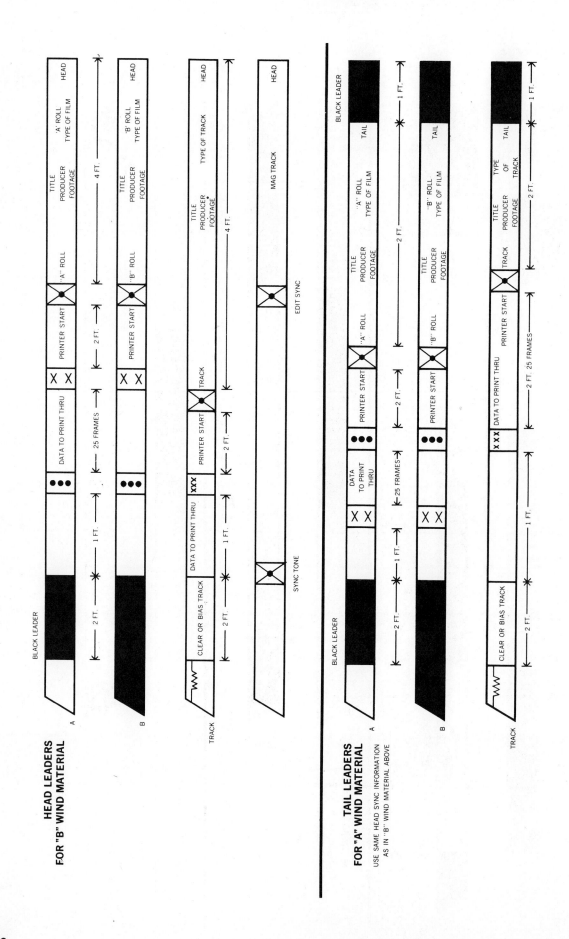

Preparation of 16mm. printing leaders. (Courtesy of General Film Laboratories.)

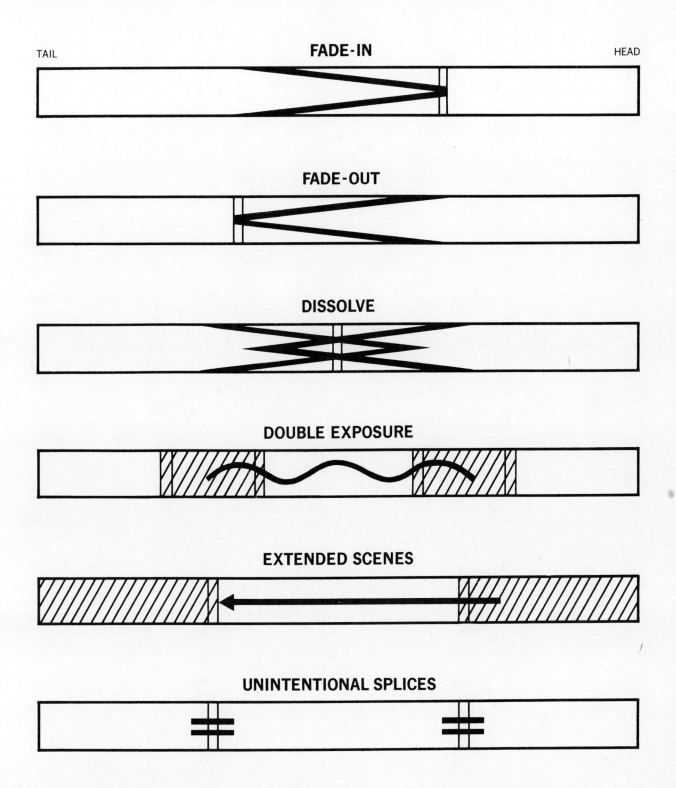

Work-print markings for special effects. (Courtesy of General Film Laboratories.)

Processing

Processing is the series of continuous, automatic laboratory operations in which the latent images exposed on film are rendered visible by treating the film with chemical solutions. Guided through a series of precisely controlled baths, the previously exposed film is developed, rinsed, fixed, and rewashed.

In the first stage the exposed film is spliced to other lengths of sprocketed film. This seemingly endless celluloid chain travels over rollers that guide the film through the developing solution. The latent images are rendered visible by the chemical bath, washed as the film passes through the second bath, fixed in a third bath, and rewashed before entering the drying chamber. At this point the tonal values in the negative are exactly opposite to those found in the original subject matter: blacks, for example, appear as clear areas on the developed film, and the polarity of the whites and light areas is completely reversed. The developed negative (the film originally exposed in the camera) is rewound on plastic cores and used to produce the positive image.

In the next stage the emulsion side of the developed negative and the emulsion side of the raw stock used for printing are placed in direct contact with each other. In this position light passing through the developed negative film exposes the printing film. The procedure used to obtain the negative image on the in-camera film is repeated for the print film. After passing through the developing solution, it is guided through a rinse bath, in which the developing-chemical residue is removed, fixed, and rewashed before entering the drying chamber. It is rewound on positive cores and returned to the production studio along with the negative roll of film.

Specialized emulsions require different types of chemical solutions. The high-contrast film types needed for optical mattes and titles require developing agents that have a higher reactivity than the chemical solutions used for low-contrast results in black-and-white negative film emulsions. Reversal-film stocks, by comparison, require special handling. With this type of in-camera raw stock the developed film yields a direct positive image—there is no negative. The film is processed to produce a negative image and reprocessed. During this second phase the developed silver on the in-camera film is bleached out, and the film is reexposed and redeveloped to yield a positive image. The fixing bath is used only after the second of the two developing procedures has produced the positive images on the print film.

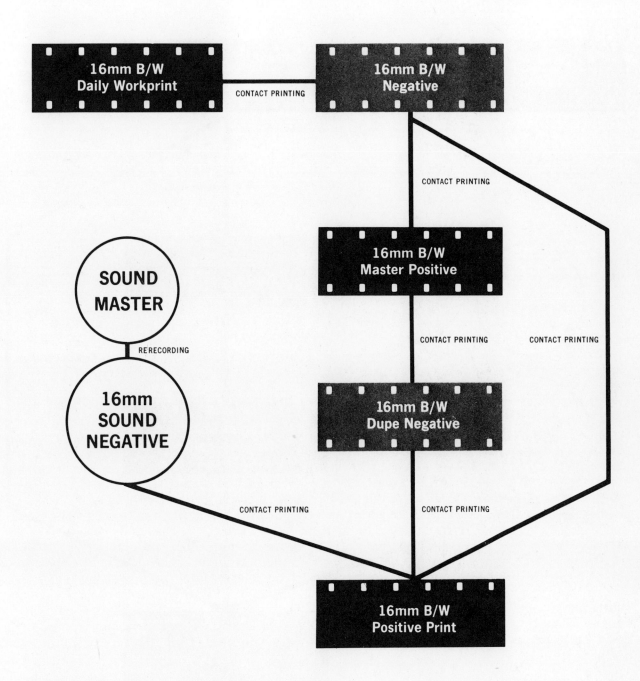

Printing-flow chart—16mm. black-and-white negative. (Courtesy
of General Film Laboratories.)

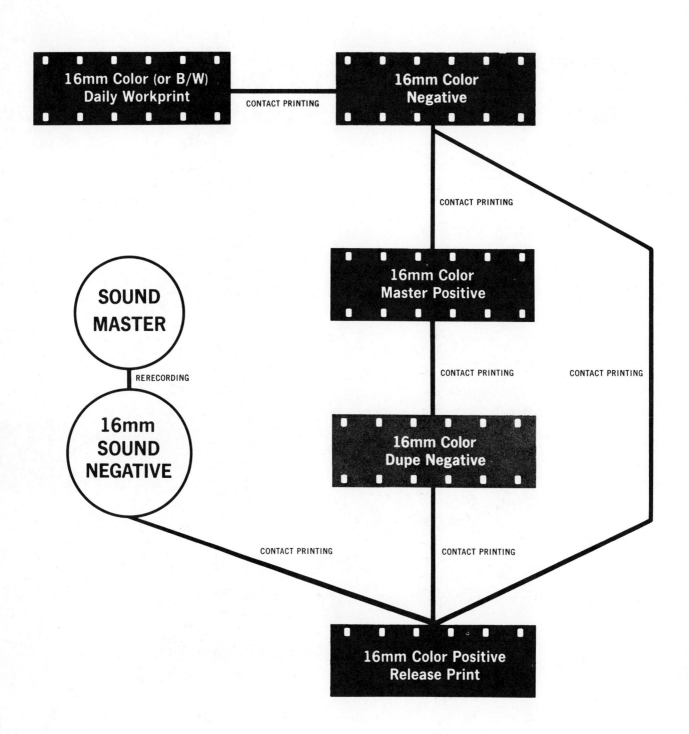

Printing-flow chart—16mm. color negative. (Courtesy of General
Film Laboratories.)

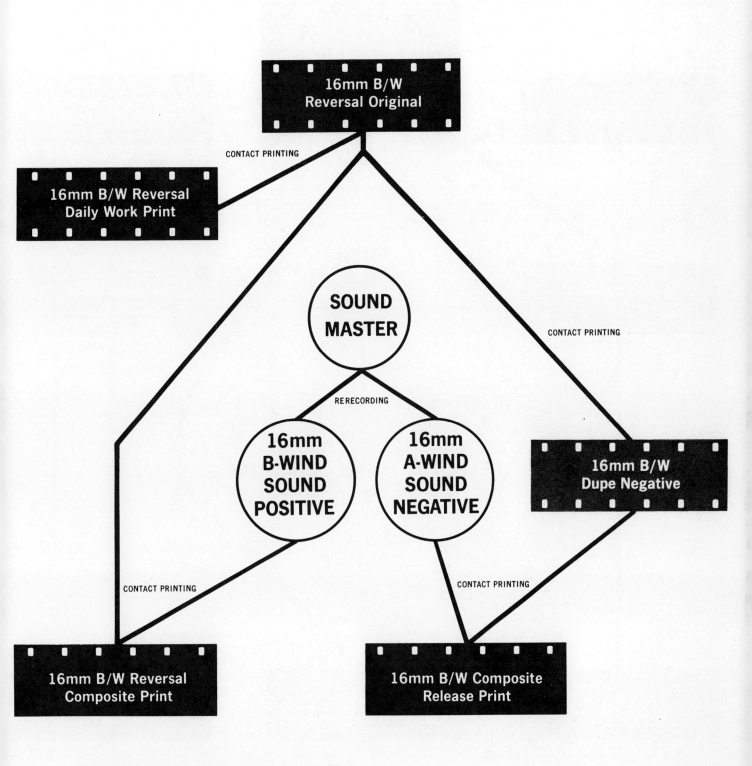

Printing-flow chart—16mm. black-and-white reversal original.
(Courtesy of General Film Laboratories.)

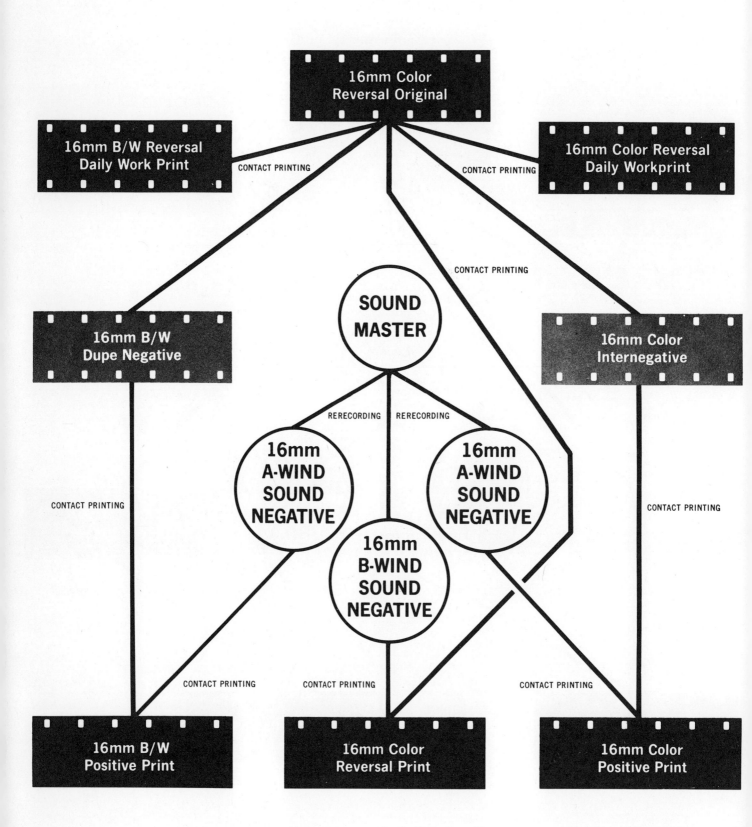

Printing-flow chart—16mm. color reversal original. (Courtesy of General Film Laboratories.)

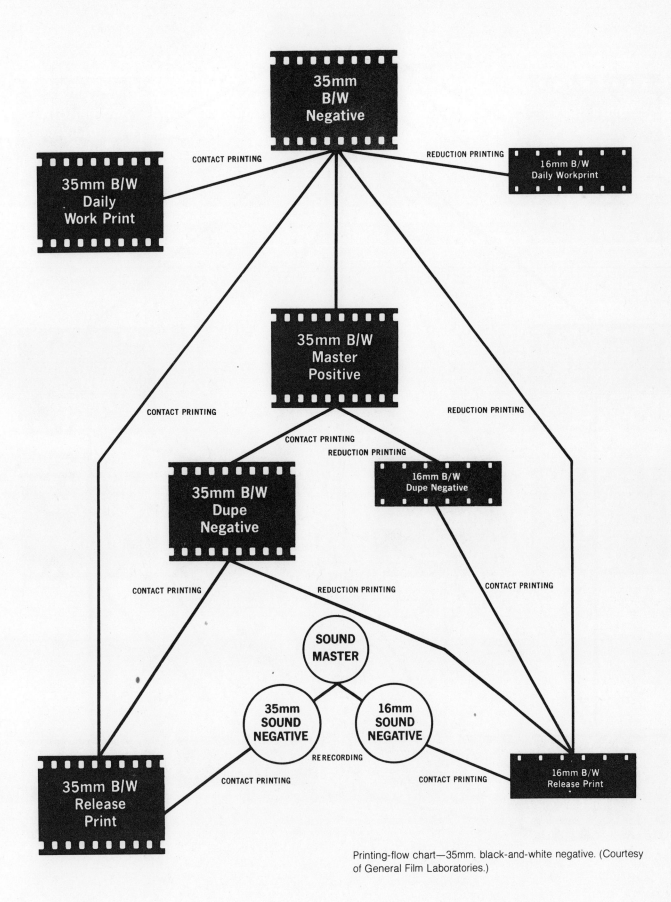

Printing-flow chart—35mm. black-and-white negative. (Courtesy of General Film Laboratories.)

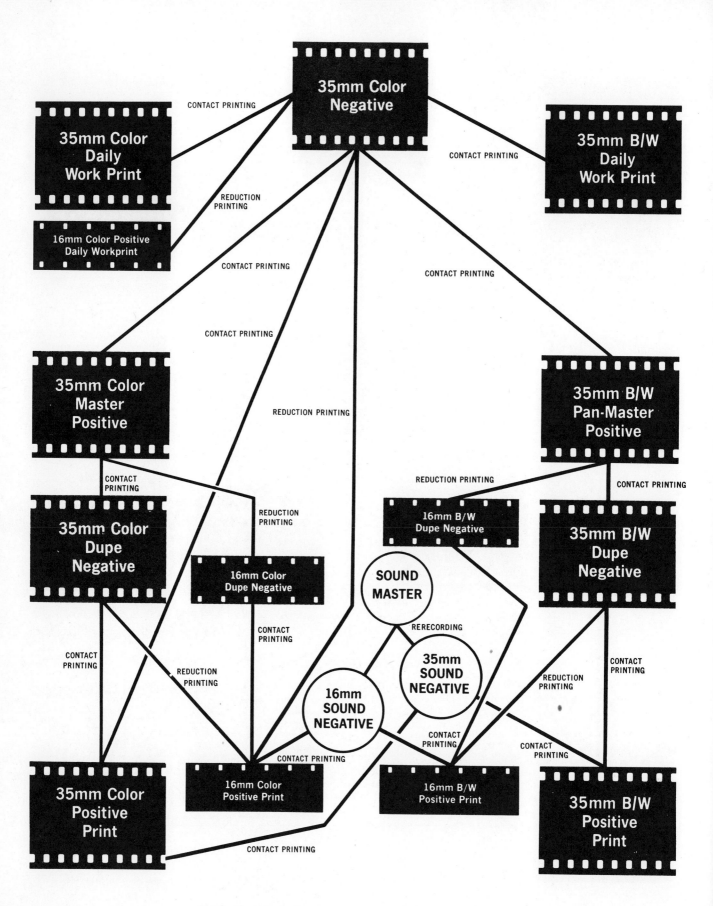

Printing-flow chart—35mm. color negative. (Courtesy of General Film Laboratories.)

The Optical Printer

The optical printer, a camera capable of photographing processed film, is one of the most important technical achievements of the motion picture industry and makes possible a great variety of effects.

The optical printer is not only capable of copying individual frames of film but can also enlarge or reduce portions of a frame. With the optical printer, an action, either live or animated, can be slowed down, speeded up, or even reversed. The latter is used to produce effects such as a swimmer returning to the diving board from the water.

The optical printer can flip or spin an entire scene or an individual frame as well as make other transitions from one scene to another. Fades, wipes, and cross-dissolves of any length are other effects achieved with the printer. One of the most frequent demands commercial television makes upon the optical printer is the superimposing of titles over live action scenes. Double exposures and combining of more than one piece of film are also everyday routines for the printer. Multiple image shots, the duplication of an action or image on the same frame of film, have also become routine functions, taken in stride by the optical printer and its operator. The uses of the optical printer are limited only by the imaginations of the directors and film editors.

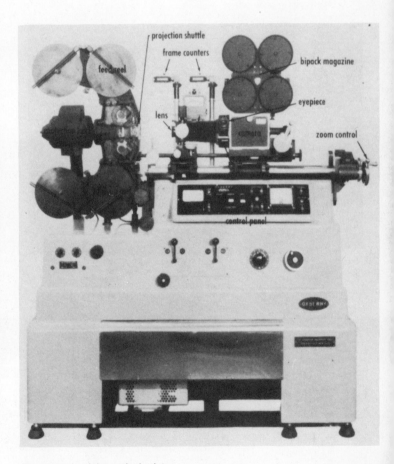

The controls of the optical printer.

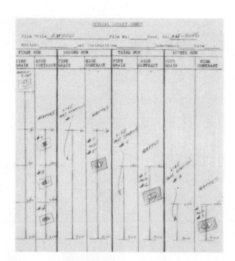

The optical layout sheet.

Similar in many ways to the exposure sheets used by the animation cameraman, the optical layout sheets serve as a guide for copying and combining the various pieces of film used during the optical photographic process. In the optical layout sheets, frame counts, indicating the exact length of scenes, effects, and transitions, are supplied by the film editor and are determined by the analysis of the accompanying sound track.

The work print is also used by the film editor as an additional check on the information and frame counts indicated on the optical layout sheets. The film to be copied, along with the film containing the mattes, titles and other effects, is placed in front of the projection housing on the optical printer. This film, during the photographic process, passes through a shuttle that is synchronized with the shuttle in the optical camera. A light source in the projection housing illuminates the individual frames of film as they pass through the projection shuttle. These frames of film are copied, or exposed, on the raw film stock in the optical camera.

The projection shuttle can accommodate several pieces of film at the same time. This multiple exposure makes possible the combination of animation, live ac-

The optical cameraman threads the fine grain film (the film to be copied) in the shuttle of the optical printer.

tion, and stop-motion scenes with mattes or other pieces of film in order to achieve wipes, superimposures, and other effects.

THE DOUBLE EXPOSURE EFFECT

In most cases, a double exposure is an undesirable effect. This composite print, however, produced for the Corning Glass Works commercial, follows the script to the letter. The scene's background was photographed on one length of film and each one of the several shots showing the woman in the kitchen was photographed in front of a black background. Each of these shots of the woman was then superimposed over the background in a separate optical camera run.

FLIP EFFECTS

This is a transitional effect in which a scene seems to rotate on a center axis until the image becomes a thin line—actually the thickness of the film itself. The incoming scene develops from this thin line into a full-frame image to complete the effect. In practice the outgoing scene is threaded into a flip device positioned between the optical printer lamp-house and the camera lens. During the filming process the cameraman rotates the flip device frame by frame for the length of the effect. Halfway through the effect the incoming scene replaces the outgoing scene in the flip device, and the stop-motion rotation continues until the scene, in the final frame of the effect, is in the normal projection position.

SPIN, OPTICAL

A spinning effect produced by rotating the processed print of the scene being duplicated in the spin mechanism positioned between the optical printer's lamphouse and the camera lens. During the filming process the cameraman rotates the spin device in which the film is threaded in stop-motion, frame by frame exposure for the length of the effect. The speed of the spin is controlled by dividing the length of the effect, in terms of frames, into the total distance the spin device will travel during the effect, and moving the mechanism incrementally for each frame. If desirable, a zoom can be added to the spin effect by moving the camera closer to or farther away from the film threaded in the spin device.

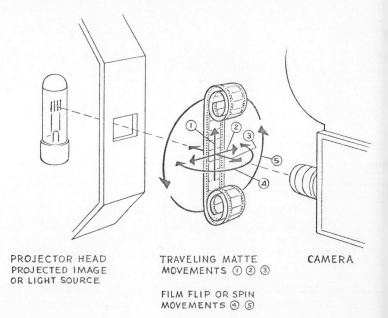

PROJECTOR HEAD
PROJECTED IMAGE
OR LIGHT SOURCE

TRAVELING MATTE
MOVEMENTS ① ② ③

CAMERA

FILM FLIP OR SPIN
MOVEMENTS ④ ⑤

TRAVELING MATTES—OPTICAL FLIPS—FILM FLIPS—FILM SPINS—RIPPLE EFFECTS—WIPES

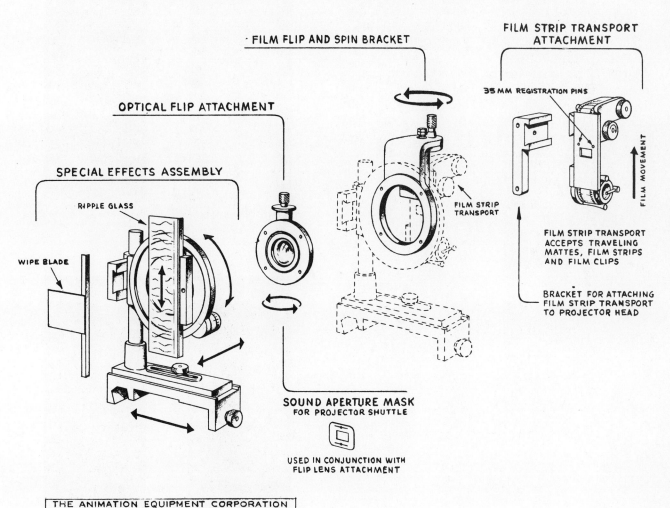

FILM FLIP AND SPIN BRACKET

FILM STRIP TRANSPORT
ATTACHMENT

OPTICAL FLIP ATTACHMENT

35 MM REGISTRATION PINS

SPECIAL EFFECTS ASSEMBLY

RIPPLE GLASS

WIPE BLADE

FILM MOVEMENT

FILM STRIP
TRANSPORT

FILM STRIP TRANSPORT
ACCEPTS TRAVELING
MATTES, FILM STRIPS
AND FILM CLIPS

BRACKET FOR ATTACHING
FILM STRIP TRANSPORT
TO PROJECTOR HEAD

SOUND APERTURE MASK
FOR PROJECTOR SHUTTLE

USED IN CONJUNCTION WITH
FLIP LENS ATTACHMENT

THE ANIMATION EQUIPMENT CORPORATION
38 HUDSON ST., NEW ROCHELLE, N. Y. NE 6-8138

THE DROPPED SHADOW

The television dial spinner and the more observant movie-goer is subconsciously aware of the fact that some projected titles are easier to read than others. This is not due to any optical phenomenon or illusion. It is merely the result of a frequently used motion picture process in which a white title is separated from the background by means of a matte. The dropped shadow effect is achieved by photographing the high contrast negative and high contrast positive titles on separate runs. During the optical process, the high contrast *negative* on the first run is photographed with the fine grain film that is used as the background for the title. The optical camera is in its normal center position in relation to the shooting field on this run.

With the shutter in its closed position, the previously exposed film in the optical camera is returned to the frame in which the title first appears. The high contrast *positive* title is then photographed for the same number of frames as the title on the high contrast negative. On this second run the optical camera is positioned slightly higher and to the left of the normal optical center.

The high contrast negative produces the dropped shadow effect and acts as the matte for the title on the high contrast positive film. The farther away from center the high contrast positive is positioned, the greater the dropped shadow effect. This dropped shadow effect is used quite frequently for motion picture titles as well as for the commercial production.

The fine grain film contains the abstract background over which the title was superimposed optically.

The white title, photographed over a black card on the animation stand, is shown as it appears on the high contrast positive print.

The same title as it appears on the high contrast negative after processing by the film laboratory.

The optically combined title without a dropped shadow.

Layouts indicate the size and position of the dropped shadow.

The first step in the optical process shows the combination of the background and the high contrast negative.

The superimposed high contrast positive title photographed in an off-center position.

The Matte

Anyone who has ever taken a photograph with any kind of camera knows that if the film in the camera is not advanced after the taking of a picture, a double exposure or double image will result when the next photograph is taken. In itself, the double exposure is an effect used quite often in motion picture production. It is necessary, however, in many instances to combine one length of film with another without getting a double exposure or double image. The accomplishment of such an effect becomes possible through the use of mattes.

The matte, as used in motion picture terminology, refers to either art work or film which is used to temporarily conceal an area of the motion picture frame.

The frequently used term "matting out" describes the function of the subject well. Practically all mattes, both art work and film, are opaque black. The word "opaque" is used here as an adjective opposed to the word "transparent."

A photographed black area will show up as an unexposed part of the frame of film. This basic principle makes possible the accomplishment of photographic effects where more than one piece of film is involved. Wipes are actually another form of matte and will be discussed later.

With these mattes it is possible to photograph a picture on an unexposed portion of the film while "matting out" that portion of the frame already exposed. More

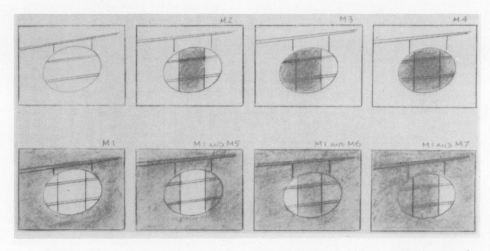

These are the guides used for making the mattes needed for the optical combination.

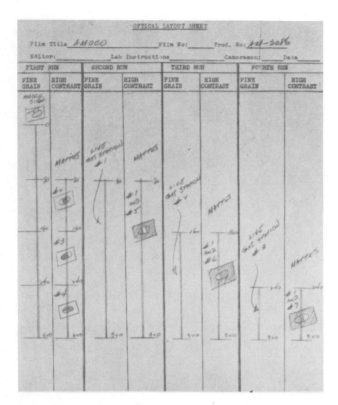

The layout sheet used for combining the mattes with the fine grain film in order to achieve the split-screen effect within the Amoco oval sign.

than one picture may finally appear on the same frame of film without double-exposure or double-image effect through this process.

For animation and other motion picture techniques, mattes are used frequently and in many ways. This chapter discusses some of the more important uses of the matte. The main function of the matte in animation is to make possible combining an animated sequence on one length of film with another scene, either live or animated, on another strip of film.

The novel montage effect in the one-minute commercial produced for the American Oil Company was made possible by a rather involved combination of mattes.

In order to achieve the unusual split-screen effect within the Amoco oval, several mattes were required. The first was needed for masking out the inside portion of the oval in the hanging Amoco sign. A second matte

The three frames in column 1 show the Amoco sign at the beginning of the split-screen sequence. Matte 1, used only in combination with other mattes needed to achieve the effect, appears under Column 1.

The first frame in each of the other columns shows the completed effect at various stages after the mattes have been combined with the fine grain film. Frame two, in columns 2, 3, and 4, shows how the mattes and live action film of the gas stations are photographed on the second, third, and fourth runs in the combining process. Frame three, in columns 2, 3, and 4, shows how the matte and fine grain film of the Amoco sign combine optically on the first run.

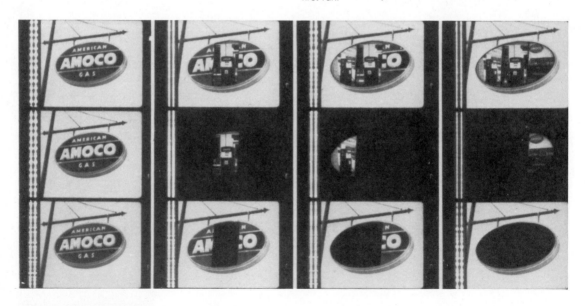

was needed for masking the entire area of the film frame around the oval. Additional mattes were needed for each of the three sections within the oval for the three live action shots of gasoline stations. Since each of the three live shots of the gas stations appeared in the separate sections of the oval at different times, it was necessary to combine and re-photograph several of the mattes on the animation stand before going into the optical process.

A tracing, from a projected frame of film containing the live action Amoco sign, was made for the positioning and subsequent production of the mattes. This tracing also served as the layout for this interesting film sequence. Each of the mattes was very carefully inked and opaqued in white and photographed over a black card on high contrast film.

In the first step of the optical process, the fine grain film containing the Amoco sign was exposed for the first 80 frames. Matte 2, the black mask for the center section of the three within the oval, was exposed with the fine grain film of the sign until frame 160. At that frame, matte 2 was replaced by matte 3, the combination of the center and left-hand sections of the oval.

Columns 1, 2, 3, and 4 show the split-screen effect as it appears in the composite print. Columns 5 and 6 show the transition to the scene that follows.

This matte and the fine grain film of the sign were both exposed until frame 240. At frame 240, matte 4, the black mask for the entire area within the oval, was exposed with the fine grain film to frame 320.

If the exposed film were removed from the optical camera after this run and processed, it would show the complete sign for the first 80 frames. On the next 80 frames, the film would show the sign with a black unexposed area in the center of the oval. The 80 frames between 160 and 240 would show the sign with the center and left-hand sections of the oval as the black area. In the final 80 frames of the split-screen effect, the entire area within the oval would be completely black.

In the next step of the optical process, the exposed film was run back to frame 80 with the shutter in the closed position. At frame 80, the shutter was reopened and the first of the live action gasoline stations, for the center section of the oval, was photographed with mattes 1 and 5. This film combination was exposed until the end of the split-screen effect at frame 320. After the film had been returned to frame 160 with the shutter closed, the second gasoline station was photographed with mattes 1 and 6. This film combination allowed only that portion of the live action scene in the left-hand section of the oval to be exposed. This combination was also held until frame 320. The shutter was again closed and the film was returned to frame

240. On this next run the third of the live action gasoline stations for the right-hand section of the oval was combined with mattes 1 and 7 and also exposed until frame 320.

The film after processing showed the three live action gasoline stations within the oval of the sign. None of the mattes was visible on this combined film.

The novel split-screen effect achieved through this optical process is an excellent example to show the versatility of the matte in motion picture production.

The matte, in the award winning Ford commercial, not only plays a featured part but takes a curtain call as well. Instead of doing its usual quiet and efficient job backstage, the matte, in this 60-second presentation, shares the spotlight with the film's subject matter.

In the commercial, the matte is used as an important part of the visual presentation rather than as the "behind-the-scenes" technical process for optical combinations. Instead of masking out or concealing an area of the motion picture frame, the matte, as used here, is very much in evidence.

The theme of the commercial is, "Ford is proportioned for you." The still photographs used in the film show a man in different positions against an abstract background. A lack of roominess in the average car is suggested by the different poses in the still photographs.

The different sizes and shapes of the matted areas not only add visual interest but help emphasize the poses in the stills. The mattes, drawn by the animator, move in synchronization with the music and dialogue on the sound track. For the positioning of the animated mattes, tracings of the still photographs are used as the layouts. After these mattes have been inked and painted with black opaque, they are photographed in sequence on the animation stand. The still photos serve as the backgrounds for the animated mattes.

The script outlines the 64 scenes used in the commercial.

These three layouts show the tracings made from the projected film clips. The positions for the mattes are indicated on the layouts.

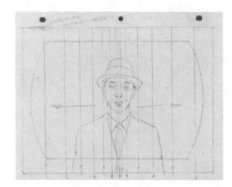

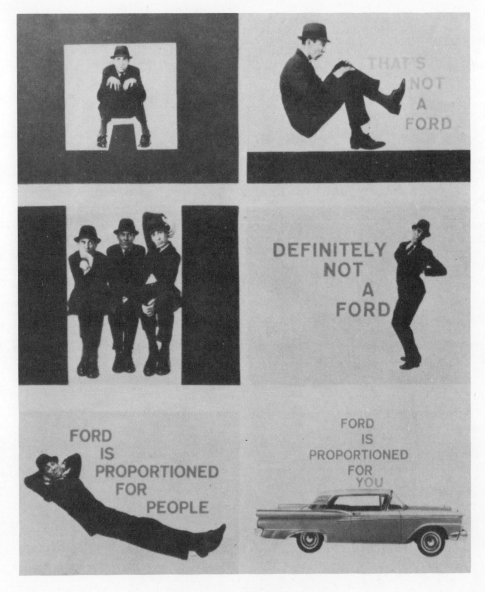

The rough (?) story board.

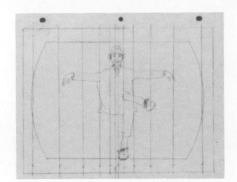

These film clips show the matte sharing the spotlight with the subject matter in the Ford commercial.

If the animated mattes were to be combined with live action instead of the still photographs, the animated mattes would have been inked and painted with white opaque. These white mattes would then be photographed over a black card on high contrast film.

The negative, after processing by the laboratory, would show the matted animation as a black area on the clear frame of film. For the optical combination, the high contrast negative would be combined with the live action film on one run.

The novel approach and rapid pace of the Ford commercial sustained interest for the entire 60 seconds. The always effective visual squeeze technique coupled with the clever use of the animating matte combined to help tell the film's story in an award winning style.

TRAVELING MATTES

Unlike the static matte, a traveling matte consists of a series of mattes on successive frames of film, corresponding with the continually changing matteing areas in the background film. In either case the matteing process makes possible the combination of animation with live-action scenes, the superimposition of titles, and the creation of a wide variety of unusual illusory effects without undesirable double exposures.

SELF-MATTEING PROCESSES

In this Dreyfus Fund commercial produced with the MPO Spectrumatte self-matteing process, the lion never left the studio. The Wall Street area, the background for the commercial, was photographed separately thereby avoiding possible panic among the bulls and the bears that normally inhabit the area. In the first optical camera run, the positive matte of the lion (5) was photographed with the background scene (8). With the shutter closed, the film was returned to the start position. In the optical camera run that followed, the film of the lion in front of the black studio background (2) was exposed with the negative matte (4) to produce the composite effect (10).

Some of the film elements shown here were used only as intermediate steps for the production of other needed matteing elements.

1. Eastman Color Negative
2. Pan Master/Fine Grain Print
3. High-contrast print made from the Color Negative.
4. High-contrast Negative
5. High-contrast Positive
6. Separation print from original Color Negative
7. High-contrast Negative from Separation print
8. Background—Fine Grain print
9. Composite Negative
10. Composite print

Mattes. This commercial for Command, a hair-grooming product, proves that it's a snap to have girls in the palm of your hand. The man and woman who starred in the commercial were each photographed at different times and on separate sets. The self-matteing filming process produced the film elements needed to achieve the composite effect.

Multimedia, or Videography

Multimedia, or videography, used in educational television, is a relatively permanent facility available for multiple-image presentations. The programmed material is either channeled to the participating schools via closed-circuit television or displayed on monitor screens by means of various projection devices. Commercial development of techniques that are capable of filling oversized screens with images from a number of sources continues at a brisk pace. Budgets for the production of multimedia presentations, in which the information is transmitted to the screen's beaded surface by as many as six projectors, are proportional to the complexity of the effort and the desired effect. The technique is quite popular with many of the nation's largest corporations and is used for in-plant sales meetings and conventions. Many professional educators have voiced strong opposition to the multimedia presentation, questioning the practicality of a technique that demands a great amount of viewer concentration and requires the absorption of information under abnormal conditions. To these critics the technique is analogous to a reading process in which the reader is asked to scan the contents of a number of pages from several books simultaneously. In a multimedia production the component picture information is usually a joint venture. Contracts for live-film sequences, for example, are assigned to studios with indoor sets, backlot facilities, and filming crews equipped to handle location work; slidefilm presentations, to studios specializing in that type of production; animation, to an animation studio.

Each of the separate efforts must be assembled, coordinated, previewed, edited, and synchronized with corresponding sound tracks—a Herculean task indeed. The use of optical processes, however, eliminates many of the problems associated with the synchronization of composite images. The combined picture information is exposed with matteing processes onto one strand of film that can be threaded into a single projector for normal viewing on conventional screens. Static artwork, slides, photographs, and documents are photographed in different areas of the film frame in accordance with the storyboard requirements. During each of the several runs needed to produce the composite effect the optical cameraman exposes each length of film with its corresponding matte. Live-action and animation sequences are also added optically.

Wipes

Most wipes, used for optical effects, are actually mattes in themselves. Originally photographed on the animation stand, wipes become an important part of the optical cameraman's library. Each catalogued wipe appears on a separate strip of film and has an identifying number so that the film editor and optical cameraman may quickly and easily select the wipe to be used in order to achieve a desired effect.

The most frequently used wipes are made in different film lengths ranging from 8 frames to 5 feet. The variety of wipe effects is limited only by the creative genius of the director.

The wipes shown on these pages are the ones used most frequently for making transitions from one scene to another.

Each wipe consists of both the positive and negative sides and is catalogued for quick and easy identification by the film editor and optical cameraman.

Although the average wipe is 16 frames, or one foot in length, some wipes are duplicated in varying lengths from 8 frames to 5 feet.

The wipe, as a visual transition from close-ups of "product shots" to subsequent scenes, is becoming an increasingly popular effect in commercial films.

An example of the "custom-made" wipe is included in the Dual Filter Tareyton commercial. In this one-minute spot, the transition from a close-up of a cigarette to a live action scene is achieved with this specially made wipe effect. In order to make the mattes needed for this wipe, a frame of film containing the close-up of the cigarette is projected onto the compound table.

The tracing of the cigarette, made from the projected frame of film, is used as the layout for the production of the mattes needed for the wipe effect.

These mattes, inked and opaqued in white, are photographed over a black card on the animation stand. The print and negative of the high contrast film, after processing by the film laboratory, are both used during the optical process.

In the first step of the optical combination the fine grain film containing the close-up of the cigarette is photographed with the high contrast negative. This negative shows the cigarette in black over the clear area of the frame. This black area grows progressively larger on each successive frame of film until the entire frame is completely black concealing the fine grain film of the cigarette.

The film in the optical camera, in the next step of the process, is run back to the first frame of the wipe effect with the shutter in its closed position.

At this frame, the fine grain film of the live action scene is combined with the high contrast *positive*. On the high contrast positive, the cigarette, in the clear area of the black frame of film, becomes progressively larger until the entire frame is completely clear revealing the live action scene in its entirety.

This optical run completes the transition from the close-up of the cigarette to the live action scene. The use of these wipe effects increases visual interest and gives added emphasis to the "product shot," the mainstay of the commercial film.

The positive and negative mattes used for achieving the wipe effect.

The wipe effect shown in the last column is achieved by combining the negative and positive strips of film in columns on previous pages with the animation or live action film. First two columns here show the partially completed wipe. Last column shows the completed wipe effect after the negative and positive sides of the stock wipe have been combined with the fine grain film.

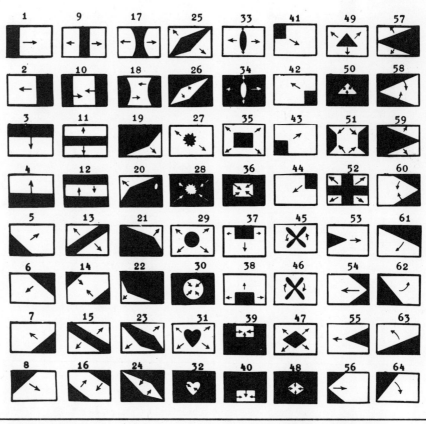

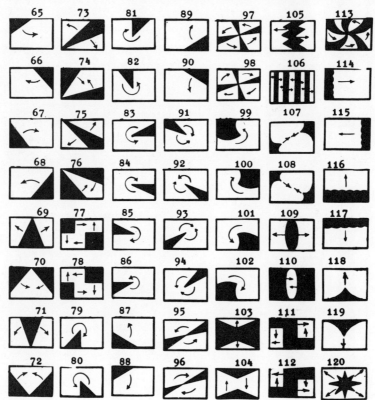

Standard wipe chart.

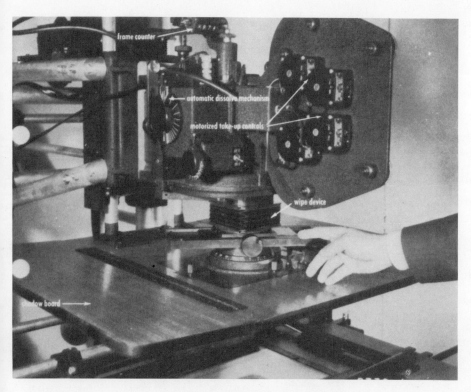

Shown in this photograph is a device used for making the more simple wipes. It is attached to the camera lens mount and fits over the opening in the shadow board.

The motorized take-up controls for the film magazine are above and to the right of the wipe device. The automatic dissolve mechanism is on the left side of the camera. The frame counter can be seen directly over the dissolve mechanism.

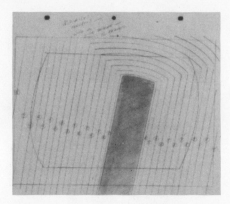

The layout used for achieving the wipe in the Tareyton commercial.

The wipe effect, from a close-up of the cigarette in the stop-motion film to the live action scene that follows, is shown in this film sequence.

Effects

SPLIT—SCREEN SHOT

As the name implies, the split-screen shot is an optical effect in which the screen is divided into a number of sections and related picture information is exposed in each segment. Similar in many ways to the multimedia or videography techniques, each one of the several areas in the film frame requires its own matte. The processed film containing the subject matter that is to be inserted in any one of the specific areas must be repositioned optically and exposed within the previously matted areas during a separate optical camera run. This multiple exposure effect usually requires pre-opticals and the combination of matteing elements.

Split-screen effect. For this "hidden" split-screen shot, a soft-edge vertical wipe hid the line of demarcation usually visible in split-screen shots. The effect, produced for an Eastman Kodak advertisement, was achieved by overlapping the leading edges of the high-contrast vertical wipe pattern during each of the optical camera runs needed to achieve the effect.

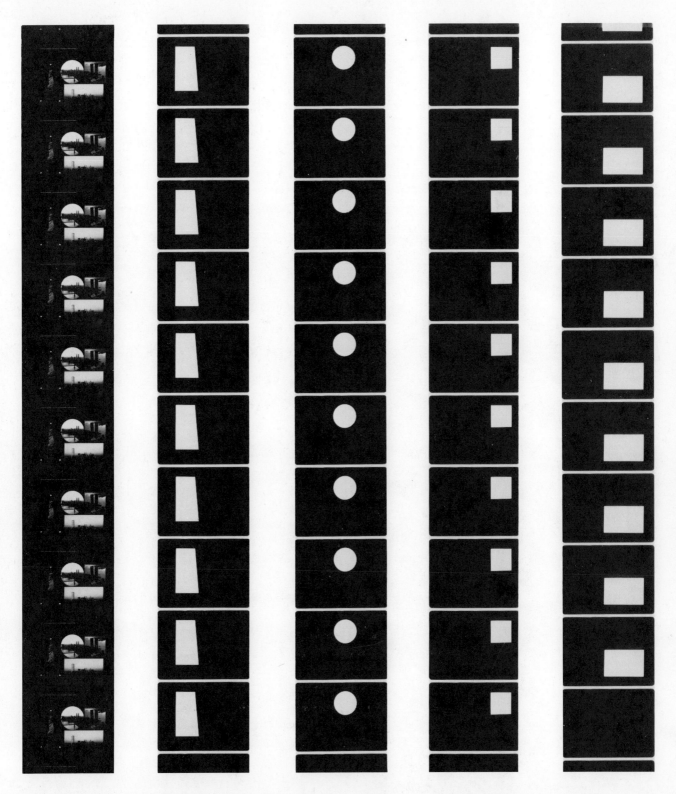

The split-screen effect and the mattes needed to achieve the multimedia effect.

THE MULTIPLE EXPOSURE EFFECT

These film clips from a television commercial produced for the Brillo Manufacturing Company shows the multiple exposure effect at its best. A variation of the split-screen effect, the multiple images are produced by means of preopticals and mattes. The composite effect is achieved by repositioning the processed preoptical film elements for each one of the several optical camera runs.

SOLARIZATION

This is a polarity-reversal effect produced by exposing an image to intense light for long periods of time. Imaginative directors and graphic artists use variations of the technique to produce unusual illusory effects. In practice solarization effects are achieved with mattes derived from the live-action color film. In the

The solarization effect and the film elements needed to achieve the effect.

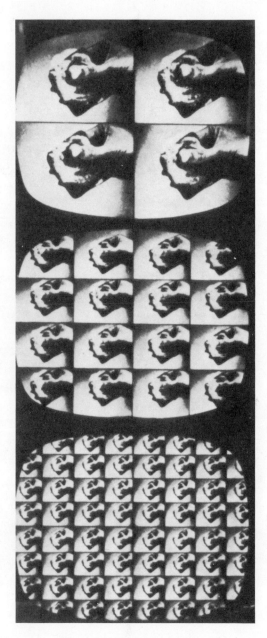

The multiple exposure effect.

first step of the process the live-action footage is duplicated on a pan master (see Editing). Its gradations from black through intermediate shades of gray to white are used to produce the high-contrast mattes needed to achieve the effect. During the optical combination the negative and print films are projected onto color film through selected filters to produce psychedelic effects.

STROBE

Strobe is an illusion that is created because of the relationship, during the filming process, between the speed of a moving object and the interval between exposures. For most viewers, wheels that seem to be turning backward while the vehicle itself is obviously moving forward provides an excellent and familiar example of the illusion. The undesirable illusion is usually predict-

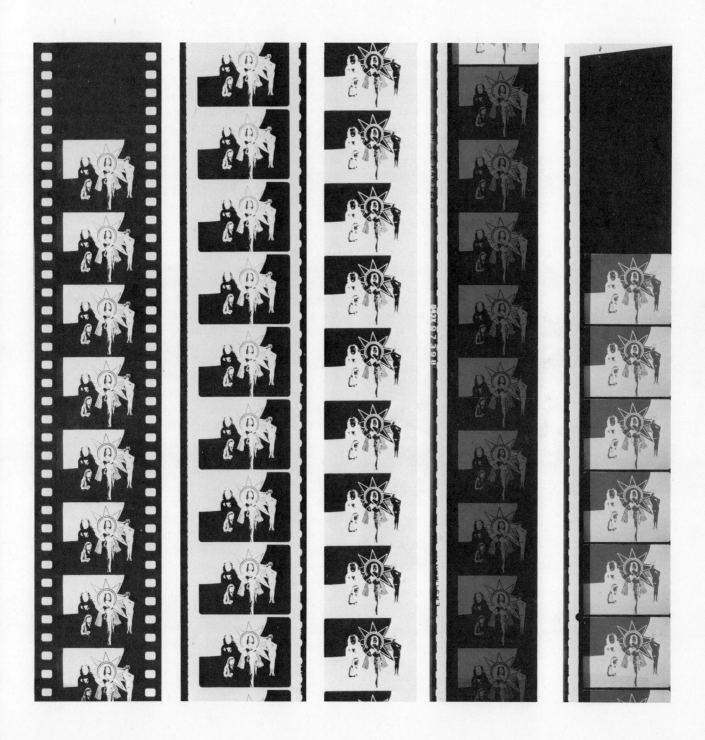

able and can, in most cases, be eliminated by controlling the speed of the moving vehicle or by changing the camera angle and the resultant perspective.

Deliberate strobe, by comparison, is regarded as an eye-arresting illusory effect. Produced by multiple exposure, the overlapping images within the film frame are produced by duplicating a sequence of action as many times as is desirable over the same length of film. During the many optical camera runs, the start frame of the action is advanced by several frames for each run and reexposed to produce the multiple-exposure effect.

OUT-OF-FOCUS EFFECT

An out-of-focus effect can be used either as a transition or to create a specific mood. As a transition, the outgoing scene is simply thrown out of focus progressively in successive frames of film until the picture information is blurred beyond recognition. The camera shutter remains completely open at all times during the single run needed to produce the effect. If, for example, 80 frames are allotted for the total effect, the outgoing scene is gradually thrown out of focus for the first 40 frames, and the incoming scene is then exposed, beginning with a completely blurred frame, for the other 40 frames, ending with completely sharp focus. This relatively inexpensive optical can be used to introduce dream sequences, create horror effects, or form abstract backgrounds for superimpositions.

Strobe. This multiple-exposure effect is similar in some ways to the illusion created by a deliberate strobe. To achieve the effect, the original scene was duplicated optically over the same length of film, the action being advanced by several frames for each camera run.

DIFFUSION AND DISTORTION EFFECTS

Optical effects in which the picture information is deliberately distorted or diffused are used mainly for transitional purposes or to establish a mood. The procedures for producing these effects are quite similar to those used for producing out-of-focus effects. The main difference between the two lies in the special materials that are needed to achieve the different effects. Special materials for diffusion include almost any substance that can be positioned in front of a lens and that allows some light to pass through unobstructed while scattering the remaining light in many directions. The diffusion, usually unpredictable, produces areas of softness and sharpness within the same film frame. The effect is used to create an air of mystery, an eerie atmosphere, or a feeling of vagueness. The materials used to achieve the effects range from commercially available glass disks with patterned surfaces to loosely woven fabrics and small pieces of metal window screening. Lenses that either elongate or flatten images in any direction are used to produce distortion effects. In most cases the special materials are supported by frames positioned in front of the camera lens. The degree of diffusion or distortion can be controlled to some degree by exposing the film being duplicated with stop-motion processes. Incremental changes in the position of the materials in front of the lens are made for each exposure. As in the out-of-focus effect, the images in the last few frames of the outgoing scene and the first few frames of the incoming scene are usually so distorted or diffused that the two scenes can be spliced as in a direct cut.

REVERSING ACTION

This is a pioneering motion-picture technique, originally introduced to elicit chuckles from the most sophisticated audiences and now used to produce a wide variety of effects for almost as many purposes. In practically all cases, the effect is produced with direct, in-camera photographic processes or with the optical printer. To photograph live action, the film is first run through the camera with the shutter closed for the required length of time; then, with the camera motor reversed and the shutter reopened, the scene is photographed normally. When the film is processed, the last frame exposed is at the beginning of the roll, and the action is reversed when the film is projected. With the optical printer the process is even simpler. The normally photographed and processed scene is merely rewound, threaded on the projection side of the optical printer, and duplicated on the raw stock in the optical camera. The film is projected normally to reverse the action.

The Computerized Optical Printer

Like the more conventional models, the computer-controlled printer accepts both 16mm. and 35mm. transport mechanisms. A provision for interchanging shuttles and sprocket assemblies makes it possible to handle any combination of raw stock and previously processed film—16mm. camera stock with 16mm. elements on the projector side of the printer, 16mm. camera stock with 35mm. elements in the projector head, 35mm. raw stock with 16mm. projector elements, and 35mm. raw stock with 35mm. elements in the projector. An added advantage not shared by conventional printers is the ability to make major changes during the actual filming by simply updating the program. The basic command language for the computer-controlled optical printer is similar in many respects to that for the computerized animation stand. The principle differences between the two computer languages center around the controls that are used mainly to achieve optical effects. Basically, the computer-controlled optical printer is programmed to respond to industry terminology.

Synchronization between camera and projector is absolute. Each unit is designed to function independently in either the forward or the reverse mode, in sync or out of sync. There is no mechanical linkage between camera and projector. Absolute synchronization between both units is maintained by the computer itself, eliminating any chance of flicker. This type of electronic drive makes it possible to program any skip-frame or multiframe effect, with any mathematical combination, quickly and accurately. The printer also has a manual override for simpler effects. And because the computer can drive both the camera and the projector at much faster speeds than are obtained with the larger motors and clutches in conventional printers, electronic

```
ZEROQU,103,32,29,29
QU,201,32,29,29
QU,402,32,29,29
QU,613,31,28,28
CU,0,0,0
TIP
SYP
AD,0,686,0
PUN
FA,0,16,IN
SH,103
PU
DI,103,16,0U
SH,119
PU
AD,103,686,0
PU
FL,DI
SH,201
PU
AD,201,1283,0
PU
SH,402
PU
AD,402,2734,0
PU
SI,920,460,480,3,BO
EA,20,460,480,3,BO
SH,575
PU
SI,1000,575,615,3,IN
WE,20,575,615,3,IN
DI,613,20,0U
SH,613
PU
SK,1,1,633
PU
AD,613,2389,0
PU
FL,DI
SH,640
PU
DI,640,16,0U
SH,656
PU
AD,640,2416,110
PU
UNTA
FL,DI
SH,704
PU
FA,704,16,0U
SH,720
AD,640,3200,0
PU
CU,640,0,0
AD,640,110,0
PU
UNTP
FA,640,16,IN
SH,704
PU
FA,704,16,0U
SH,720
EN
```

Programmed instructions.

visual-display counters are incorporated instead of the mechanical type formerly used. As a result of these innovations the printer is able to operate on a complete program, locate scenes in the various projectors, bring the proper frame into exposure position in the camera, and carry out all of the preprogrammed instructions.

In practical terms the computer-controlled optical printer means that the producer or editor does not have to compromise on a desired effect because of the complexity of the operation involved. Capable of performing 198,000 calculations per second with absolute precision, the computer-controlled printer creates incremental zoom and pan moves of any distance in any number of frames, and each move is precisely repeatable. The computer calculates image size by percentage, not by field size. A zoom started with the camera

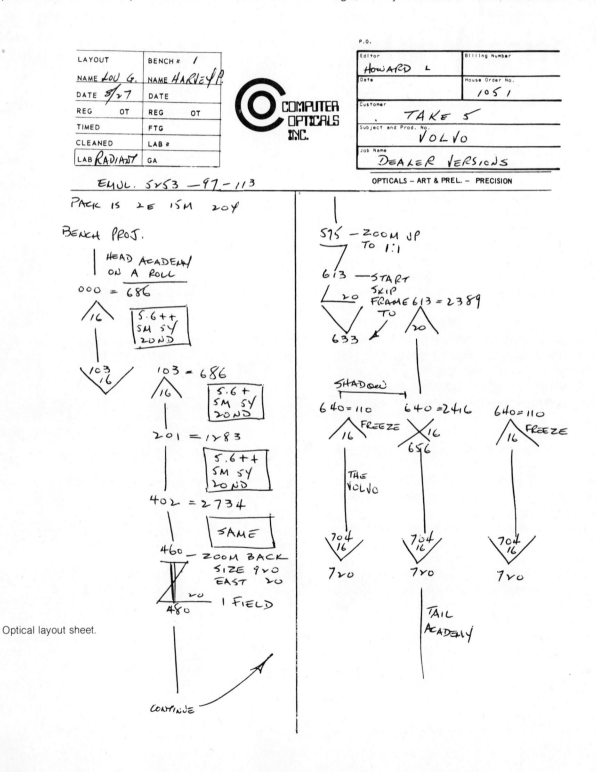

Optical layout sheet.

at its extreme position can be continued with the aerial projector to the final position with no apparent changes in speed at any point of the effect. This capability makes possible a much greater enlargement or reduction in the size of the image. And since there is no mechanical linkage between film and the lens, focus is absolute at every incremental point. Similarly, computer light-valve control assures even density from one end of the effect to the other.

For the producer of a multimedia presentation (videography), the printer allows the combination of picture information and the creation of split-screen or montage effects on a single strand 35mm. negative. The fade and dissolve mechanism can produce transitional effects of any length from four frames to infinity. Shutter opening and closing is programmed to follow the shoulder-and-toe curve characteristics of the film in use.

The computer-controlled printer is also capable of reversing a previously programmed movement. Instructing the computer to flip dissolve, for example, reverses the direction to produce a dissolve from out to in rather than from in to out—the exact opposite of the previous command. The same command can be used to reverse any effect previously typed into the computer.

Other transitional effects such as wipes or scene pushes can also be accomplished in any length quickly and precisely with no riding between scenes. 'Mattes are no longer necessary to achieve an absolute butt (a nonfluctuating line) between the incoming and outgoing scenes. Starting at any specific point, the computer repeats each of the moves in the effect with absolute precision as many times as is required. This capability assures matched moves on insert shots and background pans. A motorized lens compound driven by the computer maintains camera and aerial-projector focus at all points of a zoom movement from reduction through blow-up. In order to utilize the most efficient f-stop of any selected lens, including anamorphic lenses for wide-screen formats, a computer-controlled light valve, which maintains a constant level of light regardless of camera or aerial-image position, is incorporated in the design of the printer. A color-additive light source makes color corrections on a scene-to-scene basis, eliminating the need for corrective filters—a big plus for the computer-controlled optical printer.

In Conclusion

The reader, at this point, should be able to answer the question—"What makes them move?"

The small army of artists and technicians who created and then guided Mr. Wimple, the hero of the GE commercial discussed in Part I of the book, through each of the many "moves" and production processes, has seen the composite print and left the screening room to return to their drawing boards, animation stands, moviolas, and optical printers. With sleeves rolled up and pencils resharpened, they turn to the next script and storyboard, and analyze its specific requirements.

To these talented and dedicated individuals who have helped make my many years in the industry a completely beautiful experience, I can only say— "THANKS!"

Glossary of Terms

A & B printing   A method of combining picture information from two separate rolls of 16mm. film. Arranged in checkerboard fashion, all of the odd-numbered scenes are cut together to form the A roll, and the even-numbered scenes are similarly spliced into another B roll. Each scene is duplicated sequentially during laboratory processing. Transitional effects such as cross-dissolves and fades are added during the printing process along with superimpositions to produce the composite print.

A & B rolls   The rolls into which the scenes are separated in editing 16mm. film material. The odd-numbered scenes are spliced together into the A roll, and the even-numbered scenes into the B roll. Lengths of opaque black leader are spliced between each scene. The length of leader between scenes 1 and 3 on the A roll, for example, is equal to the length of scene 2 on the B roll; similarly, the length of leader between scenes 2 and 4 on the B roll is equal to the number of frames in scene 3 on the A roll. During the laboratory printing process the scenes from each roll are printed sequentially to produce the composite print. Effects and superimpositions, such as titles and other graphic material, are spliced into a C roll and added to the specified frames.

academy leader   A 12-foot length of film that has numbers and is spliced to the beginning and ending of each completed production.

achromatic lens   A lens system used to duplicate previously processed lengths of film. Filtering the printing light through the lens eliminates chromatic aberration and the resultant color fringing.

action   The series of events and movements that makes up an animated film.

advance, sound track to picture   The number of frames between any specified point in the sound track and the corresponding picture. In a composite 35mm. motion-picture print, the sound track precedes the corresponding picture by 20 frames; in a 16mm. print, by 26 frames. The position of the gate in the motion-picture projector, through which the picture passes while the sound-track area is scanned by the projector's exciter lamp, places the picture 20 frames ahead of the corresponding sound. Advancing the sound track in relation to the picture places each element in its proper projection position simultaneously.

aerial-image head   An accessory on the projection side of the optical printer that doubles its effectiveness. In addition to the running footage that passes through the projection head, other lengths of film threaded in the aerial head can be exposed simultaneously to create a wide variety of unusual illusory effects.

aerial-image photography   A unit used to project previously processed lengths of film onto the ground glass positioned between the registration bars on the compound table. Titles and other graphics, inked and opaqued on transparent cels, are placed on the registration pegs and combined with the projected film via stop-motion processes. The overhead-lighting units illuminate the graphics during the filming process. The film in the aerial-image unit is projected on the ground glass that is positioned over the underlighting unit. Compare aerial-image head.

afterimage   See tail.

Amici prism   A 90-degree angle prism used in conjunction with the conventional lenses on the animation stand for insert shots and tabletop photography.

298

anamorphic print   A print in which the aspect ratio is greater than the 1.33:1 standard. Squeezed or compressed by means of an anamorphic lens system on standard width film during the filming or optical-printing process, the picture information is restored to its normal proportions during projection by complementary deanamorphic lenses.

aniforms   A technique developed by Aniforms in which two-dimensional cutouts are substituted for the mountainous pile of drawings used in conventional animation. Developed by the famous puppeteer, Morey Bunin, the aniforms, or representations of the characters to be animated, are cut out of a sheet of flexible black plastic material, positioned in front of a black background, and outlined with white paint. Polarity is reversed in the television camera during the filming process. The resultant white image with a black outline provides a unique, line-drawing effect.

animascope   A system patented by Westworld Artist Productions for producing animated cartoons with live-action filming techniques. The performers are fitted with foam-rubber masks to which a flat make-up is applied, and wear specially designed costumes prepared by the art department. The actual filming process takes place on a small stage, and the performers act in front of a special black-velour backdrop.

animated zoom   A zoom effect achieved with artwork rather than with camera movement. The graphics for the effect are prepared by duplicating a title, for example, in a number of sizes, and positioning each title on a separate cel. The graphics can be moved to any size or position within the film frame.

animation   A technique in which the illusion of movement is created by photographing a series of individual drawings on successive frames of film with stop-motion processes. The illusion is produced by projecting the processed film at the standard sound-speed rate of 24 frames per second.

animation board   A standard drawing-board with minor adaptations such as registration pegs and provision for underlighting. The underlighting unit enables the animator to see the lines on a number of drawings simultaneously. Movable peg bars allow the animator to plan actions in relation to moving elements in the scene.

animation camera   A motion-picture camera mounted on columns and suspended over a compound table. The camera, driven by a stop-motion motor, films individual drawings or cels successively on a frame-by-frame basis. The columns not only support the camera and the motor, but also enable the camera to move vertically in relation to the artwork positioned on the registration pegs of the compound table. The compound table, composed of a ground-glass insert over an underlighting unit for filming transparencies, can be moved in any direction. The vertical camera movements and the horizontal compound-table movements make possible a wide variety of zoom and pan effects. Previously processed film can be projected through the camera shuttle onto the compound table, permitting graphic material to be matched to the film for mattes or rotoscope work. The animation stand includes the complex of camera, compound table, and control panel. See also matte and rotoscope.

animation, computerized   The generation of motion sequences by means of a computer, or the operation of an animation stand by control tapes produced by a computer. In a computerized system, the animator generally makes the key drawings, and the computer interpolates the intermediate drawings needed to complete the action. In a computer-controlled animation-recording system, photographic instructions are initiated by a teletype tied to a computer. The punched-paper control tape produced by the programming process directs the animation stand through the entire sequence of movements.

animation, limited   An animation technique designed to produce maximum movement with a minimum amount of drawing.

animation, multiplane effects   A process for producing dimensional effects with cel animation. The camera is mounted on a lathe bed, and the artwork is produced in the conventional manner. The dimensional backgrounds, however, are constructed from a variety of materials and mounted on a movable table. The cels for each exposure are locked in a glass frame positioned in front of the background. The distance between the animation cels and the several background planes creates dimensional effects with continually changing perspectives.

animation stand   See animation camera.

animator   The artist or cartoonist responsible for creating the illusion of motion with the drawings produced under his direction. The animator himself does only the key drawings for a motion sequence; the intermediate drawings needed to complete the action are done by the animator's assistant. See also extreme and in-between.

answer print See optical print.

anticipation A preliminary action that precedes and emphasizes the main action in an animated cartoon.

approach (also dolly, truck, or zoom).   The movement of a camera from a long shot of a scene to a close-up of the same scene or vice versa.

background A realistic or abstract scene rendered with watercolors by the background artist. During the filming process the inked and opaqued cels carrying the animation are registered to pegs on the compound table, and positioned over the background which is registered to a separate set of pegs.

background, sound Music and/or sound effects synchronized with the picture information. The background music sets the mood for the corresponding picture. The sound effects complement the visual information and accent actions needing sound support.

back lighting A light unit positioned under the compound table and used to film transparencies, drawings for pencil tests, and mattes for special effects. The light is focused on a rectangular ground glass in the center of the compound table between the top and bottom traveling-peg bars.

bar sheet (also lead sheet). A visual synopsis of the animation sequence prepared by the animator from the film editor's sound-track analysis. It indicates the number of frames allotted for a specific action, the frames in which dialogue occurs, and the position of musical beats and special effects.

beat The musical tempo used for timing or synchronizing sound.

bipack A process utilizing four-compartmented film magazines to combine artwork positioned on the compound table and lengths of previously processed film. With this simple optical printer the processed film is loaded into one of the magazine's two feed compartments, and raw stock is loaded in the other. Both lengths of film pass through the camera shuttle simultaneously on their respective routes to each of the two take-up compartments. The artwork is exposed along with the previously processed film to produce composite effects.

bipack magazine A four-compartmented film magazine with two take-up and two feed compartments. See bipack.

bloop A small, triangular-shaped piece of tape or plastic that is placed over the sound track area at splice points. The mask covers the objectionable sound that occurs during projection whenever a splice is encountered.

blowup The duplication of picture information on 16mm. film to the 35mm. width. In most cases the results are unsatisfactory because the grain in the 16mm. film is magnified proportionately.

blue backing A background used to produce matteing effects. It is exposed to color-blind or non-sensitive film. Subject matter photographed in front of this background produces self-mattes for subsequent optical combination.

bottom pegs The lowest set of pegs on an animation board or camera compound table used for registering drawings, cels, or backgrounds.

breakdown An indication that intermediate drawings are needed to complete the action. The instruction appears on the animator's key drawings along with spacing guides showing how the action should be timed or divided.

bumper footage A specified number of frames exposed at the beginning and end of each scene photographed on the animation stand. The extra footage provides added flexibility for the editor during the post-production stage.

burn-in 1. The process of superimposing titles over previously exposed film. The subject matter receives additional exposure during the burn-in run on the animation stand. 2. The combination on the optical printer of titles or other graphic material with processed film.

butt splicer A type of splicer designed to eliminate the possibility of out-of-focus frames at a splice point or of frame loss, which would throw a double-system sound track out of sync.

calibrations 1. A marking on the background indicating its position in each frame of the panning action. This information appears on the exposure sheets prepared by the animator and is used as a guide by the cameraman during the filming process. 2. The incremental moves plotted by the cameraman for zoom and pan effects.

camera projection See rotoscope.

cel A transparent sheet of celluloid, about 0.005″ thick and similar in size to the drawing paper used by the animator, used for tracing the cartoon figures before they are opaqued. Cels are punched to fit over the registration pegs on the drawing board and on the compound table.

cel level The position of each cel in the composite picture in relation to the background. To expedite the animation and photographic processes, a cartoon character is often inked and opaqued on a number of cels. If the body, for example, is not animating, it is traced separately on a hold cel, which is designated as bottom level and positioned closest to the background. The head, in turn, would be inked and opaqued on another cel and placed on the registration pegs over the hold cel. The animating eyes and mouth would be inked and opaqued as a top-level cel. With the separation of component parts into top, middle, and bottom cel levels, the head and body do not have to be retraced for each frame, and the animation cameraman has to change only the top-level cel for each frame of the animated action.

checker The person responsible for checking the inked and opaqued cels for numerical continuity and color consistency. In a dry run that precedes the photographic process, the checker places each of the cels over the background and matches the cartoon characters to props if necessary.

checkerboard editing The preparation of A and B rolls for processing. See A & B printing and A & B rolls.

china girl A relatively short length of film containing a medium close-up of a model whose skin tones, clothes, and background include all of the primary and complementary colors. Also included within each of the film frames are color patches that are used as a guide by the timer for making optical or laboratory color corrections.

cinex A series of filters positioned within windows cut into a circular disk. The device, mounted in front of the optical-camera lens, is used to expose representative frames in a scene before the actual production of the composite. The frames of processed film are evaluated by the film editor and the optical timer, who select the appropriate correction filters for the optical-printing process.

click track A cue track used by the film editor in the absence of the sound track that will subsequently be synchronized with the corresponding picture. It is recorded with little regard for quality, and used to establish a beat or to provide the timing for an action sequence.

close-up A scene or action photographed from such a short distance that only a small part of the subject fills the frame of film. A close-up of an actor might show his head only or, in an extreme close-up, perhaps only his eyes or mouth.

collage A montage effect. The subject matter displayed throughout the film frame may consist of a wide variety of graphic elements, including photographs, drawings, or abstract materials. Compare montage.

colorer See opaquer.

color model, or model drawing One of several drawings interspersed throughout a scene indicating the colors that are to be applied during the opaquing process. Since many people work on the drawings for a given scene at the same time, the color models assure color consistency.

complete drawing An animator's notation indicating that a drawing should be completed by the inbetweener. If only part of the cartoon character is in motion, for example, the animator would draw the moving part only and add the letters "c.d."

composite master positive A fine-grain composite print, either black-and-white or color, that is used for making composite dupe negatives.

composite print A length of film combining picture and sound elements.

composite reversal original An original positive print, produced by reversal processing, that contains both picture and sound track.

compound table See animation camera.

contact printing The production of a negative or positive (depending upon the polarity of the film) by running the original film in direct contact with raw stock past the printing light.

continuing zoom A zoom effect in which the subject matter continually increases in size in successive frames of film until it not only fills the frame but continues beyond the field covered by the camera lens.

cording An identification technique in which short lengths of string or tape are attached to the perforations at the beginning and end of one of the scenes wound on a reel, so that selected lengths of film can be located and made into fine-grains or dupes.

cover shot, or insurance take   The reshooting of a scene to change the performance, camera angle, or set lighting.

crawl title   The presentation of credits or other information with a panning effect. The lines of copy appear at the bottom of the film frame, pan up through the frame, and disappear beyond the upper limits of the film frame.

cross-dissolve (*abbr*. x-dissolve).   One fade-in and one fade-out, probably the most frequently used between scenes as a transitional effect. It is intended to suggest changes in both time and location. The effect is produced by fading out one scene and fading in the following scene over the same length of film. Because of the blending or overlapping of picture information, the effect is also referred to as a lap dissolve. The effect is produced by closing the shutter incrementally during the exposure of the outgoing scene for the designated length of the effect. With the shutter still in its closed position, the exposed film with the faded-out scene is rewound to the opening frame. The effect is completed by simply fading in the incoming scene over the same length of film. Cross-dissolves generally provide not only the desired visual continuity, but also are quite pleasing to the eye.

cross-fade   A transitional effect consisting of two separate cross-dissolves. In the first, the outgoing scene is faded to a color or a shade of gray rather than to black. The incoming scene is cross-dissolved from the selected color to complete the effect.

cue sheet   The frame count, provided by the film editor, which serves as a guide for the optical combination of picture elements.

cut   The abrupt end of a scene or action. The following scene is spliced at the cut point.

cutaway   A scene inserted into a sequence in order to add suspense to the flow of action. It might include, in live-action sequences, for example, a close-up of the performer's eyes or hands, or the reaction of another performer in the scene.

cutback   The scene that follows an insert shot. It represents a continuation of the story line and a return to script continuity.

cutoff area   The outer limits of the film frame that are not visible on television receivers. Titles and other graphic material prepared for television must be confined to the safety field, an area comfortably within TV transmission limits.

cutout   A drawing that is inked and opaqued on thin illustration board, cut out along the outlines, and pasted in place over the background of the scene. Cutouts are used to reduce the number of cel levels.

cycle   A series of drawings arranged to form a complete action. A walk cycle, for example, includes the drawings needed to complete one full step and lead in to the start of the second step. The first and last positions of a cycle are referred to as hookups.

dailies, or rushes   The processed results of film exposed during the previous day's photographic efforts.

dialogue   The speech, conversation, or off-stage commentary recorded on a film's sound track.

diffusion and distortion effects   Optical effects in which the picture information is deliberately distorted or diffused. Used as a transitional effect or to establish a mood, the procedures for producing these effects are quite similar to those used for producing out-of-focus effects. The main difference between the two lies in the special materials that are needed to achieve the different effects. Special materials for diffusion include almost any substance that can be positioned in front of a lens and that allows some light to pass through unobstructed while scattering the remaining light in many directions. The diffusion, usually unpredictable, produces areas of softness and sharpness within the same film frame. The effect is used to create an air of mystery, an eerie atmosphere, or a feeling of vagueness. The materials used to achieve the effects range from commercially available glass disks with patterned surfaces, to loosely woven fabrics and small pieces of metal window screening. Lenses that either elongate or flatten images in any direction are used to produce distortion effects. In most cases, the special materials are supported by frames positioned in front of the camera lens. The degree of diffusion or distortion can be controlled to some degree by exposing the film being duplicated with stop-motion processes. Incremental changes in the position of the materials in front of the lens are made for each. exposure. As in the out-of-focus effect, the images, in the last few frames of the outgoing scene and the first few frames of the incoming scene are usually so distorted or diffused that the two scenes can be spliced as in a direct cut.

documentary A film depicting historical, social, or political events, conditions, or people in real-life footage and in an objective, factual manner.

dolly A flat, 4-wheeled platform on which the camera is positioned for live-action photography. The term is also used to describe the movement of a camera from a long shot of a scene to a close-up of the same scene, or vice versa.

double exposure An effect produced by reexposing the same frame of film, resulting in a ghost image.

double printing The combination of picture information from two lengths of negative film to produce a composite print.

dropped shadow An optical-printing process designed to improve the legibility of titles. To produce the effect, the black title, which is on a length of high-contrast film, is exposed with the background film to produce the shadow. The white title, which is on another length of high-contrast film, is offset during the burn-in run to complete the effect. The offset title is usually positioned above and to the left of the black title.

dubbing The addition of sound elements, music and/or sound effects, for example, to the sound track that contains the dialogue or narration.

duping The reproduction of picture information from one length of film on a second length.

duplicate color negative See internegative.

edge numbers Identifying numbers imprinted at 1-foot intervals along the edges of the film. They are duplicated in the print material and used by the optical layout man in the production of the optical print, and by the film editor in matching the negative to the work print.

Edicomp An electronic-editing technique in which editing data is used to transfer the original sound and videotape to an edited second-generation copy.

Editec An electronic system in which the edited work print is used as a guide for rerecording the composite videotape.

editing The sorting, assembly, splicing, synchronizing, and general preparation of the various film elements into a smooth flow of picture and sound information.

editor The person responsible for assembling individual scenes, arranging them in the order indicated in the script, and synchronizing the sound elements (dialogue, music, and effects) to the corresponding picture. In addition to supervising the preparation of the work print, the editor is also responsible for the optical, special, and transitional effects produced by optical processes.

editorial synchronism The synchronization of sound and picture elements during the editorial process. The separate sound track is aligned at all points with the corresponding picture while the work print is assembled. Compare projection synchronism.

effect (*abbr*. effx) A generic term for illusory effects of any kind. The general term describes illusory images such as fades, cross-dissolves, wipes, split-screen shots, montages, matte shots, and multiple-image shots.

expose The listing of the animation drawings in their proper sequence on the exposure sheets.

exposure (*abbr*. x) The production of a latent image on film; in animation, the photographic process in which the cels are placed over the background and photographed on the animation stand via stop-motion equipment.

exposure sheet (*abbr*. x-sheet) A sheet, prepared by the animator and used by the cameraman during filming, that lists each cell, its position over the background (cel level), and the number of exposures it receives. It also shows the frames in which zooms and/or pans take place, and position of the background in every frame, as well as the location of fades and cross-dissolves. It follows the drawings and cels through every stage of development before reaching the animation camera.

extreme A key drawing, made by an animator, that illustrates the main action and contains instructions for its continuation. Spacing guides indicating timings and other notations guide the inbetweener in producing the secondary drawings needed to complete the action.

fade An effect used at the beginning or end of a sequence. A fade-in, used to introduce a sequence, is produced by gradually opening the camera shutter so that each successive frame of film receives progressively greater amounts of exposure, until the density and color values in the scene are identical to those in the original subject matter. A fade-out is produced by gradually closing the shutter, until the last frame of the effect is completely black.

feed reel The plastic or metal reel on which the original film or tape is wound.

field guide A numbered guide used by the animation cameraman for composing and aligning artwork, and for plotting zoom and pan movements. The markings are arranged to indicate the areas covered by the camera lens in use.

field size The area covered by the camera lens: an 11 field (11 F), for example, indicates a shooting area that is exactly 11 inches wide.

film A thin layer of light-sensitive material over a supporting cellulose base. Rolls of film vary in width from 70mm. with 10 perforations on each side of the film frame, to 8mm. with a single sprocket hole per frame. The perforations match the sprocketed devices in camera, projector, optical-printer, editing and laboratory-transport mechanisms, providing precise registration at every stage of production. Film expands when warm, contracts when cold, swells when wet, and shrinks when dry. Coating the film base with a gray or jet-black dye will prevent undesirable halation, and has no effect on print quality: it merely prevents light from passing through the layer of emulsion and reflecting back from the cellulose base. Films are available in roll form or daylight loading containers, and in a wide variety of types, including black-and-white, color, and reversal stocks. Special types are also available: film that is sensitive to colors beyond the range of the human eye, film specifically designed for television recording, sound-recording film, high contrast film for matteing and titles, duplicating stocks for laboratory and optical printing, high-speed rapid-reversal film, and leader stock for editing purposes. Standards outlined by the American Standards Association (ASA exposure indexes) assure a high degree of quality and consistency.

filmograph, or slide-motion film The use of zoom and pan effects over static artwork to create the illusion of motion—actually a slide-film with movement.

filmstrip or slidefilm A series of photographs, illustrations, and other graphics that is shot in sequence on successive frames of film. During the projection process each frame is visible on the screen for the length of the accompanying narration, which is carried on a disk or tape. A new audio-visual system developed by the 3M Company makes it possible to add sound to the slides themselves. With this sound-on-slide system, each slide holder carries its own detachable magnetic sound track. The slides are focused on screens by means of automatic projectors with built-in recording and playback capabilities. To update the subject matter, the sound track is rerecorded and replaced by another detachable sound track. Advertising agencies should find this system quite useful for storyboard presentations.

fine cut The assembly of a number of scenes in proper order, with each scene cut to its final length.

fine-grain A film with a finer grain than that in most raw stock. Fine-grain film is used for optical printing and for duplicating work; resultant prints have a finer texture.

flashback An inserted scene that takes place at an earlier time.

flash frame A deliberately overexposed frame of film that serves as a cue mark for the editor or optical cameraman.

flash pan, or zip pan A transitional effect in which the camera is panned away from the subject matter. The speed of the panning action and the resultant blur, during which detail is not distinguishable, is used to suggest a change in location.

flip A transitional effect in which a scene seems to rotate on a center axis until the image becomes a thin line—actually the thickness of the film itself. The incoming scene develops from this thin line into a full-frame image to complete the effect. In practice, the outgoing scene is threaded into a flip device positioned between the optical printer lamphouse and the camera lens. During the filming process, the cameraman rotates the flip device frame by frame for the length of the effect. Halfway through the effect, the incoming scene replaces the outgoing scene in the flip device, and the stop-motion rotation continues until the scene, in the final frame of the effect, is in the normal projection position.

floating pegs Registration pegs, mounted on a flat metal plate, that can be placed at any point on the animation stand compound table. They allow the compound table, along with any artwork positioned on it, to be moved without affecting the registration.

foil Pieces of aluminum foil applied to the film at specific points by the editor. They are used to locate cut points when the picture information is transferred to videotape. The pieces of foil activate a pickup device that places an electronic cue on the videotape. Generally, this technique has been replaced by the new electronic editing processes.

foot, feet A standard linear measurement for film.

footage A length of film.

frame (also X) A single exposure or picture in a length of film.

freeze frame Reexposure of the picture information in one frame of film on successive frames, for the specified length of the effect, in order to stop an action within the scene being duplicated.

gimmick A shortcut, such as a cutout devised by the animator, to reduce the number of drawings required for an effect. In most cases, the use of gimmicks is questionable: any saving in either time or effort for the animator is negated by the additional burdens placed on other production departments.

grading The scene-to-scene exposure balance throughout a film presentation.

graphics A generic term for illustrative material, generally not including animation.

guide, animation A pencil layout indicating the positioning of animation or camera movements.

guide track A temporary sound track used for synchronization purposes in the absence of the actual recording that will subsequently be combined with the film's picture information.

head out The position of the leader strips in relation to the film wound on a reel. The leaders are wound on the outside of the film roll for threading in a moviola or projector.

high-contrast film A contrast film used for photographing titles, mattes, and other elements that are combined with background scenes during the optical-printing process.

hodoscope A display panel containing a number of lights or lamps, each of which may be activated separately. Each lamp flashes for a brief interval corresponding with an action or movement occurring in front of the display panel, which activates the controlling circuits. In some cases, the individual lamps may be activated by lengths of projected film focused on the panel. Especially valuable for high-speed, multichannel data recording, a shutterless and fast-framing camera is set up to expose the rapidly changing data that passes in front of the lamps. When used for outdoor advertising displays, the technique is especially effective if the projected film that activates the panel carries an animated action sequence.

hold The term used to indicate a stop position for drawings or pan backgrounds.

hold cel A particular cel, group of cels, or background that is exposed for a specified number of frames, as opposed to the cels carrying the action, which are changed in successive frames of film. See cel levels.

hookup The interchangeable drawings for the first and last positions of a movement cycle. See cycle.

hot splicer A film splicer with a thermostatically controlled heater that maintains a constant 100-degrees temperature. Fitted with tungsten-carbide inserts for cutting, the splicer also has tempered-steel springs that position the film precisely during the scraping and splicing process.

I D (*ID*entification). The abbreviation for the commercial between regularly scheduled programs. The I D also carries the TV station's call letters.

inbetween An intermediate drawing needed to complete an action. The animator makes only the key drawings; the assistant animator, or inbetweener, is responsible for the secondary positions. See also extreme and key drawing.

inker The person responsible for tracing the lines in the animator's drawings onto transparent sheets of celluloid.

insert scene A short length of film—a closeup of a performer's hands or eyes, for example—that is intercut between two related scenes in order to help the visual continuity.

insurance shot See cover shot.

intercutting The alternation of scenes from two related sequences to give the impression of simultaneousness.

interlock The synchronous projection of separate picture and sound elements, either on film or on videotape.

internegative A negative produced from an original color-reversal print. Negatives derived from print material are referred to as duplicate color negatives.

interpositive A denser-than-normal print used for color optical or duplicating work. It has a distinguishing orange-colored base or mask.

invisible splice A type of splice used for preparing A & B rolls. The film is positioned in the splicer, and the first cut is made on the frame line. The second cut, on the film to be joined, is made in the picture area. Since scrape markings would be reproduced, the film must be handled carefully. The splice is lined up with the leader strip, and does not show in the processed film.

jump cut The shortening of a scene by eliminating a number of expendable frames without affecting the continuity of the action.

lap dissolve See cross-dissolve.

layout, animation The design of the characters to be animated and/or the plotting of the action.

layout, optical The timings and frame counts in the film editor's work print, which are transferred to layout sheets for the optical cameraman. The layouts specify the length of scenes to be duplicated, the frames in which transitional effects take place, the location of superimposures, matte runs, and other effects.

leaders Lengths of film that are spliced at the beginning and end of a roll of film. The head leader is threaded through the projector's transport mechanism, eliminating the need to handle any part of the picture itself. Numbers are marked in reverse order on these leader strips at 1-foot intervals to assist the projectionist.

lead sheet See bar sheet.

library footage, or stock shot An entire scene or length of film, from an earlier production, that is used as an insert. Commercial organizations specializing in library footage issue catalogs describing unusual locations and special-effects footage available on a rental basis. Sound and music libraries offer similar services. See also scratch print.

lily A card divided into spaces containing each of the primary and complementary colors along with a small number of tonal values in the gray scale. It is placed over the last frame of the artwork being photographed, and exposed for several frames. After the film has been processed, the lily is used for evaluating the colors and tonal values in the print.

limited animation The use of shortcuts to produce the maximum amount of movement with a minimum of drawings. The hold cel is particularly important in this animation technique, since the animator draws only the parts of the figure that are actually involved in action. See hold cel.

lip synchronization Match up of the mouthing of dialogue by an animated cartoon character with the sound track. The animation is prepared in accordance with the frame counts prepared by the film editor from the sound-track analysis. See live action.

liquid gate, or wet gate A self-contained unit that removes or minimizes the effect of scratches, dirt, dust, and surface abrasion during the optical-printing process. In operation, the film being duplicated is totally immersed immediately before exposure in an aquarium, a housing unit that contains a liquid whose refractive-index effect on film makes the salvage process possible. The liquid in which the film is immersed fills the abrasions, eliminating the light refractions that are intensified by contrast buildup.

live-action A film or sequence of film in which live performers or real objects are photographed, as opposed to a sequence of motion achieved by photographing a series of animated drawings. The synchronization of the sound track with the corresponding pictures in which dialogue between performers takes place in live action is analogous to the process in the animated production.

logo A trademark or symbol that identifies an organization. The term is used frequently in commercial film production.

long shot (also establishing shot) A scene or action photographed from a distance so that a large area of the setting appears on a frame of film, and individual actors or objects appear quite small. The opposite of a close-up.

M & E track A sound track containing music and sound effects only. The accompanying dialogue is recorded separately. Separate tracks are especially useful if the dialogue is to be dubbed in a foreign language.

magazine   A film container mounted over a motion picture camera.

magoptical print   A print containing both magnetic and optical sound tracks.

magoptical track   A length of film containing both magnetic and optical sound tracks. This type of track is arranged alternately and used for editing purposes.

marriage   The combination of picture and sound-track information in the composite print.

master positive   A fine-grain print film used to produce a duplicate negative.

matching negative   The delicate process of cutting and matching the original picture negative to the edited work print.

mattes   An opaque silhouette, conforming in size, shape, and position with a corresponding area on the film, which serves as the background for picture information on separate lengths of film that will subsequently be inserted in the matted, unexposed areas. The masking of the inset area within the background film is only a temporary measure in the achievement of the effect. In the first step of the optical process, the positive matte, on high-contrast film, is exposed with the background film. The high-contrast negative matte, in the second of the two optical camera runs needed to complete the effect, is exposed with the film that carries the picture information that is to be inserted in the matted area. Unlike the static matte just described, a traveling matte consists of a series of mattes on successive frames of film, corresponding with the continually changing matteing areas in the background film. In either case, the matteing process makes possible the combination of animation with live-action scenes, the superimposition of titles, and the creation of a wide variety of unusual illusory effects without undesirable double exposures.

mechanical animation   The construction and subsequent photography of three-dimensional models of a mechanism. The subject matter is illustrated by means of directional flow lines, which are inked and opaqued on cels and superimposed on a second camera run. Other movable parts of the mechanism are also rendered on cels and photographed on the compound table with stop-motion processes.

medium shot   A scene photographed so that the full figure of an actor or cartoon character fills the entire frame. It is between a close-up and a long shot.

mix   The rerecording of all sound elements (dialogue, music, and effects) into a single sound track that is used to prepare the composite print.

model drawing   See color model.

modulation   The sound patterns in variable-area and variable-density sound tracks.

montage   An effect in which a number of related images are visible within the film frame simultaneously. It is used in many ways for as many different purposes. In a feature-length production, the film editor may use a series of extremely short lengths of film spliced together to create an impression. There is no attempt at visual continuity: the effect is used to save time, film footage, and several pages of explanatory script. In a television commercial, montage is not only a necessity but a merchandising aid as well. In a 1-minute commercial, montage is used to increase the amount of information reaching the consumer. Compare collage and visual squeeze.

mood music   A musical background that helps to establish a mood or setting for the corresponding picture.

moviola   A viewing device used by the film editor to synchronize the sound track and the corresponding picture.

multimedia, or videography   In educational television, a relatively permanent facility available for multiple-image presentations. The programmed material is either channeled to the participating schools via closed-circuit television, or displayed on monitor screens by means of various projection devices. Commercial development of techniques, capable of filling oversized screens with images from a number of sources, continues at a brisk pace. Budgets for the production of multimedia presentations, in which the information is transmitted to the screen's beaded surface by as many as six projectors, are proportional to the complexity of the effort and the desired effect. In a multimedia production, the component picture information is usually a joint venture. Contracts for live-film sequences, for example, are assigned to studios with indoor sets, backlot facilities, and filming crews equipped to handle location work; slidefilm presentations, to studios specializing in that type of production; animation, to an animation studio. Each of the separate efforts must be assembled, coordinated, previewed, edited, and synchronized with the corresponding sound tracks—a Herculean task indeed. The use of optical processes, however, eliminates many of the problems associated with the synchronization of composite images. The combined picture information is exposed with matteing processes onto one strand of film that can be threaded into a single projector for normal viewing on conventional screens. Static artwork, slides, photographs, and documents are photographed in different areas of the film frame in accordance with the storyboard requirements. During each of the several runs needed to produce the composite effect, the optical cameraman exposes each length of film with its corresponding matte. Live-action and animation sequences are also added optically.

multiple-image shot An optical effect produced by duplicating the picture information within the film frame as many times and in as many positions as the film editor specifies.

mylar tape splicer, or guillotine splicer A splicer in which mylar tape is used to join lengths of film in either butt, overlap, or diagonal splices without losing frames. It is used only for editing purposes.

negative The developed, in-camera film from which the positive print is made. The color values in the negative are reversed so that a black area in the original subject matter appears white or clear in the print film. In color film, the values in the negative are approximately complementary to the colors in the original subject matter.

notch A cutout area along the edge of the film, used by optical technicians and laboratory timers to indicate changes in printing lights.

off-register A vibration effect produced by moving the animation camera in relation to the compound table on successive frames of film. The incremental north-south and east-west movements, in relation to the artwork registered to the pegs on the compound table, create an effect that accents violent animated actions such as explosions or crashes.

ones, twos, threes The number of exposures that each of the cels in an animated action receives during the photographic process. An action exposed two frames for each cel, for example, is twice as long and requires half as many drawings as the same sequence photographed on ones. In limited animation techniques, exposure on threes is not uncommon.

opaquer The person responsible for applying opaque colors to the outlined areas on the cels traced by the inkers. The opaquer applies watercolors to the reverse side of the cel according to the instructions on the model drawings.

optical effect The duplication and/or addition of picture information on the optical printer: any effect that is produced by optical means rather than with direct, in-camera photographic processes. Optical print, or answer print, refers to the print produced on the optical printer. It contains the duplicated scenes to which superimpositions, transitional effects, matte inserts, or special effects have been added and is complete with respect to visual continuity. The approved answer print becomes the guide for the production of the release print.

optical printer, or optical camera An optical, electrical, and mechanical device that combines the functions of the camera and the projector. It is used to duplicate the picture information in a number of lengths of previously processed film simultaneously and to create transitional and special effects.

optical recording The optical sound patterns in the sound-track area of the film. During the projection process, the modulations are electrically converted from light impulses to audible sound. See also variable-area and variable-density sound tracks.

original picture effect The negative produced by the laboratory from the in-camera raw stock used during the actual filming process.

out-of-focus effect An out-of-focus effect can be used either as a transition or to create a specific mood. As a transition, the outgoing scene is simply thrown out of focus progressively in successive frames of film until the picture information is blurred beyond recognition. The camera shutter remains completely open at all times during the single run needed to produce the effect. If, for example, 80 frames are allotted for the total effect, the outgoing scene is generally thrown out of focus for the first 40 frames, and the incoming scene is then exposed, beginning with a completely blurred frame, for the other 40 frames, ending with completely sharp focus. This relatively inexpensive optical can be used to introduce dream sequences, create horror effects, or form abstract backgrounds for superimpositions.

outtake A duplicate of a scene not used in the final film.

overlay   A piece of artwork rendered on thin illustration board and hinged to the background. The overlay and the background sandwich a portion of the inked-and-opaqued cels, creating the illusion of depth.

pan   An effect in which the camera is moved horizontally from one point of the set to another. See also tilt.

pan background   A panoramic background designed so that it can be moved in relation to the cels on the registration pegs of the compound table.

panchromatic master positive, or pan master   A black-and-white print produced from a color negative on panchromatic film and used to make black-and-white duplicate negatives.

pantograph   A small, tablelike unit attached to the side of the compound table. A pointer, indicating the camera center in relation to the field guide positioned on the registration pegs, moves in conjunction with the compound table. The pantograph makes plotting and executing complex compound-table moves a relatively simple procedure.

pegs, registration   Fixed pins on the various types of drawing boards used by animators, inbetweeners, inkers, and opaquers. The same peg setup is also used on the compound table for registering drawings, cels, and backgrounds.

pencil test   The photographing of an animator's drawings in order to check the fluidity of an action. The drawings are reviewed by screening the processed film on the editor's moviola. Corrections can be made before the drawings are inked and opaqued.

picture duplicate negative (also dupe negative)   A negative produced from positive materials such as black-and-white, color, or separation master positives.

platen   A frame-enclosed piece of optically clear glass, which is attached to the compound table to lock the cels in position over the background during the filming process.

position   The registration of drawings, cels, or backgrounds in relation to the compound table's normal center peg position.

positive   The print produced from the original in-camera film negative. The colors and gray tones in a positive print are the same as those found in the original subject matter.

post-synchronization   The recording and synchronization of a sound track with the picture after the filming process has been completed. The film editor must provide arbitrary timings for animated actions and lip sync sequences. Compare pre-synchronization and reading.

pre-synchronization   The recording of a sound track before the filming process takes place. In animation, the recording of the sound track usually precedes any of the actual production processes. The film editor provides the animator with frame counts, derived from the sound-track analysis, which show the number of frames allotted for an action and the frames in which dialogue takes place. Compare post-synchronization and reading.

print   A positive picture produced from an original or dupe negative. The colors and tonal values of the original subject matter are reproduced in the processed print.

probe   A device used to measure and check the intensity of the light source in an optical printer.

process camera   A camera with a stop-motion motor, specifically designed for animation stands and optical printers.

processing   The production of visible images, by means of laboratory printing processes, on lengths of previously exposed film. Normal development of a length of black-and-white motion-picture film yields a negative image. The tonal values in the developed film are exactly opposite to those in the original subject matter. With proportionately greater silver deposits in the lighter areas, black areas become clear in the negative-film frame, and the lighter areas appear proportionately denser. In the processed print, the tonal values are similar to those found in the subject matter at the time of exposure. By comparison, in-camera reversal stock yields a direct positive. To produce the positive image, the film is developed in two stages. In the first stage, the developed silver in the emulsion is exposed and bleached away by chemical action. In the second step, the remaining unexposed silver is reexposed, redeveloped, and fixed to yield the positive picture information. A chemical reaction, referred to as coupler development, is the basis for the reproduction of color values. The exposed silver halide in the color film forms metallic silver during the first stage of the developing process. The oxidizing developing agent combines with the chemical coupler to produce insoluble dyes, which are proportional to the amounts of metallic silver formed during the first stage of the developing process and which reproduce the colors in the original subject matter. The color values of the negative images are complementary to those in the original. When the coupler components are extracted from the developing solutions, the positive images produced by color reversal processing are obtained by developing each of the three emulsion layers separately. If the couplers are added to the emulsion layers of the original in-camera, color-reversal film by the manufacturer, however, the film is developed in a single solution to produce the direct positive images.

production   The phases or processes used in the making of an animated film or feature-length motion picture. Also, the completed film.

projection printing, or optical printing   The process of duplicating film by projecting it through an optical system similar to that in an optical printer. The projected film is exposed on the raw stock in the printer's camera.

projection shuttle   The shuttle through which lengths of previously processed film are projected. It is capable of accommodating several thicknesses of film simultaneously, and the projected images are exposed on the raw stock in the printer's camera.

projection synchronism   The alignment of sound and picture information on the same length of film. The sound precedes the corresponding picture by 20 frames in a 35mm. print and by 26 frames in a 16mm. print. Compare editorial synchronism.

puppet animation   A stop-motion technique in which the subject matter consists of three-dimensional figures and backgrounds, which are moved incrementally for each frame of the action sequence.

quick cut   A moving montage effect produced by splicing together a number of short lengths of film. In most cases, despite the related subject matter, there is no attempt to establish visual continuity.

raw stock   Unexposed film.

reader, sound   A device for reproducing sound that is used for editing and analyzing sound tracks. It has a revolving drum over which the track area passes to make contact with the reproducing head.

reading   The film editor's analysis of the pre-recorded sound track for synchronization with the animation. The frame counts indicate the number of frames al- lotted for a specific action and a breakdown of each word of dialogue into syllables.

reduction print   The duplication of picture information on 35mm. film in the narrower 16mm. width. The size of the grain is not as important in reduction as in enlargement. See blowup.

register   The positioning of the animated drawings, the inked-and-opaqued cels, or the background on the registration pegs in the drawing board or the compound table.

reel   A plastic or metal spool used for winding film.

release negative   A negative, containing both sound and picture information, from which the release print is produced.

release print   The final version of a film, complete with respect to sound and picture information, that is distributed to theaters for exhibition.

repeat   The reexposure of an action. See cycle.

rerecording   See mix.

reversal original   A positive picture image produced from in-camera raw stock by reversal processing.

reversal processing   A laboratory process that produces a direct positive image from the in-camera film instead of the usual negatives.

reversing action   A pioneering motion-picture technique, originally introduced to elicit chuckles from the most sophisticated audiences and now used to produce a wide variety of effects for almost as many purposes. In practically all cases, the effect is produced with direct, in-camera photographic processes or with the optical printer. To photograph live action, the film is first run through the camera with the shutter closed for the required length of time; then, with the camera motor reversed and the shutter reopened, the scene is photographed normally. When the film is processed, the last frame exposed is at the beginning of the roll, and the action is reversed when the film is projected. With the optical printer, the process is even simpler: the normally photographed and processed scene is merely rewound, threaded on the projection side of the optical printer, and duplicated on the raw stock in the optical camera. The film is projected normally to reverse the action.

rewind A device attached to the film editor's table that is capable of supporting a number of feed and take-up reels.

rock, camera See off-register.

rotoscope One of the first techniques for duplicating human action graphically. To produce the effect, live actors, made up and costumed to resemble animated-cartoon characters, are photographed in front of neutral backgrounds. The processed film, positioned in the animation camera shuttle and projected onto the compound table, is traced by the animator. The outline and detail of each figure on the successive frames of film are redrawn on separate sheets of drawing paper registered to the pegs in the compound table, and each of the drawings is traced on transparent cels and hand-colored (opaqued). In the final stage of production, the cels are photographed over appropriate backgrounds prepared by the art department. The processed film is synchronized with the corresponding sound track by the film editor. The projection process is also used to produce mattes for subsequent optical work: areas within the film frame in which new material is to be inserted are carefully traced by the graphics department, and the mattes are photographed on high-contrast film for optical combination.

rough cut A temporary arrangement of scenes, cut to their approximate length, used to check the visual continuity in the early stages of the post-production process.

run The exposure of film during any part of the photographic process. A double run indicates that the same length of film is exposed twice; two or three runs are often needed to produce multiple-image effects.

rushes See dailies.

scene An action or incident, filmed in an appropriate location or setting, that forms part of a related sequence in a film presentation.

scraper The device on the splicer that is used to remove the emulsion from the part of the film frame in which the splice is to be made. Film cement is applied to this area, and the length of film that is to be joined is pressed into position to complete the splice.

scratch-off An operation in which sections of the artwork on successive frames of film are scratched away, removed, or concealed during the photographic process. The camera operates in the reverse mode. When the processed film is projected normally, the artwork appears progressively on successive frames of film.

scratch print Library footage or stock shots made available by commercial organizations. Stock footage of every conceivable subject can be leased by the editor. The film is deliberately scratched to prevent unauthorized duplication. Unscratched footage is produced from the original negative. Some libraries specialize in music and sound effects.

scratch track A temporary recording prepared for synchronization purposes only. The film editor works with this type of sound track if the original recording is not readily available.

segue A musical transitional effect.

self-mattes See mattes.

separation positive A black-and-white print produced from a color negative. Each of the primary colors in the negative is reproduced through the appropriate filter in the corresponding shades of gray on a separate length of film. The lengths of film are used to produce a color-corrected negative for printing purposes.

sequence A grouping of related scenes that are spliced in proper order and complete with respect to visual continuity.

shot A specific scene or the action occurring within the scene.

shutter A part of the camera used for controlling the degree of exposure or the amount of light reaching the film in the camera.

single-concept film An abbreviated documentary film, usually covering one specific aspect of the subject matter and used as a teaching aid. It is generally distributed in self-threading cartridges, and a continuous loop makes it possible to rerun the film as many times as necessary, or to stop at any point for discussion. The film may be run with or without sound.

skip frame An optical effect, used to speed up an action, in which designated frames are omitted during printing.

slidefilm See filmstrip.

slide-motion film   See filmograph.

slides   A 2 by 2-inch transparency mounted between two pieces of glass for projection purposes.

sliding cel   Cels, approximately two or more fields in width, that are used for ·cycle actions in which the animated-cartoon character pans through the scene.

slit-scan, smear, or streak photography   A photographic process in which exposure takes place through a masking slit that is moved in a horizontal plane over the subject matter. Each successive frame of film photographed in this manner provides a time reference relating to a movement, condition, or phenomenon. The technique was originally designed to obtain data pertaining to stress-and-strain conditions, explosive phenomena, and movement patterns normally exposed with high-speed photographic processes. Variations of this masking technique are currently used to achieve unusual abstract-lighting effects in commercial productions. This adaptation requires a motion-picture camera driven by a stop-motion motor. The camera is mounted so that each frame in the sequence of movement—the panning of subject matter behind the slit and the movement of the camera itself—is precisely repeatable. Animation stands with underlighting are ideally suited for this purpose. During the photographic process a light source directed on the portion of the subject matter that is visible through a slit is moved across one plane of the film frame. During each of the multiple runs needed to achieve the effect, the position of the slit in relation to the subject matter is changed incrementally to allow exposure on different planes. The abstract-light patterns in the composite effect create the illusion that the camera is moving through the subject matter along a rainbow-lined route. The technique was developed by Trumbull Film Effects and used in the Stanley Kubrick production *2001: A SPACE ODYSSEY*.

solarization   A polarity-reversal effect produced by exposing an image to intense light for long periods of time. Imaginative directors and graphic artists use variations of the technique to produce unusual illusory effects. In practice, solarization effects are achieved with mattes derived from the live-action color film. In the first step of the process, the live-action footage is duplicated on a pan master. Its gradations from black through intermediate shades of gray to white are used to produce the high-contrast mattes needed to achieve the effect. During the optical combination, the negative and print films are exposed on color film through selected filters to produce psychedelic effects.

sound effect   Any sound that helps lend credibility to the corresponding picture.

sound reader   A device used by the film editor to reproduce a recorded sound track. The unit is used to analyze the sound track and to provide the animator with frame counts showing the number of frames allotted for an action and/or the frames requiring lip-sync animation. See reading.

sound track   The recorded sound that complements the corresponding picture information. The composite sound track contains dialogue, musical backgrounds, and sound effects. In 35mm. film, the sound track is positioned longitudinally in a narrow area on the left side of the film; in 16mm. film, it is reproduced along the right side of the frame. See advance, sound track to picture.

sound track advance   See advance, sound track to picture.

sound work print   A sound track containing sections of dialogue, music, and effects. The intercut track is synchronized with the corresponding picture information in the work print.

spin, camera   A spinning effect produced by rotating the animation-stand compound table and the artwork positioned on it.

splicer   An editing accessory used to join lengths of film.

split reel   A spool used for winding film. One section of the reel unscrews from the other, enabling a roll of film to be removed from the reel without rewinding.

split-screen shot   A shot in which the film frame is divided into a number of sections, each of which contains different picture information. Mattes and multiple runs are used to mask each part of the film frame in turn and to add the insert information in the previously matted areas. A hidden split, in which no definite line of demarcation between the separate picture areas is visible, is achieved by offsetting the wipe patterns on high-contrast film. The invisible-split effect is produced by overlapping the leading edges of the wipes that are used as mattes, resulting in a narrow, gray, out-of-focus area.

squash and stretch   Exaggerated changes in the proportions of an animated figure. Squash is a flattening or compressing action that usually results when a moving body strikes a solid surface. Stretch, or elongation, indicates a body traveling at great speed. The exaggerated proportions follow physical principles and lend realism to the cartoon figures.

standard field The field that is used for most of a studio's filming assignments. It is used for composition, to film titles and other subject matter for optical printing, and to rotoscope previously processed frames of film for matteing. Each studio sets its own standards, based on the equipment in use; in most cases, the 12 field is the accepted norm. See field guide and field size.

start mark, or sync mark An X drawn with grease pencil across specific frames in both the sound track and the corresponding picture to indicate a common synchronization point.

station identification (also I D) The commercial between regularly scheduled programs that also carries the TV station's call letters.

step-contact printing The reproduction of picture information from a length of previously processed negative or positive film that runs in direct contact with the raw stock. Depending upon the polarity of the film used for printing, either a positive or a negative image is produced. Each frame of film, traveling intermittently through the transport mechanism, is exposed to the printing light in turn.

still background A rendered background that remains in a fixed position on the registration pegs of the compound table during the entire photographic process. Compare pan background.

stock shot See library footage.

stop motion A photographic process in which the subject matter is exposed on successive frames of film on a frame-by-frame basis rather than continuously, as in standard motion-picture photography. Between exposures, the subject matter is moved incrementally to create the illusion of movement.

storyboard A number of illustrations arranged in comic-strip fashion with appropriate captions. It is an extremely popular method for showing the visual continuity of an animated cartoon or television commercial.

superimposition See burn-in.

sync mark See start mark.

synchronism The alignment of the sound track with the corresponding picture which is on a separate reel. See editorial synchronism and projection synchronism.

synchronization The precise relationship between the sound track and the corresponding picture information.

synchronizer A sprocketed device used by the editor to measure lengths of film.

tabletop photography See Amici prism.

tail, or afterimage An undesirable trailing or secondary image caused by improper phasing of the camera shutter and the transport mechanism.

take 1. In animated cartoons and feature-length motion pictures, a reaction indicating surprise. 2. One of several similar shots of a live scene, the best of which is edited into the print.

take-up reel The reel on which the film is wound after it has been run through a synchronizer, moviola, or projector shuttle.

technamation A stop-motion technique that uses light-polarizing filters to create the illusion of motion. The filters are mounted on a disk positioned between the camera lens and the artwork, usually a large transparency placed over the underlighting unit in the compound table, and rotated incrementally for each exposure. The polarizing axis of each filter changes constantly as it rotates in relation to the other filters. When the axes are parallel, light is transmitted to the artwork; when they are at right angles to each other, little or no light is transmitted. The light source is focused on the ground glass set into the center of the compound table. The transparency is mounted on the registration pegs. Polarizing materials are cut and fitted into position over each of the action-carrying areas within the transparency. A wide variety of commercially available materials are used to produce an equally great number of motion effects—wheels turning, smoke billowing, or water running, for example. As the filters are rotated and the axes change in relation to the transparency, the density of the applied materials changes continually to create the illusion of motion.

technical animation An animation technique used for educational and training purposes. Instead of animated figures, the graphics consist of diagrams, charts, symbols, directional flow lines, and dimensional models of mechanisms with superimposed moving parts. Graphic explanations of intricate mechanisms, demonstrations of new production techniques, or simulations of situations that have no physical counterpart are best left to specialists. The preparation and superimposition of cel animation over a device positioned on the compound table are considered routine by technical animators, who can reduce a complex problem into understandable graphics so that communication with the viewer is established from the first frame to the fade-out at the end of the film.

technique   A style or method for handling the subject matter in a film presentation.

tightwinder   A guide roller and hinged metal spring-tension arm used for winding film quickly on cores or hubs rather than on reels or flanges.

tilt   An effect in which the camera is moved vertically from one position in the background or set to another. See also pan.

title   Verbal information relating to the accompanying picture information. In the industry's infancy, captions were substituted for dialogue. Titles can be used to establish a mood or reflect the film's subject matter both in full-length feature films and 1-minute television commercials; the variety of treatments is unlimited. See also burn-in.

top pegs   The upper set of pegs on an animation board or camera compound table used for registering drawings, cels, or backgrounds.

trace back   A notation on an animator's incomplete drawing indicating to the inker that the missing portions are to be traced from another specified cel within the scene.

transfer   The rerecording or duplication of a magnetic sound track on sprocketed magnetic sound film.

transitional effect   An effect, such as a cross-dissolve or wipe, designed to create a smooth flow of visual continuity between scenes. A fade is similar to a transitional effect, but is generally used at the beginning or end of a sequence.

traveling pegs   Movable bars, set into tracks on the animation stand compound table, that are equipped with registration pegs for positioning sliding cels and pan backgrounds.

traveling matte   See matte.

trim   An unused portion of a scene.

truck   See zoom.

ultrasonic cleaner   A device in which film is cleaned by ultrasonic energy. The solvent residue resulting from the cavitation, or boiling, effect as the film moves through the cleaning solution is removed by a forced-air, flash dryoff.

variable-area sound track   An optical sound track. The modulations, corresponding to the variations of audible sound, form irregular patterns in the sound-track area. Compare variable-density sound track.

variable-density sound track   An optical sound track in which the modulations form constantly changing light gradations, ranging in density from intermediate shades of gray through black. Compare variable-area sound track.

variable-speed motor   A drive, used on animation and optical cameras, that enables the cameraman to select a convenient filming speed by simply turning a controlling dial. The camera can deliver full power at all speeds and operate on a stop-motion frame-by-frame basis.

videography   See multimedia.

visual squeeze   An animation technique in which the subject matter consists of short animation sequences, still photographs, abstract forms, and a wide variety of graphics designed and arranged to produce the illusion of movement. An unusual amount of visual information can be compressed within the 1,440 frames of film in a 1-minute television commercial.

wet gate   See liquid gate.

wide-screen print   A print in which the picture information within the film frame is wider than the standard 1.33:1 aspect ratio. Unlike an anamorphic print, in which the image is squeezed and returned to normal proportions during projection by means of a complementary deanamorphic lens, a wide-screen print need not contain a squeezed image.

wild track   A temporary sound track, containing dialogue and/or music, that approximates the contents of the recorded sound track that is synchronized with the corresponding picture. This time-saver is used by the editor for postsync productions, or as a substitute for the actual track if it is not available.

wipe An optical effect in which one scene is gradually replaced by another in the same length of film. Unlike a cross-dissolve, in which the images in each scene are blended and more or less visible throughout the entire effect, the picture information in both scenes of a wipe is visible but separated by a definite line of demarcation. The shape of the line varies with the wipe pattern used to achieve the effect. Wipe patterns, animated and then photographed on high-contrast film, serve as mattes, and conceal progressively larger areas of the outgoing scene on successive frames of film. These same areas are progressively revealed during the second camera run until the incoming scene is visible in its entirety. Again, unlike a cross-dissolve, in which the exposure varies throughout the length of the effect, the exposure during a wipe remains constant at 100% during each of the two camera runs. The negative and positive high-contrast mattes that are used to produce the effect are carefully catalogued and identified by number in wipe charts used by the film editor and the optical cameraman. Depending upon the wipe pattern, the transitional effect not only adds visual interest but also suggests changes in both time and location.

There are two types of wipe effects available to the filmmaker: in the more common hard-edge wipe a visible line separates the areas between the incoming and outgoing scenes; in a soft-edge wipe the line of demarcation is nonexistent. Instead of a visible line, the scenes are separated by a narrow, gray, out-of-focus area conforming with the leading edge of the wipe pattern. In either case the effect is produced by first exposing the positive wipe pattern on high-contrast film together with the out-going scene for the designated length of the effect (wipe patterns are available in various lengths); then, in the second camera run, rewinding the film to the opening frame of the effect with the shutter closed, and exposing the high-contrast negative wipe pattern with the incoming scene. Both camera runs receive 100% exposure. Unlike the hard-edge wipe, in which the leading edges of the negative and positive wipe patterns are precisely aligned during each of the two camera runs, the soft-edge wipe is produced by slightly overlapping the wipe patterns. This offset produces the soft, out-of-focus effect that separates the outgoing and incoming scenes. Except for the lines of demarcation or the out-of-focus areas, the wipe patterns are never visible to the viewer. If they were placed over each other in the optical printer's projection shuttle, the leading edges of the two lengths of film would match precisely and result in a completely black, opaque frame of film.

wipe effect The replacement of one scene by another by means of matteing processes. The mattes, actually wipe patterns, are animated transitional effects that are photographed on high-contrast film on the animation stand.

work print The assembly and orderly arrangement of scenes, cut to length and marked with a grease pencil to indicate the location of special effects, transitions, and superimpositions. It is synchronized with the accompanying sound track, and used as a guide for the production of the optical, or answer, print.

X The abbreviation for a frame of film.

X-dissolve See cross-dissolve.

X-sheets See exposure sheets.

zero cut A method of hiding splices in A & B roll editing. Each scene is extended by two frames at the beginning and end, and black leader is spliced between the scenes. Cuts between scenes are smooth because the overlapping footage eliminates splices. See A & B rolls and A & B printing.

zip pan See flash pan.

zoom An effect in which stationary subject matter within the shooting field is made to appear progressively larger (close-up) or smaller (long-shot) in successive frames of film by moving the camera closer to or further away from it. See also calibration.

Index

RECEIVED

MAY 2 1981

Mission College
Learning Resource
Services